For Sachio and chilli enthusiasts across Chilli Britain

www.chillibritain.com

First published in Great Britain in 2014
by ngo.media limited

Chilli Britain
A Hot & Fruity Adventure

Copyright © Gideon Burrows, 2014

A catalogue record for this book is available
from the British Library.

Paperback ISBN: 978-0-9553695-8-2
Also available on Kindle and other ebooks

Published by ngo.media limited
Austons, Layer Road, Abberton CO5 7NH
Company registration number: 04916846

2 4 6 8 10 9 7 5 3

Cover design: Chandler Book Design
www.chandlerbookdesign.co.uk

Printed and bound in Great Britain by
CPI Group (UK), Croydon, CR0 4YY

Chilli Britain
A Hot & Fruity Adventure

GIDEON BURROWS

Prologue

IF YOU CAN'T take the heat, there are three simple ways to pull out of a chilli eating competition.

Simple way number one: Stand up and walk away. Just go back to the audience and your pint of beer. Continue to enjoy the show from the outside looking in.

Simple way number two: Take a swig or more from the glass of milk sitting there in front of you. The rich fat inside the milk will bind with the burning chemicals in the chillies. You'll get at least a little respite from the scorching in your mouth and throat.

Simple way number three: Throw up. In front of your friends and family. In front of hundreds of spectators. On camera. Medical volunteers will even hand you a little cardboard receptacle in which to do it.

I take my position alongside nine other contenders as the compère explains how the competition will work. The ten of us will be presented with a different chilli for each round. We have to eat the chilli right down to the stem, chewing it properly and then swallowing. We then have to hold the stem above our heads to show we've finished it. That we're still in the game. For each round, the chilli we have to eat will be hotter than the last. Then hotter, then hotter, then hotter. The last man or woman standing wins.

I look out on the crowd that has gathered to watch the competition at a country club on the outskirts of Bushey in Hertfordshire. The whole chilli festival has stopped and gathered for the show.

They're a picture of modern Britain: fat and thin; white, Asian and black; men holding babies, women rubbing their pregnant bellies. Viewers with pints of beer, others clutching chilli plants or bags of sauces; swag bought from the stalls around the event. Most of the stallholders have left their stations and joined the audience too. Many people – too many – are holding up camera phones, fingers poised. Along the front, three rows of children sit looking up with innocent and expectant eyes. As if the ten of us are about to do magic tricks or produce colourful balloon animals.

As the compère gets the crowd warmed up and then begins counting down to the start of the competition, I stare down at the first chilli we've been given to eat. A Bullet chilli. There are two things going round in my mind.

The first is the chant my kids were practising in the car on the way here: "Come on Daddy, don't do a sick; come on Daddy, don't do a sick."

The second is: How the hell did it come to this?

"Three. Two. One... Eat!"

In search of Chilli Britain

I'VE ALWAYS CONSIDERED myself a bit of a chilli-head. And my friends and family have too.

A bottle of chilli sauce, some chilli jam, a tub of chilli stuffed olives, a slab of chilli chocolate, a bag of chilli nuts or crisps, all wrapped up in chilli greetings paper and presented with a chilli adorned card and that's my birthday sorted for another year.

Wherever my family is invited for lunch, there's usually a hot sauce offered as a side dish. In Indian restaurants I ask for a hot curry and for good measure a side plate of chopped fresh chillies to eat with each forkful. If it's pizza, give me chilli flakes to sprinkle on top. If it's Chinese, it has to be Szechuan. If it's Mexican, a hot sauce smeared burrito or enchilada. If it's Thai, it has to be red jungle curry. And if it's British food? Sausage and mash, or fish and chips, or shepherd's pie? Well, a bottle of hot sauce by the side will do nicely.

When my Japanese friend Sachio calls round he often brings a jar of something hot. Thanks to the Japanese label, I have no idea what it is. But I'm sure the fermenting cabbage and rotting seaweed inside would taste just delicious if it wasn't overpowered by the strong chilli oil it comes in.

On the birth of my daughter, our friends presented her with a chilli themed babygro, and gave me a catering tub of spicy mango chutney. At Christmas dinner my mother-in-law places a bottle of Tabasco next to the cranberry sauce.

My four-year-old son has declared that when he grows up he's going to eat chilli with every meal too. Good lad.

For me, two decades of eating chillies has been all about the heat: the head rush, the challenge, the sheer bloodymindedness of it. Let's be honest, it's been an addiction. Without chilli, there's always something missing in a meal.

But I'm nearly forty now and perhaps I'm just about starting to grow up. There's something more subtle developing in my chilli interest, something more akin to a hobby. I've started to try to grow chillies, I've tried mixing my own chilli sauces, I've even tried to pay attention to see if I can tell the difference between the flavours behind the scorching heat of different chillies.

The thing is, I've not been particularly good at it. My chilli sauce has turned out too vinegary and wet, the heat destroying any more subtle flavours. My plants have often turned out dry, spindly and unimpressive. My tastebuds have been clumsy and flat, unable to distinguish at all between any different tenors except hot, very hot and stupid. I've concluded that I need help.

A chance visit to a chilli festival two years ago – simply somewhere to take the kids on a bank holiday – revealed something I might before have suspected but never experienced.

There were dozens of stalls, with keen and friendly cooks all presenting their own chilli sauces and chocolates and chutneys and powdered rubs to massage into meat before cooking. There were advice sessions and cooking presentations. There were hundreds of chilli plants and seeds on sale. There were raw chillies to try, books to read. There were chilli eating and curry cooking competitions. And the festival was packed. Despite being just a small local event, it was bursting to the rafters. You couldn't move for the hundreds, perhaps even thousands of people there. People like me.

I was not alone. I discovered that Britain has a burgeoning community of chilli growers and tasters, sauce, chocolate and chutney producers; fanatics, fans and weekend after weekend of festivals dedicated only to these fiery fruits. Where once supermarkets offered a choice of chillies in 'green' or 'red', they now offer a wide selection including some of the hottest fruits and sauces you can get. Now there are the chilli connoisseurs: those who swear different chillies have different subtle tasting notes, complex flavours and textures; telltale signs of origin as if they were fine wines or artisan cheeses.

There are dozens of chilli farms, hundreds of sauce and chilli food producers; there are small kitchen affairs, medium sized commercial producers, and even million-pound growing and processing operations. There are chilli appreciation societies, awards for the best sauces and most prolific plants, websites selling hundreds of chilli flavoured foods, as well as T-shirts, caps, badges, posters and even Christmas decorations with bulbs in the distinctive shape of chilli fruits.

And let's not forget the rich seam of British immigrant communities: the Indians, Pakistanis and Bengalis, the Jamaicans and Thais, Latin Americans and Chinese. They've each brought their own hot and tasty chilli based dishes to British shores, into our homes and into restaurants on every high street.

And then there are the real chilli-heads. Chilli chomping nuts that would eat me for breakfast with a side of red hot Nagas. That particular breed for whom the hottest is never hot enough. Those in a continual competition to grow, cook and eat the fiercest head-busting chillies and curries that the Guinness Book of Records can register. Usually in front of a camera, sharing their pain on YouTube for us all to enjoy.

Despite the unlikely British weather for growing the plants, there's no doubt that in Britain right now chillies are hot. Where better to seek the help I need?

The chilli growing season runs roughly from February to September each year. I've decided to spend it on a journey of learning and discovery. It'll be no less intrepid than when Christopher Columbus set off across the Atlantic more than five hundred years ago and returned with probably the first chillies to reach European shores. I'm going in search of the characters, the experts, the sauces and sorcerers for whom a taste for something hot is not just a hobby, but an obsession, a business, even a lifestyle.

I'm on a mission to learn everything there is to know about planting, growing, harvesting, cooking, brewing, tasting and enjoying chillies in all their wonderful variety. No longer will my palate be single toned. No longer will my plants be more often barren than blooming. No longer will I mistake my Ancho for my Arbol, or my Jalapeño for my Jalokia.

Chilli Britain is on the up in all its saucy, crunchy, colourful, searingly hot goodness. And I want in.

I should cacao

I'M ON THE banks of the River Orwell near Ipswich in Suffolk, on the outskirts of the village of Wherstead. Here, the imposing Orwell Bridge carrying the A14 over the river and down towards the port at Harwich looms above everything. From below it's an awesome arch of cream, stretching over the water and into the distance. From above it's a noisy, grubby A-road from which you can't even see the picturesque estuary because of high grey walls either side.

But on the western bank of the Orwell, sitting meekly beneath the bridge, is the Suffolk Food Hall. It's a huge converted barn stuffed to its timbers with cheese and chocolate counters, an on-site organic bakery, traditional butchers and fishmongers. There are food islands crammed with twenty varieties of posh pastas, fifteen pressings of herb infused olive oils and shelves of local real ales and home-made cordials. There are corners packed with the little pink trinkets, Cath Kidston aprons and Joseph Joseph cooking nicknacks that seem to me a waste of good food space, but to my wife are the very epitome of a good shopping experience. The place has a decent coffee shop and a restaurant that has recently outgrown its little corner roof space in the main shed and moved to a mezzanine floor in a new purpose built barn across the field.

But today it's not the restaurant, the coffee shop, the converted barn, the awesome bridge or even the fridges packed with tubs of taramasalata that I'm here to see. Under the restaurant in the new barn are a series of dinky commercial kitchens. And tucked into one among shelves stacked high with tubs of spices and powders, and surrounded by empty glass bottles, jars and food packaging, sits the Red Hot Chilli Fella.

Andy Roshay describes himself as a bit of a mad professor when it comes to chillies and spices. He likes to throw a few things together in his lab to see how they work. Some come off and become his leading food products: sauces, jams, ketchups, mixes, rubs and even chilli flavoured liqueurs. Red Hot Chilli Fella is one of the best known names on the local chilli scene, with Andy's products selling well in delis, at food and chilli festivals, at East Anglian market town stalls, and over the internet.

Today the mad professor is far from crazy looking. He's a silver haired, softly spoken fortysomething from Hartlepool, dressed in a smart black chef's uniform, and he's experimenting with new flavourings for one of his leading products: spiced chocolate. Every sorcerer needs an apprentice and today that apprentice is me. We're going to be making pepper chocolate together. I can't wait to sink my teeth in and it isn't long until I get the chance. I've barely pulled my apron on before Andy is handing me a slab of chocolate he'd made the day before: sea salt and lime with whole red peppercorns. The pepper is doused liberally in the chocolate, the corns bubbling crimson over the surface of the bar. Creamy melt meets peppery sting, with the salt emphasising the richness of the citrusy chocolate that surrounds it.

"I'm not so sure," he says. "Too much salt. More lime. It does look good though."

After travelling around the world spending months away from home, Andy felt he'd missed the first seven years of his son's life. He didn't want to miss the next seven. This kitchen is the result. From photography assignments across Latin America, Andy had acquired and then returned with a love of hot foods, particularly the amazing variety of fresh and dried chillies he'd discovered in Guatemala and Mexico. Twenty years ago, home cooks and even restaurant chefs had barely even heard of the chilli. Celebrity chefs had not yet been invented. Andy brought back his own stash of dried and powdered chillies to use in his own cooking, but quickly ran out.

"The only place I could get the kind of chillies I was used to was to go to a shop in London on Portobello Road where the chillies I wanted cost an arm and a leg."

Andy started looking around for ways to import chillies for his own use, but also started selling his home invented chilli products – jams, curry blends and meat rubs – from a basket on the bar of his local pub. The pub loved his Cheeky Mango Chutney so much they began buying it in bulk from him. Andy also started selling from a market stall in Colchester. He met other chilli enthusiasts and started asking customers what flavours they'd like to taste.

Andy started his business after years working first as a professional photographer, then as chief executive of a local media company. Like the red pepper chocolate bar, the visual aesthetic of his final products shows his background in the visual arts. A bubbling pot on his kitchen stove in 2010 turned into a mini-kitchen in his garden shed by 2012 and Andy packed in his old job. The following year he moved into Suffolk Food Hall, giving him space and inspiration to start experimenting for real.

My own experience of cooking with chocolate extends to melting down bars of Tesco cooking chocolate and smearing them into cornflakes before letting my kids lick the bowl. So

I'm a little surprised when Andy presents me with what appear to be chunks of dirty white chalk from the fridge.

"This is pure cacao butter made from the oil of cacao beans, and this," he says, pulling out a bag of delicate light brown powder, "is pure raw organic cacao solids. It has to be kept at below room temperature, so it doesn't all stick together."

Cacao butter makes up about half of the fist sized cacao beans that chocolate comes from. The butter is essentially a fat which melts at just above room temperature. Cacao beans are fermented and roasted to extract the butter, and what remains – with the gunk and husk removed – is ground into a fine powder to produce cacao solids. In Andy's kitchen we're putting the two back together, along with a natural sweetener, to create silky smooth chocolate. It seems we're not making cornflake cakes for the school fête. These will be high-end artisan spiced chocolate bars, retailing at £5 each.

And they will sell. Chilli chocolate is big news in Britain, and every chilli product seller has their own version. But we're far from the first to mix chocolate and chilli. The native people of Latin America have been consuming chocolate as a drink for 4,000 years and there's evidence that the Mayans were drinking chocolate and chilli together at least 3,000 years ago. They even had their own cacao god. The drink was certainly widespread by the time the Incas dominated parts of Latin America for much of the fifteenth and sixteenth centuries. Brits, however, can at least claim the invention of the chocolate bar. Joseph Fry of Fry's Turkish Delight fame created the first marketable one in 1847. By 1873 the Frys were selling that great British gift to the world: the chocolate Easter egg.

Andy puts the chalky lumps into a silver mixing bowl and places it over a pan of hot water. It immediately starts to leach oil and I give it a gentle stir, smelling the buttery but bitter chocolate waft up as it melts. It's a process that has to be slow so Andy takes the opportunity to show me around his kitchen. Stacked against the walls are towers of plastic tubs marked with the names of spices: cinnamon, mango powder, yellow mustard, paprika noble, green cardamom; and rows upon rows of dried and powdered chillies.

Andy plucks a tub marked Szechuan Pepper from the shelf, snaps open the lid and holds it up to my nose. It has an earthy and tangy smell. He takes a few peppercorns and crunches them between his teeth so I do the same.

"Szechuan isn't strictly a chilli, it's a berry, but it's exactly right for what we're making today."

He then offers me berbere spice, a mix so strong I jerk my head back from the tub. He's not surprised: this is the stuff that Ethiopian nomads would smear on the goat meat they dragged around the hot desert to disguise the rotting rancid taste. Soon Andy has me sticking my nose into boxes of spice and is holding up dried chillies for me to sniff. He pulls out a chocolate-brown dried and wrinkled fruit, the size of a large tomato. It's a Chipotle chilli. Andy pronounces it *chip-ot-lee*, not *chip-bottle* which is how I've always read it. Chipotle is the name generally used for any kind of smoked and dried chilli, but strictly speaking – says Andy, and he should know – it's a smoked Jalapeño pepper. He pronounces that with a *jal* rather than the expected guttural *khal* I've always used when ordering pizza.

Over the next few months, I am to hear all kinds of pronunciations of all kinds of chillies, but I don't know this yet so I decide to follow the master's voice. He also offers me a smoked and dried Naga to sniff; as well as a Poblano chilli which is called Ancho in its dried form and has a lovely glossy, chocolaty sheen.

"They're beautiful things," he says wistfully. "Just beautiful."

Andy then stuffs under my nose the plump squatness of a smoked Habanero 7 chilli. He tells me it was developed in the Caribbean and is a relative of the better known Scotch Bonnet. It is so called because the chilli is so strong you can flavour seven pots of Jamaican stew with a single fruit.

"You prick it with a needle and drop it into each pot for a while. But you have to remember to take it out, so no-one gets a nasty surprise."

The talk of heat prompts the Red Hot Chilli Fella to spring into action again. As well as learning about chilli chocolate this is what I've really come for: tasting. Andy pulls bottles and jars off shelves and lines them up on the brushed steel bench before me.

First up is his raspberry, lime and chilli jam. It's sugary and slightly acidic from the lime, with a deep but mild chilli aftertaste in the throat. Perfect for a pimped-up cream tea, if you're of the chilli persuasion, though I suspect few in the chilli world spend their afternoons eating scones and drinking tea from quaint china cups. I then taste the jar that started it all: Cheeky Mango Pickle. It's soft and seedy, with a much stronger but later burn than the jam. There's none of the sharp bitterness of the mango chutney I've heaped on papadums in Indian restaurants. This is smoother and more refined.

"And this Oh My God chilli sauce is one of my best sellers," says Andy. It's made with dried and smoked Naga chillies, which does indeed make me think: "Oh my God, wasn't Naga once the hottest chilli on Earth? Can I really take this?" But the flavour is actually rich and tastes like a good barbecue smells, backed up by an incredible but certainly not inedible heat. Nevertheless, I'm starting to sweat now. Friends laugh about how much I sweat when I eat chilli, as if I can't take it. But sweating on the face, chest and neck are natural reflexes to burning sensations in the mouth from the chemicals in chillies. Meanwhile, the stomach doesn't actually absorb much of the stuff that makes chillies hot.

Andy hands me a wooden tea stirrer which indicates there'll be no more teaspoon tasting and we should proceed gently from here. He made a small batch of his Suffolk Sauce to celebrate moving into the new kitchen. It's brewed using a grilled red pepper and tomato base, then spiced with fresh Scorpion chillies. "The Scorpion is very new," he says as I put the spatula into my mouth and take a suck. "And very, very hot."

First I taste the freshness of the fruit. Following so quickly on the heels of Oh My God, it's the first time I've been able to distinguish between dried and fresh chillies in a sauce. But then the heat kicks in. My throat begins to feel scorched and my tongue is tingling. But despite being far hotter than the Oh My God, I prefer this because of the fruitier taste. I sweat some more.

Andy places a small cup of milk on the table then unscrews the lid from a small test tube sized glass bottle. The liquid inside is iodine-orange and Andy scrapes a few drops from the lid onto a spatula. "Now, don't suck it. Just touch it on the tip of your tongue."

Immediately, I feel an incredible burn across the front of my mouth that quickly washes around as my saliva reflexes try to get rid of the fire. I swallow and the action turns into uncontrollable hiccups. Andy smiles and I notice he's not trying the brew for himself.

"This isn't a sauce, it's just a pure chilli extract. You'd only use a drop for flavouring, you'd never taste it neat like that." He hands over the milk and offers me a paper towel to wipe away the sweat streaming into my eyes.

"Thanks," I manage to croak. There's no flavour to describe, just intense burn that seems in no rush to go away. He turns back to the cacao lumps which are now just about melted into a thick, silky gloop. I take the opportunity to collect myself. I actually need the toilet, but I'm afraid to say so in case Andy thinks I'm going to throw up or to wash his painstakingly brewed sauces out of my mouth. I stay put and try to keep a smile on my face.

A few minutes later the hiccups have died down and I'm ready to join Andy at his stove again. He gently folds the pure cacao solids into the melted cacao butter and ends up with a pleasingly stiff deep brown goo. He thins it with a good few glugs of thick agave syrup, a natural sweetener. He tells me it's packed with good stuff like antioxidants. I steal a sticky finger worth from a dribble down the side of the bottle. It's like a thin honey, fresh and grassy.

Andy uses a pestle and mortar to crush the Szechuan pepper, which he's lightly fried to take out any remaining moisture. With some dried strawberry shavings, he adds the pepper to the mix and gently stirs it all in. It's ready for the moulds which he's lined up on another bench. I love the sight of the chocolate as it thickly folds itself out of the bowl and into the moulds, releasing a gorgeous waft in my direction.

We now have to wait for the chocolate to cool, which gives me an opportunity to ask Andy why he would give up his job to do this for a living. He leads me outside and indicates the panorama of the River Orwell, the estuary beyond and the smooth curves of the bridge as it feeds into the steep banks either side. It looks as if the bridge has been there for thousands of years and is a view that says satisfaction, a slow pace of life.

His dad was a chef and Andy was always in and out of his kitchen when he was cooking at home. When Andy returned from Latin America with all these new flavours, British cuisine was in an early eighties gutter where a chunk of pineapple, a fan of melon slices or a bowl of prawn cocktail was still considered edgy. But now, he says, something really exciting is happening in British cooking. Spain, Italy, France – they've all been famed for their food, but they don't have the variety we have.

"How many Spanish families are eating home-made Chinese food one night, home-made curry the next? Every TV chef is using chillies, the supermarkets are stocking different varieties, we've developed our tastes and we're being more adventurous. I love being part of that."

Andy is clearly no hot sauce brewer for its own sake. He doesn't look down on producers that try to make the most head-banging sauce, but that's not what his cooking is about. This is gastronomy and it shows. Andy gets excited about the possibilities in a handful of spice. He's keen to try a little of this and a little of that to make his products work. He's raising wasabi plants on his kitchen windowsill just to see what he can do with the ginger-like rhizome, which is growing in the soil beneath. Wasabi can be as hot as some of the hottest chillies, he says, and gets up your nose like a very pungent English mustard. He says if people can be persuaded to try new and unexpected flavours, they can often catch on. The secret is using really good ingredients, treating them with care, being passionate and getting right up close to the people who are tasting what you produce. They'll tell you what they like and what you should be trying to create next.

"I was doing a catering gig for a fortieth birthday party

the other day and the host was taking me around the tables introducing me as a professional chef. It was if I was some famous personality. It gave me a real buzz and reminded me why I do this."

"But what if a Sainsbury's or a Tesco came knocking, and wanted you to supply them thousands of jars of sauce or slabs of chocolate every month?" I ask.

Andy looks out over the river again and says simply: "I'd tell them: on your bike. For the cost they'd want it, in those quantities, you couldn't get the quality of product I want to produce. You can have too much of a good thing."

There's a knock at the door and in pops Dave who owns a sweet shop down the coast. He's come to visit the Outrageous Cake Company who have a kitchen a few doors down. But he's been attracted into the Red Hot Chilli Fella unit by the display of sauces and chillies and the huge sparkling silver paella dish in the window. Andy offers him a selection of chocolate to taste and they speak authoritatively – Dave in his gruff Essex accent, Andy in his softer northern one – about sweets and flavours, and what would and wouldn't work in a seaside town sweet shop. Dave thinks the salt and red peppercorn might be a bit adventurous for his customers, but definitely feels he can sell a dozen or more bars a week of a more traditional chilli variety. It's a window onto the community of small, specialist and artisan food suppliers these units were set up to support.

"We're developing five new flavours right now," Andy tells Dave. His 'we' indicates me, as if I'm a member of his gastronomical team. I try to look busy and expert with my notebook as if I'm jotting down tasting notes for our latest invention. "When we're done I'll get some over to you to taste."

The two shake hands, Dave goes on his way and I

suddenly feel the pressure. The chocolate we've developed that morning could be the next big thing in Clacton. This is the moment of truth. Andy taps a bar of our Szechuan and strawberry chocolate out of its mould, snaps off a row and hands it to me: "That, my friend, is chocolate."

And it is. Proper chocolate. Silky as it melts, the chocolate is rich and dark with a tang from the strawberry. I expected to be overpowered by the Szechuan, but Andy agrees that though a little peppery it's not quite enough. When you're selling artisan chocolate bars at £5 a piece, there's no room for a mere strawberry flavoured bar, however rich. It appears Clacton will have to wait, but Andy is already considering what to add to bring the pepper out. Perhaps a splash of something citrusy. He's not disappointed, he's already excited about trying something else.

Perhaps to lighten my spirits, he pulls a tall twisted pyramid bottle off the shelf. It's limoncello, the Italian after dinner liqueur. We pour a tasting-cup each and savour its light and fruity lemonyness which is followed up by a not inconsiderable – but certainly not unwelcome – burn from the Habanero oil he's infused. Andy packs up a bar of our chocolate into a gold gift box and presents it to me. Then suddenly something occurs to him. He moves across the kitchen again.

"Each year I brew a special sauce which I present to my clients as a thank-you for their business. This year's was a chutney made with eighty percent Maruga Scorpion chillies, pepper, fenugreek, spinach, a whole load of spices, all marinaded in oil. I've got a half finished jar of it left. It's a real beauty."

We both taste the chutney and the reaction is immediate. It's deliciously varied in taste, a little onion, a little pepper, you can taste the roasted bitterness of the fenugreek, but the heat has us both hiccuping and I'm spluttering with a deep guttural cough. "Wow! That's much hotter than it was a few months ago," says Andy.

Now he's coughing as much as me and reaching for a drink. He has been bested by his own special sauce. My endorphins kick in as the heat chemicals hit my immune system, offering a full body rush. The sauce is so tasty and smoky I can't help but try a little bit more. I'm afraid the rough bittiness of the chutney might get stuck in my teeth and leave me with mouth burn for the rest of the afternoon, but I don't care. This is what I've been looking for. A mix of great taste and feel-good rush that lasts. And has you uncontrollably crying out for more.

As I cycle the 25 or so miles back to Colchester, I stop halfway to refuel, having eaten little but chilli sauce and chocolate all morning. I order beans on toast. But no matter how much brown sauce I heap on top, there's something missing. I know what I'm really craving. Just another dash or two of that Maruga sauce... followed by a little Szechuan and strawberry chocolate.

To be honest, I am perhaps the world's most unlikely chillihead. Hold your nose now great and the good of Chilli Britain, but I'm vegetarian. Yes, all that sales patter about your chilli sauce being a perfect accompaniment to barbecue-grilled meats or as the base for a beef curry just doesn't ring my bell. I don't salivate over a chicken or lamb vindaloo. A Thai prawn curry isn't quite my cup of jasmine tea either.

And talking of drink. Well, I don't. Now I know there's nothing that washes down a hot (vegetarian) chilli and rice or a super hot Indian than a pint of near freezing lager. I know that a strong, chocolaty real ale, served at room temperature, complements the warmth in any hot dish. I know that a glass of chilled Chianti is a perfect companion to a rich chilli and tomato penne all'Arrabbiatta. There's nothing I used to love more than these combinations. But these days I don't have much of a choice. That's because of the medication. I live on a drugs cocktail that would put Pete Doherty to shame and my tablets clearly state they shouldn't be mixed with alcohol.

Because there's another thing that ought to be standing in the way of my chilli eating (but doesn't). I have a mild form of epilepsy. Mini-seizures that seemingly – though we're not quite sure – can be brought on by overstimulation. Too much coffee, hormones generated by very strenuous exercise, endorphins naturally released by the body from eating hot and spicy foods. My tendency to have mild epileptic seizures also means I can't drive, at least not on the motorway. That means my journey around Chilli Britain is to be conducted mainly by train, bicycle and bus. But a slow public transport meander across England, Scotland and Wales in search of hot flavours sounds – to this vegetarian epileptic teetotaller at least – like the perfect way to spend a few months.

And there is just one more thing I maybe should mention. I have a stomach ulcer. One that was so crippling when it first made itself known that I was crawling on hands and knees around the living room for eight hours, before eventually heading for A&E. It doesn't take a genius to work out that possibly, just maybe, eating large quantities of strongly spiced food, or even chillies in their glorious naked rawness, isn't necessarily the best thing for someone with a stomach ulcer of this severity. It's an old wives' tale that hot food can *cause* ulcers, but chillies can aggravate them once they're there. So I kept my penchant for chilli a bit quiet from the A&E doctor as he was busy looking for a vein to pump painkiller directly into my bloodstream.

In short, I'm a bit of a wrong-un when it comes to sporting a solid constitution. But I love public transport, don't mind alcohol-free beer and am even partial to Quorn. Stop eating chillies? No way. I like a chilli, I love chilli sauce, I like growing chillies, I like talking about chillies and as I'm discovering right this minute I like writing about chillies. With the help of my prescription for Lansoprazole gastric pills, I shall not be defeated. So with all these provisos noted and digested, let us continue.

Unfinished business

FIRST, WARM YOUR compost.

It's a cold Sunday afternoon in mid-February and there's a gale blowing outside. I'm shivering in the conservatory as trees rock outside and threaten to drop onto the polycarbonate roof above me. Three fruit trees already came down in the winds last night, a couple more look like they're on the way. The garden is flooded, as is most of the south of England. Yet, surrounded by glass that looks like it could shatter any moment, I'm in Mexico. Or at least I'm pretending to be.

I'm determined to get it right this time. On Saturday I could hardly contain my excitement as the package from Simpson's Seeds dropped onto the doormat. Carefully – there are fragile goods inside – I tear open the package and there they are. Sitting in tiny white envelopes like neatly labelled pouches of diamonds. My chilli seeds. A handful of wonderful potential. The beginnings of this year's crop.

Like a croupier, I fan out the envelopes one by one on the table, reading the labels with welling excitement. Friar's Hat, Joe's Long Cayenne, Lemon Drop, Purple Tiger, Red Missile, Etna, Masquerade, Prairie Fire, Vampire, Sweet Pepper Mohawk, Sweet Pepper Sunshine and Habanero 7.

Ah, Habanero 7. Me and Habanero 7, we have unfinished business. For three years now I've been trying to grow chillies on my conservatory windowsill. Year one started with just a couple of plugs I'd picked up from B&Q.

The next year I went crazy and bought some seeds. Most did eventually sprout but then didn't do that much of interest. Last year was different. I was given a propagator for my birthday. I carefully, lovingly selected the seeds from the catalogue, choosing which to order based on the delectable descriptions it offered.

Joe's Long Cayenne: "the pods dry well and make a fine, hot paprika". Lemon Drop offers "bright yellow chillies, with a strong lemon flavour to them". Friar's Hat is "much admired for its striking appearance, slow to mature but worth it". Masquerade "starts purple then turns yellow, orange and finally red". Etna, "a very hot compact ornamental". And Habanero 7: "pale green fruit mature to bright red, wrinkled in appearance, handle with care".

"I'm going to make an exhibition," I told my wife. "You know, a talking point. A talking point you can eat." The idea was to start growing a mix of chillies that would not only satiate my desire for something hot and provide an ingredient for meals, but would have guests gasping in admiration. A pristine, varied and colourful collection of chilli plants, arranged in neat little rows on the conservatory shelves. All in matching pots with little wooden labels, the chilli's name written out in swirling letters.

"Wow," they'd say. "I didn't know you were green fingered. What a display! What variety! What colour! Please talk to me in obsessive encyclopaedic detail all about the different varieties and their culinary properties." Of course, what they actually said was: "Oh, are you growing peppers?" Then they'd carry on with their conversation as if I hadn't spent months carefully nurturing and raising, watering and watching as my chilli collection bore fruit. But last year, I didn't do too badly. By luck or by accident, last year's seeds gradually became chilli seedlings. My chilli seedlings became little green and purple plants. Then those plants bore a few fruit, and I harvested them and – oh joy! – I tasted them and thus my life was fulfilled.

Actually, it wasn't as easy or successful as that. Some of my chillies had to be dragged into maturity like recalcitrant teenagers, all spindly and limp like they couldn't be bothered. Others remained stubby and broad, like the fat kid at the back of the class. There were a few times when I'd, you know, forgotten that plants needed watering for a week (OK, maybe two). Then there were a couple of occasions when I'd near drowned them, water spilling over the sides of the pot, trickling down onto the conservatory shelves and then onto the floor. But they all fruited. Some were probably as hot as they were supposed to be, most didn't have the heat I'd been promised. Some had only a few crinkled chillies on them, while others grew but then rotted on the stems.

Anyway, come late summer there *was* a display of sorts. A riot of colour and height, of green and purple leaves. There was only a dusting of nasty little black flies flitting from the soil and determined greenfly tucking themselves into the crevices where the branches met the stalks. I had successfully grown a wonderful exhibition. An exhibition that you could eat.

All apart from Habanero 7. It was supposed to be the cream of my crop. The hottest chilli I was growing. The talking point of talking points. The exhibition plant you could eat, but only if you had the stomach for it. Habanero 7 was to be the one my friends would gather round in awe and amazement. They'd be scared to touch a fruit in case it leaked heat onto their fingers and they couldn't go to the toilet for a week.

Yet despite my best efforts, Habanero 7 was the runt of the litter. Even from germination, it took an age to show itself and then when it did eventually poke a sprout above the compost, it didn't like what it found there. Cold, grey British weather. Only the occasional hot day magnifying the conservatory into a stifling sauna by its double glazing. Reluctantly, painfully, Habanero 7 did gradually put on weight and height. Moodily it threw out a few branches here and there, topping them with leaves like it was an obligation rather than what a plant is supposed to do. But Habanero 7 remained barren. Not a flower, not a bud. And definitely no hot Habanero 7 chilli peppers.

I'd told Andy Roshay about my Habanero trouble, and he gave me a sympathetic look. "Yes, they are very difficult to grow because they just need so much heat and light." He made me feel a bit better about my failure. "Only a few farms managed to grow them at all last year because the summer was so poor." I then felt bad again, because if the pros can't coax a Habanero into life, what chance do I have?

Like I say, unfinished business. But this year, I'm determined. This year there will be light. There will be watering in the correct proportions. There will be no neglect. No destructive access allowed to my children. No cold spells or sauna hot days capitulated to. For every one of my chillies this year – for the Lemon Drops and Etnas, for the Friar's Hats and the Cayennes, even for the leftovers of the packet of old B&Q seeds simply labelled 'chillies', and especially for Habanero 7 – I'm going to be like a loving father. It's going to be forensic, scientific. I'm going to tend them lovingly, bringing each of them up to make the best edible exhibition the great Essex Bungalow Conservatory has ever known. I'm going to respect them so much they shall be referred to and written about henceforth with a capital letter. All chillies will be much too special to begin with a mere lower case. I check my neatly written notes from a YouTube video again.

First, warm your compost. If you want your chillies to have the very best start the seeds must be sown into warm compost, not mashed into handfuls of cold dirt grabbed from a plastic growbag. Before you even take your seeds out of the packet the compost needs loving care.

But what does 'warm your compost' even mean? The microwave? Ladle heaps of compost into a huge pan and stir through like porridge? I have a large propagator given to me by mum after she'd been informed last birthday that my chilli interest was entering new dimensions. I put the propagator on to warm, while I set about getting the compost ready.

I've opted for single cell seed trays and I slowly sprinkle in compost from the bag. It was recommended by the professional compost consultant at the local garden centre (or at least, the teenager who told me: "Er, just any compost really" and pointed to a big pile on offer the garden centre was clearly trying to get rid of).

This is where I hit my first problem. I want to create a moist bed of compost on which I can gently rest my seeds and then I'll sprinkle more compost over the top. But if I'm to warm my compost first, how's that going to happen? Won't I have to sprinkle the seeds onto the compost I've carefully warmed only to then contaminate their cosiness with the cold compost I've reached out of the bag?

I lay my plug tray out on the conservatory table, fill each little cell with compost and decide that before warming, the soil could do with a little drink. OK, my notes don't say that but everything living needs water doesn't it? I go to the kitchen in search of a jug and can only find a delicate ceramic one which my wife would call precious but for my purpose I'll call functional. Now what? Hot water? Cold?

This is getting complicated and I wish I'd made better notes. I opt for the in-between, mixing the two into lukewarm and head back to the conservatory.

Gently I pour a little into each cell and watch as the dry compost comes up to greet the water with a welcome rise in the middle. It then settles down again with a contented sigh. It's only as I'm filling cell seventeen that I notice the brown water leaking out of the bottom of the seed tray, staining the wooden table and dripping onto the floor below. Quickly I transfer the seed trays into the propagator and run to the kitchen for a tea towel. And while in the kitchen I spy a tupperware bowl. The answer to my topping-soil warming problem becomes altogether clearer.

Back in the conservatory, with the muddy water just about mopped up, I fill the tupperware with more compost and place it on top of the seed tray. On goes the propagator lid and in goes the electric plug. "I'll just give that an hour or two," I say as if I'm a TV gardener, "and it'll be ready for the seeds." Only, when I come back to them a couple of hours later nothing's happened. No condensation, no heat. I've forgotten to turn on the switch, it's already dark and nearly time to put the kids to bed. No matter. I switch the propagator on and decide to leave it overnight. The soil will be good and warm by the time I come back in the morning. With everything set up, I'm dying to show someone. The kids are bouncing on the sofa, clearly a much more interesting activity than looking at soil. So I drag my wife into the conservatory.

"Look," I say proudly.

"Er, what's with the tupperware bowl?"

"Oh, you have to warm the compost," I say. The expert.

"Yes, you've told me that a dozen times. I mean, why have you filled our kids' lunch box with soil?"

"Well, you have to warm the compost to sprinkle on top too." She shakes her head. Then she spots the big brown water stain on the dining table. She walks away.

The next morning, with kids packed off to school, it's time for seed sowing. I spread myself across the kitchen table with my neat pile of twelve seed packets, the propagator, the bowl of top soil and a sheet of graph paper all laid out in a tidy row. Yes, of course graph paper. If I'm to keep track of which seeds are planted into which cells, I need to create a record. The two trays are four by six cells each, perfect for my purposes. So I draw a little plan of the trays on the graph paper, 24 separate squares. Some might call this obsessive but I'm just getting started.

Gently, I take each seed packet, tear open the top and shake out four seeds from each. The differences between the seeds are stunning and satisfying. "You can tell the subtle differences even at this stage," I whisper to myself as if I'm on *Gardeners' Question Time* (but don't want to be heard by my wife). "And those differences will grow to show themselves first in the leaves, then into the fruits themselves, and oh, the taste sensations and subtle differences when those fruit are picked. Absolute heaven." The audience applauds and people shake their heads in wonder at my touching narrative.

The beautifully named Sweet Pepper Sunshine has bright little yellow points of seeds, delicate to the touch. Purple Tiger's seeds already live up to their name with a little hue of crimson around the outside. The Lemon Drop's seeds are satisfyingly lemon coloured and you can almost smell the citrus. Habanero 7. Well, those plain straw coloured circles just sit there unremarkable and challenging, as if to say "come on then, give us your best shot."

I gently drop one seed into the centre of each tray, one

variety per line of four. I note its name on each row on my graph paper. Then I use a spoon to sprinkle the compost from the tupperware on top. I now realise how ridiculous I look, bent over a seed tray with a spoon full of soil and a tupperware bowl of compost. My wife takes a photo or two, as if we'll look back on this scene in a few years' time and reminisce on how embarrassing beginnings can mature into something so wonderful. Or at least they'll be something she can show to the men in white coats when they cart me away when I'm spending my days doing nothing but staring blankly into a propagator.

The next question is where to put the propagator while the seeds germinate. I can't leave the whole thing in the conservatory. It has the requisite light but in February with a gale still blowing outside, it's not necessarily the best place to start off the plants. Habanero 7 taught me that lesson last year. Anyway, the propagator will have to work harder in the cold conservatory and frankly I'm a bit too tight to foot the larger electricity bill.

I consult my notes: seeds must be kept warm in a propagator, around 24 degrees, then in a sunny position as shoots begin to show. The obvious choice is our bedroom. There's loads of light because it's south facing, it's warm and – except at about 6.30 every morning and after bath time – it's the place our kids are least likely to wreak their havoc. I'm reminded of the books we read during my wife's pregnancy. Baby should sleep in the parents' bedroom for the first six months, in case of difficulties and so they can be closely nurtured and a strong bond can be created.

Exactly. And I am just about to express the same to Sarah when I catch myself. I'm not sure how receptive she'll be to the comparison between a tray of soil and the two newborns she spent the combined total of about 48 hours giving birth to. Instead I settle for the spare room. It's exactly where I'd have ended up myself if I'd pushed the idea of our own bedroom too hard. There's nowhere near enough sun but the little guys haven't germinated yet. Maybe when they do start to show leaves my wife will start to bond with them too. Then maybe she'll allow them in. Next to our bed.

In the spare room there's no windowsill or shelf to speak of, but the floor is too vulnerable to four- and six-year-old shenanigans. They're bound to try to play with it, or fall on it, or knock it over, or touch it or breathe near it. I drag in a chair, stick the propagator on it, press the plug into the socket (switching it on this time) and kiss my little babies goodnight. I mean, I pat the propagator to make sure it's warming up and leave the room. Hoping my pre-warmed compost will work its magic.

Chillies and sweet peppers are from the family of plants called *solanaceae*, which includes tomato, aubergine and, less obviously, potato and tobacco.

There are actually around twenty different root species of chilli, scientifically known as *capsicum*, all with their own subspecies. But five main root species are in widespread cultivation. The *capsicum chinense* are the bulbous and scorchingly hot peppers which include the Scotch Bonnet and Habanero. (They're called *chinense* because of a balls-up in 1776 by the Dutch botanist Nikolaus von Jacquin who thought they originated in China.) The *capsicum frutescens* produce shedloads of fruits, usually pointing upwards like little lanterns, and include the Birds Eye chilli (Piri Piri) and Tabasco.

In Europe, we're most likely to encounter *capsicum annum*

in our day-to-day cooking and eating. They're the rounded, easier-to-grow varieties and include what we in the UK generally call 'peppers': the fat and round red, green and yellow Sweet (or Bell) Peppers that have no heat at all and that we stick in stir-frys or stuff with rice. But *annum* also includes the hotter Jalapeño chilli, the much hotter Prairie Fire and the Spanish tapas chilli Padron. Around one in eight Padrons is super hot; when you eat a *tapa* of the delicious sea-salted fried Pimientos de Padrón in a Spanish bar you never quite know what you're going to get. Lesser known are the *capsicum baccatum*, including the weirdly shaped Bishop's Crown variety and the Lemon Drop; and *capsicum pubescens* which – snigger – tend to have hairy leaves and stems. They often have purplish leaves and some fruits grow darker rather than redder as they ripen.

But to the untrained eye at least identifying a chilli's heritage isn't easy because they cross-pollinate so readily. Stick three, or in my case twelve, varieties in a conservatory, open the windows to introduce some bugs or a breeze and you never quite know what seeds they'll produce. Perhaps some amazing new super hot strain. Perhaps something so genetically buggered it won't even grow.

8th March – I come back from my chocolate making day with the Red Hot Chilli Fella to find shoots. I have shoots! They're shy, but tiny little two-leaf shoots are appearing all over my seed tray. There's nothing from Sweet Pepper Mohawk or Purple Tiger yet and Habanero 7 sits resolutely below the soil. But that's cool. I know Habanero 7 likes to take its time. But for each of the other seeds, we have growth in at least two cells. Etna has erupted in all four.

20th March – *My seedlings are putting on some weight now, with about half sporting more than two leaves. Masquerade leads by a long way, with all four cells sprouting into tiny many leaved plants. Sweet Pepper Sunshine is doing beautiful things too and most of the others are starting to spread their wings. Vampire, I'm liking your work. Beautiful, purple tinged leaves and stalks and growing at a cracking rate. My hard work and slightly obsessive bringing the propagator in at night, then putting it back into the conservatory during the day (every single day of the week), is beginning to really pay off.*

And yes, can it be? Yes, I do believe Habanero 7 has sprouted. Just a couple of cells have tiny leaves reaching above the soil, but they're definitely there. It's great to have got this far. Purple Tiger is struggling with only one seedling, but it's Sweet Pepper Mohawk I'm most worried about. There's nothing. I plan to keep a close eye.

Searching for Scoville

AN EMAIL PINGS into my inbox: "Hi Gideon. This week isn't good for me, but afterwards I don't think I have anything I can't work around. That's until the 20th when I'm talking at a carrot meeting."

Andrew Jukes is clearly a man with a wry sense of humour about his job. He's a crop scientist at Warwick University and has offered to show me the scientific process for measuring the heat of chillies and to let me watch him as he tests one of the dozens of chillies, chilli sauces or other chilli based products he gets sent every year. If you've got something hot and want to know exactly how hot it is, Andrew Jukes is the man to tell you.

But first I have to find him. Warwick University is not, as you might imagine, in Warwick. It's in Coventry. Or rather on the outskirts of Coventry, requiring a half-hour bus trip from city to campus. But the problem is this: when I get to Warwick University (in Coventry) I can't find the Crop Sciences department. After wandering around aimlessly for a while in the rain, I decide to make a stab in the dark and head to the department that sounds most similar – Life Sciences.

"Oh," says the receptionist with a puzzled look on her face as she pulls Andrew up on her computer. "You want Crop Sciences, not Life Sciences."

"That's right," I reply. Crops are a kind of life aren't they? "Can you point me in the right direction?"

"Oh, no," she says as if it's a crazy question, "it's Warwick University. But it's not here. It's in Warwick."

"Actually," she corrects herself, "it's in Wellsbourne. I suppose that's more like Stratford-upon-Avon. I'll do you a map. Where did you park your car?"

It turns out there is no shuttle bus between the two Warwick University campuses, neither of which are actually in Warwick. In fact, the Wellesbourne Crop Science department – sixteen miles away – isn't served by public transport at all. It's obvious, now I think about it, that the Crop Sciences department is buried deep in rural Warwickshire. You know, where all the farming and harvesting of crops takes place. Whatever, I'm going to be late for my meeting and am stranded in the wrong place without an easy way of getting to where I'm supposed to be.

Having already travelled by bike, train and bus for five hours, I'm not going to give up easily. I wander around the Warwick University (in Coventry) campus a little longer, wondering what to do next. I was just about to offer a student a tenner to borrow their bike – maybe an hour's ride at a fair pace? – when a bus turns up heading for 'Stratford, via Leamington Spa and Warwick' and I hop aboard. At least I'm out of the rain and will be heading in *kind of* the right direction. I can make a plan when I reach Stratford which, I'm informed by the driver, is just another hour's bus ride away. On the way, my smartphone has just enough battery left to enlighten me. If I jump off the bus as it passes a crucial roundabout a couple of miles out of Leamington Spa, I'll only be about five miles away from the rural campus.

And that's how I – a grown man of nearly forty – end up standing at the side of the A429 with my rucksack on my back, my thumb out and a desperate look on my face trying to cadge a lift off any passing driver. Like I'm a student. After ten minutes' wait a kind driver for the interestingly titled Whale Ale Company saves me from my roadside plight and plonks me at the front door of the Warwick University Crop Sciences department. If you're intending to travel there, then you should be aware it is neither in Warwick nor Coventry, nor for that matter in Stratford-upon-Avon or Leamington Spa. Go by car.

Actually, I would have liked to spend more time in Royal Leamington Spa, rather than just shooting through it on the number 16 bus looking for a roundabout at Junction 15 on the M40. The market town was one of the first provincial locations to have an Indian restaurant, which a visitor in 1975 suggested had led to "a level of luxury and extravagance to tempt the fate of Sodom and Gomorrah". Which seems a bit harsh for serving a lamb dopiaza with a side of pilau rice and a naan bread.

Even today, this relatively white town on the edge of the Black Country is regarded as one of the UK's pioneering centres for Asian cuisine. It's probably a legacy of the 1970s influx of Bangladeshi and Pakistani immigrants who came to join their families who had been working in the car, motorcycle and bicycle factories around Coventry since the 1950s. Leamington boasts a huge array of posh and not-so-posh curry houses, which must be a boon to the hundreds of Warwick undergrads who live there, as well as the more well-to-do country folk living in its rural surrounds.

It doesn't take long when I finally do meet Andy to realise his email about the carrot meeting wasn't a joke. Studying, researching, writing and talking about vegetables is pretty much what he gets up to every day.

"To be honest, I try to fit testing chillies around everything else I'm really supposed to be doing. I might be counting aphids on a lettuce one day, looking at a soil sterilising solution another, and every now and again I get a half-day when I'm doing nothing much and think: I'll get my chillies out."

There's no real element of humour in what I think is a very funny job. In fact, he seems quite surprised he's become the chilli heat expert. It's a calling he fell into by accident after the BBC's *Gardeners' World* called eight years ago asking if he would develop an accurate process for comparing their heat.

"I was expecting to show some researcher or producer how to do it and that would be that. But they came down with Monty Don and the rest and I had to give the results on television," he says. "It took all day and was really inconvenient."

Andy isn't a man particularly impressed with the glamour of the hottest chillies or the competition to breed the most brain busting fruits. For him it's all about the science and he doesn't see what all the fuss is about. There's a strict process he goes through. He gives a smile as he shows me the three sauces he's been sent that morning: Extreme Prejudice, Who Dares Burns and another mystery bottle marked only with an X in biro. I look at him questioningly.

"It looks like it's had its label ripped off," he says as if receiving top-secret mystery bottles of condiments is something he deals with all the time. The X could show that a sauce maker is working on a concoction so secretive even Andy can't know what's inside. Or it could be a competitor's sauce that the supplier wants to measure against their own. Or maybe they just haven't thought of a clever name or designed a killer label yet.

It turns out that in the world of chillies and chilli sauces there can be quite some competition between suppliers.

Breeding the hottest chillies and producing the most mind blowing sauce – and being able to tell your customers you have done it – gives you a significant edge over another supplier. For that reason, Andy has to be rather coy about what he says. When I ask him about the hottest products he's ever tested, he clams up and promises to send me a list.

"I wouldn't want to miss anything out or it to look like I'm showing favouritism. I have to be careful what I say and who I'm testing for. Some producers can be quite protective."

He does tell me that Sainsbury's have asked him to test their chillies to ensure there's consistency from one month to the next. Apparently, the supermarket gets complaints that the chillies they sell sometimes aren't hot enough. Which makes me think: what kind of person has enough time on their hands to write to a supermarket about the heat of chillies? And, anyway, you'd think it would be the other way up – when your usual mild chilli con carne has had the kids in tears, Granny's false teeth dropping out and even the dog whining from a dodgy tummy.

It's not just chillies and sauces Andy's tested. "People send me all kinds of things. I've done pizza, sausages, burgers, cocktails." He lets his guard down and smiles. "The cocktail was the most horrible thing I've ever come across. It was disgusting, a mix of vodka and chilli oil, but the oil sat on the top and who knows what was floating at the bottom."

"Did you taste it?"

"No! It smelled like the contents of an ash tray. It was extremely hot and I don't think they knew what else to do with it but send it to me."

I'm not sure what I expected from Andy's set-up. Perhaps an alchemist surrounded by bubbling cauldrons into which he'd throw handfuls of weird and wonderful chillies?

Little red beakers of sauce into which he'd dip chips or crisps, tasting them and then marking his estimation of their heat up on a wall chart? Warning labels on fridges, phials of black liquid marked with a skull and crossbones? One of those nuclear test stickers? But this is the chilli world stripped bare of its boasting and brashness. Andy likes hot food more than the average bloke but clearly doesn't go in for chilli craziness. What he likes most is the science.

"The process of testing is pretty boring really, and it's really quite simple," he says. What then follows is the most fascinating and complex bit of scientific testing I've ever encountered. Granted that isn't saying much. I don't think I've ever worn a white coat in my life.

We go into a real-life scientific laboratory, all test tubes, whirring machines, rows of strange bottles and posters of varieties of cabbage. Again I think the posters are ironic, but as I spy further posters for types of corn, bird species and – yes – carrots, I realise they're for real. Andy pulls out from a fridge a tiny phial marked 'H Naga' – another secret code? – and drop-pipettes a tiny quantity into another yet smaller phial. This is the concentrated chilli extract that has to be created before the testing begins. Andy dries a specific quantity of the chilli for hours in an oven at exactly eighty degrees centigrade, then powders it using a kitchen coffee grinder.

"We used to use a special technical grinder but the powder would come out so fine it got everywhere. You couldn't come back into the lab for hours and it would get all over your skin. The trick is not to get the powder onto your hands." He shakes his head. "That's when the trouble starts. This can be really unpleasant work."

Next he adds the ground-up chilli – or for that matter ground-up dried sauce, pizza or burger – and adds an exact quantity to ethanol, which he again heats for four hours until the concoction is well mixed. Then the ethanol is evaporated off to leave the extract.

"It's important that the process is the same for whatever I'm testing and each time I end up with exactly the same thing." He waves the little glass phial of chilli extract: "This."

We go over to a machine that looks like it's been mocked up from an old photocopier. For good measure it has a Hewlett Packard logo on the side. Here, finally, are my expected bulbous glass jars of potion: transparent acids and solvents, each with plastic tubes reaching far into the depths of one part or another of the photocopier.

Andy slides the chilli extract into a slot and presses a few keys on his laptop. After a reluctant warming-up a tiny mechanical hand pops out of the machine and grabs the sample. This is serious science, but I can't help but think of those claw-a-teddy arcade games you get at the seaside. It drops the phial somewhere deep in the machine and the testing has begun. A little whirring later and a graph begins to appear on the laptop screen. The machine has taken a tiny drop of the extract and is now busy doing yet more extracting and then stretching the compounds inside. Once separated, an ultraviolet light is shone through tiny drops of each compound to measure its density, creating little peaks on the graph.

"The chemicals that count in a chilli's heat are these," says Andy pointing to three peaks on the screen. Nordihydrocapsaicin, capsaicin and dihydrocapsaicin. Together, these chemicals are called capsaicinoids and are what give chillies their heat. The chemicals hit the pain receptors in different parts of the mouth and throat, making you feel a burning sensation. No actual burning takes place.

Capsaicin and dihydrocapsaicin are the biggest killers in terms of immediate heat, but another sneaky little one called homodihydrocapsaicin is responsible for a delayed heat that, once it comes in, is much harder to get rid of. Before the words get any longer we'd better move on.

"What about Scovilles?" I ask Andy. "I thought chilli heat was measured using the Scoville Scale."

"Ah," he says with a knowing look. "That's essentially a made-up measurement. No other fruit or vegetable has a separate scale like that. You don't get a scale for the amount of a particular enzyme in a tomato, do you?"

I thought the Scoville Scale was the biggest thing in chillies, chilli sauces, chilli growing and chilli eating, so what gives? In 1912 a chemist called Wilbur Scoville developed a less than complex way of measuring how hot chillies were: he and his mates tasted chilli extract in raw form, then progressively watered it down with sugar water until they could no longer detect a trace of heat. The dilution became the now famous Scoville Heat Unit (SHU). If he diluted the extract so it was one part chilli extract to 1,000 parts sugar water, then he'd get 1,000 on the Scoville Scale. If it's one part extract to 20,000 parts sugar water then it's 20,000 SHU. And so on.

No wonder Andy was dismissive of the decidedly non-scientific Scoville method. Different panel members would naturally have different tolerance for heat. And once Wilbur and his pals had downed who knows how much chilli-sugar-water cocktail, their ability to taste microscopic traces of heat would have burned out too. Let alone the problems of accurately reporting something as subjective as taste. So sometime in the 1970s serious scientists sat down and started carrying out a measuring process similar to what Andy had shown me. They tried as best they could to measure chillies already chalked up on the Scoville Scale. They mapped Scovilles to the actual parts-per-million of capsaicinoids in the extracts, and eventually came up with an equation to convert between the two.

"Actually, after around 650,000 Scovilles the comparison becomes very weak because that's about as hot as Scoville had ever tasted. Anything above this is extrapolation, which may or may not be accurate."

The super hot chillies around today couldn't have been tested by Scoville anyway, because they simply didn't exist back then. Like little fruity Frankensteins, we've been breeding and cross-breeding chillies for their heat only in more modern times. These freak chillies don't exist in the natural world. The hottest chilli ever recorded so far is the Carolina Reaper at around two million Scovilles. Andy says the hottest theoretically possible for a fresh fruit is around six million because chillies have so much other stuff to do than just be hot. If a chilli was entirely made of capsaicinoids and didn't have to do other stuff – things like reproduce and grow and produce sugars and consume energy – it would measure sixteen million SHU. Almost pure capsaicinoid extracts are on the market at that level and they're pretty intense.

We turn to the results of our test and Andy shows me a printout. The sample comes out at around 65,000 parts-per-million of the hot compounds that count. That means, he says, around six or seven percent of the dry chilli has gone into making it hot. Given the hottest possible for a fresh chilli is probably fifteen percent of its dried weight, that makes ours pretty hot indeed. Nearly a million on the Scoville Scale.

After all this testing, Andy leans in to reveal a few trade secrets of the chilli industry. First, when someone tells you their sauce is one million Scovilles they may sometimes be being a bit naughty. As if it's an offence against chemistry itself, he says they're likely to be talking about the heat of the chillies used in the sauce, rather than the sauce itself. The sauce is going to have tomato and sugars and salt and other flavourings in it and those dilute the heat of the chillies in the bottle. If the sauce was boiled down, ground and extracted in the way Andy and I have this afternoon, its results in Scovilles or parts-per-million would likely be nothing like the boast on the label.

He also reveals that even chillies from the same plant can vary widely in their heat. Just because one chilli has scored highly on Scoville doesn't mean every one of them will. Sometimes producers send him a single chilli, so he can't get a fair measure. Another shake of the head.

"It's not up to me to tell suppliers what to do, or how to grow hotter chillies or make hotter sauces," he says. "I just measure their chillies and give them their numbers."

Finally, he tells me that the heat of a chilli depends not only on its species or breeding. He estimates that at least half of the heat comes from being grown in the right conditions – warm, dry, good soil, plenty of light – and also depends on when it is picked. What he calls 'environmental factors' can change a chilli's heat two- or probably even ten-fold. Those growers who spend their time trying to cross-breed the hottest chillies to produce super hot chillies might better spend their time worrying about the time of picking, the soil, the amount of sunlight or any other of the umpteen factors affecting plant growth.

And Andy should know. After all, investigating the environmental factors that help fruit and vegetables to proliferate, as well as working with pesticides, complementary crops and other magic potions to make each crop grow better is his full time job. At which point I make my excuses, keenly aware I don't want to get all Monty Don on his busy schedule. But after thanking him for making the time, I do have just one question left.

"Do you know if there's a bus stop anywhere even close to here?"

Chilli Britain

No.	Symbol	Name	Scoville
1	Bp	Sweetbell	0k
2	Pi	Pimento	0k
3	Cy	Cherry	0k-0.5k
4	Pe	Pepperoncini	0.1k-0.5k
5	El	El-Paso	0.5k-0.7k
6	Sf	Santo Fe Grande	0.5k-0.75k
7	Co	Coronado	0.7k-1k
8	Es	Espanola	1k-2k
9	Po	Poblano	1k-2k
10	An	Ancho	1k-2k
11	Mu	Mulato	1k-2k
12	Pa	Pasilla	1k-2k
13	An	Anaheim	0.5k-2.5k
14	Sf	Sandia	0.5k-2.5k
15	Nu	NuMex big Jim	0.5k-2.5k
16	Ro	Rocotillo	1.5k-2.5k
17	Pu	Pulla	0.7k-3k
18	Mi	Mirasol	2.5k-5k
19	Gu	Guajilo	2.5k-5k
20	Ja	Jalapeno	2.5k-8k
21	Cp	Chipotle	5k-8k
22	Hw	Hot Wax	5k-10k
23	Py	Puya	5k-10k
24	Hi	Hidalgo	6k-17k
25	Se	Serrano	8k-22k
26	Ma	Manzano	12k-30k
27	Sh	Shipkas	12k-30k
28	Da	De Arbol	15k-30k
29	Jo	Jaloro	30k-50k
30	Aj	Aji	30k-50k
31	Ta	Tabasco	30k-50k
32	Ca	Cayenne	30k-50k
33	Sk	Santaka	40k-50k
34	Sc	Super Chile	40k-50k
35	Pq	Piquin	40k-58k
36	Ya	Yatsafusa	50k-75k
37	Ci	Chiltepin	60k-85k
38	Th	Thai	60k-85k
39	Tb	Tabiche	85k-115k
40	Ba	Bahamian	95k-100k
41	Cc	Carolina Cayenne	100k-125k
42	Ku	Kumataka	125k-150k
43	Jh	Jamaican Hot	100k-200k
44	Be	Birds Eye	100k-225k
45	Te	Tepin (Mild)	80k-240k
46	Dt	Devil Tongue	125k-325k
47	Fa	Fatalii	125k-325k
48	Oh	Orange Habanero	150k-325k
49	Sb	Scotch Bonnet	150k-325k
50	Ch	Chocolate Habanero	200k-325k
51	Rs	Red Savina Habanero	350k-577k
52	Bj	Bhut Jolokia	1m
53	Ts	Trinidad Scorpion	1.46m
54	Cr	Carolina Reaper	1.56m-2.2m

Walter Scoville in 1912 was far from the first European to have his fun with the chilli munching. Indeed, the Spanish and Portuguese in particular have been gnawing on the fiery beasts for 600 years. And that's a lot longer ago than the first branch of Nando's opened.

In 1492 the rather proud Italian-born but Spanish-sponsored explorer Christopher Columbus set off west from Spain in search of a sea route to Asia. We Europeans had been doing a roaring trade in spices and silk from India, China and the Middle East long before that, but he thought by going west by sea he'd find a shorter and less treacherous ocean route than going round the bottom of Africa.

Only problem was he bumped into America on the way. Actually, on the first voyage of four he bumped into the Caribbean islands. Whether he was fooling himself or just couldn't admit he'd got it wrong Columbus declared he'd reached India and named the islands the *Indies*. (Later, they were renamed the *West Indies* to distinguish from the *East Indies* which were the Pacific islands we now know as Indonesia.)

The native people he'd found in the West Indies, he named *indios* which is Spanish for *Indian*. They were nothing of the sort, being Latin American in descent. Anyway, he also discovered they had a penchant for growing and cooking with a fiery red fruit they called *aji*. Here comes another Columbus mistake: he reckoned the fruit was part of the pepper (think salt and pepper) family we were already bringing over by land and sea from Asia, so he called it *pepper*. Well, it is spicy isn't it?

It was chilli, but the name stuck. That's why chillies are

still known as peppers across much of Europe and why most of us in the UK often call them chilli peppers. On later voyages Columbus reached mainland Latin America (still not India then, Chris?) where he found other varieties of his *pepper,* along with other fruit and veg. Grumpy ten-year-olds forever pushing beans, sweetcorn and pumpkin around their plates have never forgiven him (though to give him his due, he also indirectly invented chips because he also brought back the potato).

Within fifty years, chillies had spread all over the world as Europeans continued their conquests and trade route expansion. The Africans, Thais, Chinese and Asians lapped up the new hot fruits the Europeans brought. They were already used to eating spicier foods like black and white pepper and ginger. The Spanish and Portuguese ended up with a taste for something a little hotter too.

But back in Britain we were a bit more coy. In fact, we much preferred to use them as pretty little ornamental plants. It was only in the late nineteenth century that the first British recipes using chillies emerged. So when we breathlessly talk about a brand new interest in chilli flavours in Britain, it's worth remembering we originally had our chance five hundred years ago and couldn't take the heat.

After my visit to Andrew Jukes and my own Columbus-like intrepid journey around Warwickshire, I eventually reach my dad's house in Wolverhampton.

When I arrive there (a mere three hour journey to go about 35 miles) he hands me a present. It's a packet of Scorpion chilli seeds and a packet of Bhut Jolokia seeds. I sow them both into warmed compost as soon as I get home the next day. A few days later, when Andy sends his list of the dozen hottest chillies he's ever measured, I'm just a little bit afraid to see them both on the list. The Viper strain of the Bhut Jolokia/Naga is the very top. It's going to be some rush if I can get those babies to fruit and have the guts to try them.

Chillies are hot because they contain capsaicinoids, and when those compounds hit the receptors in our mouth and throat they cause a burning sensation. Endorphins are produced by the brain to neutralise pain receptors, so the more pain we put ourselves through the more endorphins are released. And since endorphins and morphine are close cousins, it's no surprise that chilli freaks who eat the very hottest fruits report not only massive rushes but sometimes even hallucinations. Step aside acid, we're off our heads on Carolina Reaper. No wonder hot food sellers do so well at festivals.

But it's only the endorphin rush, not the capsaicin compounds, that's mildly addictive. In other words, chillies are probably no more addictive than the buzz of going for a run, riding a roller coaster, watching *The Exorcist* or having an orgasm. In fact, scientists are – somewhat ironically and surprisingly – messing around with capsaicinoids as a potential painkiller. The chemicals in chillies cause you pain, but the endorphins they release as a result have a painkilling effect. So they're trying to figure out how to get the same endorphin release without giving you the burn. A team at the University of Texas have also discovered capsaicin-like chemicals at sites where patients are experiencing pain, so they reckon blocking the production of these chemicals could also act as a painkiller.

Researchers are also using capsaicinoids to *intentionally* put people in pain just so they can test new painkilling patches on them. And finally, I kid you not, scientists have found that extract of Bhut Jolokia could be used to treat arthritis. And that smearing eight percent capsaicin cream on your skin helps with the pain of shingles. "Capsaicin, once applied to the skin, causes a brief initial sensitization followed by a prolonged desensitization of the local pain nerves," say the folks in the white coats. In other words, it hurts like hell before it numbs the pain.

But chillies have yet more uses, too. Chillies are also used for colouring food and even colouring birds. If I had to be an animal, I'd be a flamingo. Usually it's their diet of shrimp that makes them pink, but zoo flamingos don't have a ready supply. So they feed flamingos chillies instead to give their feathers a lovely puce tinge. I'm not suggesting you should give your kids handfuls of Piri Piri instead of stale bread to throw to the local ducks to see what happens. But theoretically it could turn the white ones light pink.

22nd March – A random sunny day and some of the edges of the leaves on Vampire, Joe's Long Cayenne and Etna have gone all grey and crispy. Strange, because they're not dried out. I consult my chilli growing bible which tells me my early seedlings have to be introduced to the sun very slowly. Just a few hours a day. I thought it was the more sun the better. But it seems the leaves need to slowly build up a waxy coating before they spend whole days in the sunshine. I've gone and scorched them. A quick internet search also advises me to try not to get the leaves wet when I water them. A little bead of water can act like a magnifying glass, burning the leaves just like you used to fry ants in the playground on a sunny day at school. Don't pretend you didn't. I decide to move the propagator out of direct sunlight and into a more shaded area of the conservatory.

24th March – No, no, no. Another random sunny day and my chillies are trapped in the conservatory with the windows closed while I'm out for the day. When I get back my inch high seedlings are sagging over with thirst. Some of the leaves have shrivelled up completely, exactly what my book says you should never let happen. It's 35 degrees in there. I think I caught them just in time. The soil is bone dry and leeches the water I offer, but it eventually takes on a little drink. By night-time the seedlings have started perking up again. A close call.

25th March – The very tiniest sprig of Sweet Pepper Mohawk has finally broken through. I knew you could do it.

26th March – Oh Sweet Pepper Mohawk, how have I wronged you? I thought the green shoots in one of your cells yesterday were early leaves breaking through, but a closer look revealed it was just a bit of grass.

5th April – We've been blessed with a windy, but very sunny and warm early April. And that means the seedlings have gone from strength to strength. Any time now, Masquerade and Vampire will be breaking for the border. There's not much room left for them under the propagator lid. All the other plants are looking really good too, only Sweet Pepper Mohawk is having none of it. I think it's a lost cause. I've taken to leaving the propagator lid off most days now, only replacing it at night. The warmth in the conservatory is more than enough. Plus, I'm told allowing a breeze to ruffle the plants a little helps them grow stronger stems.

Exploring the dark side

"THE VERY BEST thing you can do for yourself after you've swallowed a really hot chilli or chilli sauce is to purge as soon as possible."

"Purge," I say. "You mean, be sick?"

"Yeah, it's called the poke and puke. If you're going to take on heat in that quantity, you need to throw it up right away so you don't get stomach cramps. That's where the trouble starts, let alone when it gets down to your intestines."

I can't believe I've travelled for three hours to throw up in a stranger's house. Fifteen minutes before, as I cycled from Fareham station to meet internet chilli sauce reviewer Darth Naga, my biggest worry was how to greet him: Mr Naga? Too formal. Darth? Too familiar. Now my biggest fear is whether I'll make it back to the station alive. Or at least without frequent stops at the side of the A27 to chuck up. Tony Ainsworth – aka Darth Naga – has already promised he won't hurt me too much when I come to meet him. But he never mentioned anything about purging.

Fareham, sitting on one top of the western flank of Portsmouth harbour, used to be the main thoroughfare between Portsmouth and Southampton and reaped the rewards to become a major Hampshire market town. That was until the M27 came along, skirting the town and leaving it somewhat desolate.

"Call me Tony," says Darth as I arrive at his door. I'm here for an interview, followed by what Tony says will be 'a little challenge'. We're going to make one of his popular YouTube chilli review videos, tasting a hot chilli sauce. It could be blisteringly hot, it could be disgusting. Either way, Tony wants me to be prepared.

"We've got two pints of milk," his girlfriend Lisa shouts from the kitchen. "Do you want me to swill the mop bucket out, just in case?"

"Don't worry," says Tony, "even if you do spew, you still get a massive endorphin rush which is the best thing about it. And if you're lucky you may get to taste the sauce on the way out again."

Darth Naga is one of the biggest personalities on the chilli scene. His chilli tasting videos are a major online destination for chilli lovers. Chilli growers and sauce brewers from all over the UK and even beyond send him their stuff hoping he'll do a video review. Even if his review is bad, it can boost sales. Actually, what does good and bad even mean in hot chilli tasting?

"There are two types of viewers of my videos," says Tony as we chomp on a lunchtime sandwich in which the pesto is as challenging as it gets. "There are those who are genuinely interested in the sauces I'm trying. They want to see what new things are being produced and value my opinion before buying something they think they'll like. Then there are the others…"

"Sadists," Lisa chips in protectively.

"They're the people who want to watch my reaction to the sauces and chillies, to watch me suffer," says Tony. "I think we have this innate instinct in human nature to watch people experiencing pain."

Embarrassingly, I know he's right. Ahead of my visit I spent the best part of a day watching Darth Naga's videos, cringing and laughing as I watched him travel to hell and back to taste some of the world's hottest sauces, chillies and chilli extracts. Usually from his bedroom with a skull and crossbones flag behind, he speaks directly to the camera and tries sauces, raw chillies and whatever else he's sent. Then he tries to describe the taste and burn in real time.

In *Darth Naga vs The Carolina Reaper* he and his mates taste the world's hottest chilli, which burns their fingers even before they stick it in their mouth. Darth then throws it right back up again before dancing around his garden spitting and swearing, genuinely uncomfortable. By the end of the video, all three are drinking milk and then throwing up milky-white puke into buckets jammed between their legs.

In *Darth Naga vs 20 Minute Burn*, a hot sauce made with 7.3 million SHU chilli extract, he has to spend fifteen minutes off camera because it hurts so much, for so long. "Never do this neat," he concludes. "It's not something I want to ever, ever do again."

After testing raw Naga Viper chillies – green then red in quick succession – he vomits again right there on screen. Then he has to dash off to pour vegetable oil into his eye because he's accidentally touched it with chilli-fingers from his own vomit.

In most videos there's a frequently recurring theme: Darth has to cut the video so he can go off and *purge* before coming back to offer his verdict. Sometimes he doesn't quite make it off camera in time. This is the guy who's generously invited me to taste a hot sauce with him today.

So I'm not sure what I expected when Darth Naga opened the door. OK, not a bloke in full Darth Vader costume. But probably someone full of boastful machismo, rubbing his hands together about the pain he's going to put me through. But Tony is a super down-to-earth and friendly guy of 34, of a certain (admittedly not unexpected) build.

He's wearing an Ironman T-shirt: the Marvel Comics character, not the swimming/cycling/running thing. He and his girlfriend meet me with great big grins and a cheerful terrier jumps up at me demanding I ruffle her fur. They all seem as delighted that I've shown an interest in Darth's 'work', as I am at being invited into their lives to find out what makes the UK's premier chilli taster tick.

Tony says he's been surprised how popular his tasting videos have become. He's just an ordinary guy, with an ordinary job (tech support – why doesn't that surprise me?) who likes hot food and started his video channel as a hobby. Now he's recognised at chilli festivals, is frequently asked for his autograph or to have his photo taken with fans, has been on TV and has even been recognised in supermarkets. One chilli producer, the Mr Vikki's brand based in Cumbria, has created a limited edition sauce called The Emperor Strikes Back which has Tony's face leering out from the label.

"I think my channel has become so popular because on the videos you get to see me as me," he says. "There's no character or fake personality, it's just me and my real reactions to what I'm trying. My body doesn't actually react that well to chillies, so you're getting a very real result: the tears, the hiccuping. Occasionally I taste a sauce and I can't take the heat. That's when I end up throwing up."

Tony has been a fan of hot foods since he tried a hot phall Indian curry as a teenager. But he fell into chilli reviewing after visiting a chilli festival on a whim and writing up his experiences with the sauces. He remembers his first official review which he did before he started posting videos on YouTube. It was a heaped teaspoon of puree made of pure Naga chillies. Like a drug user talking about a dodgy acid trip, he says he "had a really bad time on that one." He tasted the sauce, suffered for a bit, then passed out. He woke up lying in the foetal position on the bathroom floor, totally naked with his clothes folded neatly by his side. He reckons – before he later got used to the rush – he'd overdosed on endorphins. Soon after he adopted the Naga as part of his nickname and started regularly posting on YouTube. He now has over 2,000 channel followers. Tony affectionately calls his subscribers his *chilli padowans.*

I look up from my notebook puzzled.

"I guess you don't know so much about Star Wars?"

"…"

"It's OK," he says. "Padowans are apprentice Jedi. They're learning about the Force. They're just getting into the whole Jedi thing."

I nod. Tony is my Luke Skywalker, is that right? Or Darth, or Ewok, or something. But I'm here to learn and he reaches for a selection of hot sauces while Lisa goes off to find the sick bucket.

As Tony describes his tasting method, it occurs to me that he is a little like Andrew Jukes at Warwick University. Tony too insists on testing a relatively exact measurement of sauce – a single tablespoon – and on doing it 'blind', having never tasted the sauce before. That way his followers get to see his real reaction and can compare it fairly with the other sauces he's tried. He even makes sure he has a week long break before each tasting. He doesn't want to build up a tolerance to chilli heat which would throw his reviews off kilter.

"There are a lot of reviewers out there whose tolerance is through the roof because they're doing a review all the time. But I like to maintain my tolerance at a low level, so I'm going to a sauce fresh."

Tony offers me a choice of sauces for our tasting test. We can go for Burning Desire Foods' 7-pot Scorpion Insane Hot

Sauce. We can try a Grim Reaper sauce made with the Carolina Reaper chilli, officially recognised by Guinness World Records as the world's hottest fruit. Or we can do Darth Naga's own challenge: tasting a steaming Dorset Naga-based concoction from Twisted 7 sauces called The Organ Grinder, followed immediately by tasting The Organ Grinder Monkey – which is essentially the same sauce but with an 800,000 SHU extract added. For fun.

Before we choose, I finger each bottle in turn and tell Tony I need a bit more information. Essentially, which of these is most likely to make me nearly die? Because I don't want to nearly die. We decide to discard the Carolina Reaper sauce. It really would be jumping in at the very deepest end.

Lisa prepares us a couple of glasses of milk. The fat in milk binds with the capsaicinoids in the chillies, stopping them from reacting with pain receptors in the mouth. It is far better than water for relieving the burn should it get out of hand. Water can make it worse because it washes the chemicals around your mouth and also carries them down to the stomach in a purer form. Milk, yoghurt and ice cream work, but butter and cheese don't because they lack the right fats.

Chillies don't actually do any physical damage, Tony assures me, but they will give your stomach a good churn. I secretly think of my ulcer. If you don't purge, he says, they can ruin your day and it can be a horrible feeling. Actually, he adds, chillies are packed with vitamin C and the hot chemicals inside them can help to detox the body. *Yeah, particularly if you're purging after eating them.* But a search of scientific papers later confirms capsaicin's antioxidant properties.

"But that's only on the inside," I say, before adding a

fearful: "what about the backside?"

"Yeah," he replies. "They do say it's hot on the way in, hot on the way out."

Lisa is listening in. "Can they make your arse bleed?" she offers sweetly, as if talking about anal injuries is normal Sunday afternoon chat between the two. I offer her a grateful glance because I didn't have the guts to ask.

"Oh, I have bled a few times," says Tony sadly, a sage old man looking back on his life as I shift my own arse uncomfortably on the sofa. "I bled when me and Andy did that sixteen million extract. It was pure crystalline capsaicin dissolved in vodka, far above and beyond anything I've ever tasted and sent me into a panic attack. It was insane."

Lisa too always liked hot food and says her dad used to trick her into tasting hot sauce when she was a kid. The two met between mutual friends and when Lisa asked them what he was really like, they told her to take a look at his videos: "he'll be the one being sick." Quite an introduction, but the relationship stuck. They recently celebrated Valentine's Day with a special love themed YouTube review, all dressed up in best suit and frock. They tasted a sauce called Widow's Tipple from the Chilli Hunter brand. Darth starts to sweat but Lisa barely blinks and looks comfortable throughout. Thankfully, there's no Valentine's vomiting. In another video it's a family affair with Tony, Lisa and her uncle as they taste chilli chocolate. This time it's Lisa that looks distinctly uncomfortable and just a little bit sweaty. She can't help but reach for the milk by the end. Meanwhile, her uncle can't even speak.

Lisa is doing more and more videos with Tony and now his padowans have started to ask 'Where's the missus?' when he posts up a review without her. "People want some eye candy because, let's be honest, I'm nothing special to look at," he says.

It's all very chummy, but I can put it off no longer. Tony sets up the camera and we make our final choice of sauce. We're going to taste the Burning Desire 7-pot Scorpion Insane Hot Sauce. Tony wants to test something he's never tasted before and I'm keen to avoid the double pronged hit of two sauces straight after each other, which is what his Twisted 7 challenge would involve.

Scorpion Insane is made of fresh 7-pot Scorpion chillies, not extract. I should be able to taste the chilli fruit itself, says Tony. It should have a really full flavour to it. I'm to swill the sauce before swallowing. I'm looking for heat, but also the notes of red pepper, onion, perhaps some celery or lemon. It might be sweet, it might be savoury, it might be searingly hot. We won't know until we taste it. The label, as most of them are, is all hell and fire and burning and stuff. On the back it urges me to 'explore your dark side'. It comes in a container not unlike an old-fashioned opaque medicine bottle, reminding me of TCP.

Tony is going to take a tablespoon, but I decide on just a teaspoon because I'm still a padowan. We look at the camera, Tony introduces me, reads out the ingredients and it's down the hatch.

It's hot, there's no doubt about that. It's really hot. I swill the teaspoonful around my mouth and feel the heat spread out and concentrate at the upper back of my mouth. But it's a slowly growing heat, a pleasurable one that brings on a quick sweat but otherwise allows me to really find the flavour of the sauce. It is savoury with overtones of grilled red pepper and celery. As I start to relax and breathe, the heat spreads more and engulfs my whole mouth. When I swallow it hits the back of my throat. But still – relatively speaking, of course – it's pleasurable rather than painful. And not the hottest thing I've ever had.

I look across to Tony and he's hiccuping and burping. He's taken on four or five times as much as me and I imagine given it a really good wash around his mouth, probably a full-on TCP gargle. Between stuttered moments to catch our breath, we discuss the sauce on camera. It is hot but really tasty too. Both of us could imagine the sauce dolloped at the side of a meal, something we'd dip chips into. I think both of us are surprised that I seem to be taking the sauce better than he is. I'm sweating, for sure, but no hiccups and certainly not the purging we'd prepared for.

"Perhaps you need another teaspoon," he says.

"Yes, I think I do," I say fairly. Tony pours me another helping, this time filling the spoon right to the brim. I taste again and there's certainly more burning heat but alongside there's more great flavour. Still a really good balance. I'm starting to understand why both the Red Hot Chilli Fella and Darth Naga say they're interested in the flavour of various chillies, not just their heat. It might just be the endorphins, but I'm having a really good – am I really saying this? – culinary experience. I can pick out the different ingredients behind the heat. Rather than terrifying, the combination is moreish. And I try to articulate this in my first ever online chilli sauce review.

Five years ago chilli sauce tasting was all about the heat, Tony tells me after we've signed off the video. ("May the sauce be with you, my chilli padowans!") They were so hot they were just for psychopaths. But now the industry as well as chilli sauce connoisseurs have moved on from the pure heat and are really exploring what can be done with the flavours. A good chilli sauce, he says, is about creating a combination of ingredients that work together, and ensuring the taste and heat of the chilli work with it rather than masking it.

"It's embarrassing to say it," says Tony embarrassed, "but I think Levi Roots has a lot to do with it. He did that Dragons' Den thing and got his Hot Reggae Reggae sauce into the supermarkets. People tasted it and then they just wanted more."

The Levi Roots effect inspired other sauce makers to try creating their own hot concoctions, but also helped create a growing market for what they were producing. "People are fed up of the swill that gets sold in supermarkets. And now there are hundreds of sauce makers out there, producing hundreds of sauces, and they're all easy to order over the internet."

And that's the true power of Darth Naga. Use the internet, Luke. His reviews always carry web addresses for suppliers and Tony's delighted to promote them. In fact, in the social media world chilli enthusiasm is massive. YouTube has allowed Tony and reviewers like him to evangelise about chilli products but at the same time it forces producers to raise their game: in terms of flavours, in terms of balanced heat and in terms of presentation and marketing. It's creating a healthy competition between chilli sauce manufacturers which has led to lots of flavours on the market, as well as an entertaining array of packaging. Tony shows me bottles sealed with wax or which come in test tubes, lots of labels with pictures of fire, the Devil and hell, sauces and producers with names like Heavenly Heat, Dare Ya, Unleash the Beast, Bunny Burner and, my favourite name, Shit Habens. There's even a sauce made up in a mock plastic medicine bottle, with one of those clicky childproof lids.

"There can be a little competition between suppliers and there have been some fallings out but they're all resolved relatively quickly," Tony tells me. "There are a lot of sauce makers now but the market is quite big too so there's enough to go around. They're more like a big family, all with something a little different, a little unique to bring to the table."

And it's clear they respect Darth Naga's opinion. Some home-kitchen sauce makers have taken a thumbs-up from Tony as a strong enough boost to start producing sauces commercially. One home-kitchen brewer got Darth to taste his sauce at the Brighton Chilli Festival a few years ago. He was so encouraged by his reaction that he went away and came up with his own brand and is now selling profitably. That brand is Twisted 7 who produced the The Organ Grinder and its wicked little sister The Monkey that Tony had invited me to try on camera.

He says everyone's palate has different tastes as well as different tolerances to heat. But Darth Naga's seems to be one palate many in the industry care about. So the guys over at Hot Headz – a leading chilli sauce maker – have reason to be very happy indeed. Their Who Dares Burns is his favourite sauce. It's the same sauce Andrew Jukes had been sent on the morning I met him in his lab.

"It has a really nice smoky flavour but a really good background of heat. Even though it's so hot, the flavour just keeps you coming back for more." Tony leans over, rolls up his sleeve and shows me the Who Dares Burns logo. The producer gave him permission to tattoo it onto his bicep. You don't see many blokes wandering round with the HP Sauce or Coleman's Mustard logo inked under their skin. Darth really does like this sauce.

"I don't regret getting it done. It's a really good motto," he says, as if it's the most normal thing in the world.

Naturally, Tony's favourite chilli is the Naga, also known

as the Bhut Jolokia or Ghost chilli. Tony likes it in a sauce after it's been dried to bring out a caramel and smoky flavour. But it still carries a heat he says is acceptable enough to accompany an evening meal. I recently watched an American extreme-eater called The L.A. Beast taking on a whole fresh Bhut Jolokia on YouTube after boasting, while flexing his own biceps, that he could take any chilli, any time. He ended up rolling around on the floor crying for his mama. Just for good measure, his buddy – for some reason dressed as Eeyore from Winnie the Pooh – kicked him in the nuts while he was down.

For the most part, Darth Naga doesn't go in for that macho nonsense. For him, the Naga is all about that deep flavour, while it's a heat that needs to be taken in (relative) moderation. Though he does later admit to a drunken escapade at the West Dean Chilli Fiesta where, after one thing led to another, he ended up having pure chilli extract sprayed on his own knackers. As you do.

Tony gives me the Burning Desire sauce we've tried as a parting gift. At home later, I stick my finger in the bottle to rekindle the fire. I suggest my wife does the same, but a sniff is plenty to persuade her it wouldn't be a good idea.

Tony has tasted the best of the best, and as I cycle back to the station it's with some regret that we'd gone for the Burning Desire sauce rather than the Grim Reaper or Darth's Twisted 7 challenge. Or maybe it was just my body craving another endorphin rush from a hotter sauce. As I push the pedals a little harder to get over a slight rise in the road, there's a twinge in my stomach followed by a burning belch from the back of my throat. It reminds me that a padowan's initiation cannot be rushed. The parting words of the master echo clearly in my head.

"I'm going to see you at some chilli festivals over the

summer and when I do, I'm going to get you on camera again." My encounter with Darth Naga isn't quite over yet. The Emperor is waiting to strike back.

"How do you fancy a long weekend in Sussex this year?" I say to my wife out of the blue, after an evening on the internet not long after visiting Darth Naga.

Sarah looks up from her book with a suspicious look on her face. It's a face that says: I've been suggesting a holiday down that way for four years and you've always said it would be too expensive, too far to drive and would clash with your cycling commitments.

"Go on," she says hesitantly.

"Well, August could be good couldn't it? I thought a nice weekend away, somewhere near, say, West Dean. It'd be good for the kids. It's picturesque, we could go hiking, there's a chilli festival on, we could swim, go to the beach at West Wittering, maybe take a boat tour off Hayling Island."

"I'm not spending three days at a bloody chilli festival," she says.

"Oh, no, of course not. Definitely not. It just happens to be on."

That suspicious look again.

"We'll just pop into the festival, buy some jam and stuff, *definitely* some gifts for your parents. Maybe I could go a second day, if it's lively…"

"OK, so we're going on holiday and you're going to go to a chilli festival and the rest of us are going to do what exactly?"

Silence. She goes back to her book. Then I have a moment of inspiration.

"We could stay in one of those olde worlde stone cottages, with wooden doors, distressed furniture, probably an Aga. I could take a look on the internet right now, book something up?"

"You're on," she says. She actually holds out her hand for me to shake. I'm surprised she doesn't spit on it first to seal the deal.

I spend the rest of the evening browsing just out of her view, trying to work out if it'll be cheaper to stay in a Premier Inn, a Travelodge or to go the whole hog and plump for the Holiday Inn. The latter is more expensive but it does have a swimming pool. That'll help sweeten the pill when I announce that a cottage really would be quite expensive for the weekend. And anyway, they're all bound to be booked up by now. After all, there is the UK's premier chilli festival taking place just down the road. And anyone who's anyone in Chilli Britain will be there.

Every morning, as I look out of my kitchen window, still blurry eyed making a cup of tea, I see my nemesis. A big fat grey squirrel leans down from the branch of the tree in our back garden to nibble away at the nuts and seeds we've left out for the birds. I swear he looks up at me with a grin on his face.

Now I like animals more or less as much as the next guy. In fact I'm even a little proud that down the road on Mersea Island there is a smattering of red squirrels that have managed to keep their tougher grey relatives at bay after a reintroduction programme a couple of years ago. And I like watching the array of goldfinches, chaffinches, jays, pied wagtails and particularly the great spotted woodpeckers that visit our hanging bird feeders. We've even had the rarer green woodpeckers nibbling around for bits of seed under the feeders.

But they're all scared off by that fat grey oaf of animal vermin that steals all the grub. I bang on the window, throw things, I've even tried to hose him down. But nothing shakes him. He's that super squirrel from those old Carling Black Label adverts. He's even bitten right through the solid metal of my bird feeders to get to the nuts inside.

Nuts.

I'm just brewing up on a Monday morning when it occurs to me. Over the weekend, my wife had brought home a packet of red hot Scorpion chilli nuts manufactured by the Red Hot Chilli Fella. She'd been nicknack shopping at the Suffolk Food Hall again and brought me back a present. I'd tried them the night before and they were delicious, but way too hot to pile into your hand like you do when you neck peanuts at Christmas. A couple at a time is the most you can stand. At that rate I'll be nibbling from this bag for weeks.

I look down at the packet of nuts and up at the fat squirrel. Andrew Jukes' words ring in my ear. When I'd asked him what other uses chillies were being put to – apart from making head banging chilli sauce, chocolate and jams – he'd said that chilli was also being trialled as a natural pesticide to protect crops from mammals like rabbits. (In India, farmers grow hot chillies around their fields in a kind of chilli burn alternative to electric shock fencing.)

As anyone with a rudimentary understanding of natural selection knows, plants need to spread their seeds as far and wide as possible. Let mice, shrews and other… *small rodents* eat all your fruit and you and your genes are a goner. But get birds to carry the seeds away before the animals get the chance and you're in the successful reproduction business.

Birds can't detect the heat in chillies, nor can snails and frogs. But mammals can. Mammals like squirrels.

Now, I'm not cruel. If I was cruel I could have just slammed the whole packet of Scorpion nuts onto the bird table and watched my nemesis try to stuff them greedily into his cheeks to carry off to his drey. That would have been bye-bye squirrel for good. But I don't want to kill the bugger. I just want the woodpeckers to come back.

Instead of getting my kids' porridge ready, I find myself grinding up a handful of Scorpion nuts and mixing them with the birdseed. It's a very small handful, members of the RSPCA take note. I pour the concoction into melted lard and ladle the gloop into half a coconut shell. This will be scientific; Andrew Jukes would be proud. I hang out a half-coconut of unadulterated birdseed on one branch and the fiery squirrel propellant half-coconut on the other. Then I spend the rest of the day waiting for tomorrow morning and our kettle-boiling/nut-stealing face-off to begin.

And the next morning? Nothing. No squirrel. The morning after that, nothing again. Same the next day. I've won. The birds are pecking away happily at the nuts and seeds, but there's no sign of my little friend. I can only suspect that on one of his early morning forays he took a full Scorpion hit, got the fright of his life and went to bother someone else's bird tables.

Then the next day, my wife hands me a clipping from the *Colchester Gazette* with a shake of her head: *"Devastating fire at historic building may have been started by a squirrel... The fire may well have been caused by animals chewing through electrical wires causing them to short out."*

Could it be my fat furred friend had taken fiery revenge on his human tormentors by trying to start the great fire of Colchester? But then explain this: the next morning my wife calls me into the kitchen and points out the window. The half-coconut of Scorpion chilli laced seeds and nuts is on the grass. And eating from it, occasionally peering up to look me dead in the eye, not even moving an inch when I dash to get a camera, is the squirrel. He has a smile on his face again. And he doesn't move until every nut and every seed has gone.

I put the kettle on and briefly consider stepping up the dose. I must have something stronger than Scorpion nuts in my bag of tricks? But then I think of all the chilli fans, growers and extreme eaters of Great Britain and I – metaphorically at least, I'm not crazy – doff my cap to the fat bastard. If you can take the heat, then you're one of us.

7th April – There are tiny shoots in both the Scorpion and Bhut Jolokia pots. These, I'm starting to learn, are some seriously hot chillies. I just have to make sure they fruit. But Habanero 7 is starting to behave like a petulant child. There are just two seedlings and they're both reluctant growers. And now the other plants around them are getting so tall in the propagator they're stealing all the sunlight. I must re-pot some of them real soon. Sweet Pepper Mohawk is gone. Dead and buried. Compared with that, Habanero 7 is doing well.

9th April – OK, this is out of hand now. Vampire, Masquerade and a particularly keen Friar's Hat are officially too big for the propagator. MUST POT-ON. I'm just so busy enjoying myself around the country meeting chilli-heads. Tomorrow, tomorrow. Plus, something is having a nibble at Masquerade. Just one leaf but enough to have me worried. Another reason to freshen them all up into individual pots. Meanwhile I have three full-on seedlings of each of my Scorpion and Bhut Jolokias. I'm on my way to a fulsome crop.

10th April – With the somewhat chaotic help of my kids, I finally repot my chillies. It took some doing, but my four- and six-year-old managed not to mix the labels up. At least I hope so. There are 11 pots of various shapes and sizes (RIP to Sweet Pepper Mohawk). The finished product is a wonder to see and I pile them up onto small tables. One of which is the little wooden table my kids do their colouring on, I'm sure they won't miss it. I'll drag them in and out of the conservatory, depending on how hot a day it's going to be (the chillies, not the children). I need to keep them nice and warm at night.

I decide now is a good time to start feeding the newly repotted plants. With each water, I'll put in some specialist chilli plant food called Chilli Focus (it's not cheap, but it is good). When the plants start to fruit, I'll up the dose. The internet tells me that feeding helps the plants grow strong, encourages flower growth and produces more fruits. Rather like in those 'before and after' photos you get in Weight Watchers adverts, there are loads of chilli comparison pictures on seed retailers' sites. They show that plants which get extra nutrients do far better than those that don't. A chilli cannot properly prosper on water and compost alone.

By the end of the day, I can already feel the chillies spreading their deep green wings. Bhut Jolokia and Scorpion are still sitting pretty in their germination pots, but even those two are now growing a second stage of leaves. It's a happy time.

A taste of Africa

I'M IN CHOCOLATE box Suffolk in search of a food
festival. It's only early April and to my reckoning the chilli
festival that forms part of the Framlingham Country Fair is
the first chilli event of the season. It's a warmish day and
thanks to a complex and traffic packed one way system, I get
a good look at Framlingham. It's a market town of the
independent shops, flower stalls and afternoon tea variety.
We didn't mean to go into the town, but I experienced that
familiar 'I'm going to a food festival and I have not a penny
of cash' problem and ended up stuck on the gyratory.

The market square has the grand total of one cash
machine, entailing a long wait before we could head around
the one way system again and towards the fair on its
outskirts. As these places do, Framlingham has an eleventh
century castle run by English Heritage and other historic
claims to fame including a guildhall, a church clock and, of
course, a rather unremarkable water pump of a couple of
hundred years old. Fascinating.

In the grounds of Framlingham College the chilli festival
is pretty tiny, absorbed into a larger countryside event: all
shire horses, birds of prey displays and that bloke who has
his sheepdog chase Indian runner ducks over little bridges.
On one stand, next to a tent selling wool lined Wellington
boots and parka jackets, a stall is flogging animal traps. I
have to turn my kids away before they spot the poster of six
dead Bugs Bunnies all lined up next to one of the devices.

The chilli festival amounts to ten stalls at one end of the tent packed with the other kinds of gourmet food sellers you tend to get at these things: ginger wine, ostrich burgers, exotic cheese, pushy olive sellers. None of the chilli stands are doing that well. The demographic of the country show is perhaps a little old, conservative and possibly too cautious to be dipping their Jacob's cream crackers into a sauce named Hell Hot Habaneros or snacking on a pile of Chilli Mafia Naga Nuts.

The director of ChilliFestUK, Alexander Mustang, has invited me to the festival to get an impression of the events he organises. Over the phone we'd agreed I'd help him at a much larger event in Merthyr Tydfil later in the year. After asking around I'm directed to an enormously fat Asian chap with flyaway grey and black hair proffering curry soaked tortilla pieces at uninterested passersby from behind his sauce stand.

I introduce myself and my friend Sachio, and Alex asks Sachio if he is Chinese or Japanese – which I think is a bit of a forward greeting. He then bows and says *konichiwa* – which I think is even worse. But then he continues a conversation with Sachio in Japanese and it's all egg on *my* face for being a judgemental dumbass.

We chat amiably and try a few of Alexander's curry sauces. These will be the ones I'll be selling in Merthyr and we make our final arrangements for meeting up in June. As we leave the stand, a woman from behind the Aunty Jee curry stand – perhaps even Aunty Jee herself – leans over and says to Sachio: "Oh, the Chinese like their hot food don't they?"

"He's Japanese," says Alexander with a shake of the head and a tut-tut.

Looking around the chilli stands I'm pleased to greet

Andy Rochey, the Red Hot Chilli Fella, with his (our!) chilli chocolate as well as a selection of his jams, oils and sauces. Sachio buys a bar of chocolate for his wife and kids who are patiently waiting outside watching the Indian runner duck show.

We meet the East Coast Chilli Company, another chilli producer from East Anglia. Tim Chapman runs it out of his home in Ipswich. After being made redundant, he's decided to spend his first year of unemployment giving chilli sauces a go. He says he's doing quite well: "It's been the best year of my life."

Next to him is Mr Vikki with samples of mild, medium and hot chilli sauces lined up in a row. They include their The Emperor Strikes Back sauce – the one with Darth Naga's face beaming out from the jar label. I can't help but try the Darth sauce. It is indeed warm, but taste-wise pretty indistinguishable from the other sauces around it. Sachio goes for something more fruity: a banana and Habanero sauce which to me does taste like bananas but leaves poor Sach surprised by its kick. It is, he declares, as far as he was willing to go up the Scoville Scale that day.

Next to Mr Vikki is Safari Sauces, an African inspired chilli sauce range with names that each have a story behind them. The Tokoloshe made from a terrifying mix of Naga, Scorpion and Bird's Eye chillies is named after a South African demon guilty of a range of evil deeds. Muti, a dark spiced sauce, is derived from the name for medicine in one of the South African traditional languages. With Bird's Eye chillies, I imagine it sits at the 'kill or cure' rather than the dab-of-germoline-on-a-grazed-knee end of medicine.

As with many chilli producers, a story or fable behind a sauce or company seems to help products to sell. Safari Sauces is all done out with a desert sunset backdrop (think

The Lion King), traditional African looking tablecloths and wooden figures. There's a zebra pattern van parked out the back. I guess in an increasingly crowded market of chilli sauces, each supplier has to find a way to make themselves unique, over and above the sauces themselves which surely can only differ so much.

Tucked behind the main presentation on Safari Sauces' stall sits a small jar labelled Cetewayo's Hell Fire. The label says it's made from the world record holding hottest chilli – the Carolina Reaper. I've only heard of the Carolina in respected hushed tones so far and resolutely rejected it when Darth offered it for our YouTube review.

"We keep it behind the other stuff so customers don't get a really nasty shock," says James behind the stand. His accent is a strange mix of South African and Scottish which, to me at least, comes out as Northern Irish. "We do try to keep our sauces flavoursome but you do need something very hot too. That's when you start doing things with Carolina Reaper."

The chilli is a relative newcomer and pretty hard to come by in the UK. It was bred by the PukkerButt Pepper Company in South Carolinia, USA, and rather typically has been plastered with registrations, patents and intellectual property rights. In other words, it should be written Carolina Reaper®, but I think that's just a bit obsessive. It's claimed the fruits average at 1.5 million SHU, but ones have been registered by Guinness World Records at a full-on 2.2 million. As Paris Hilton said (and indeed tried to trademark herself): That's Hot®.

Of course, I'm keen to try it which – duly warned by James – I do. The paste is salty and sharp and very, very hot. Essentially it's so fiery it doesn't have much identifiable flavour. But it brings on an immediate sweat and slight hiccuping that remains for ten minutes. I can't imagine eating anything with it. Possibly I'd cook a masochistic curry with it if the family were away. But with no real flavour what would be the point? I know if I'd dipped in more than a wooden spatula it could have ruined my day.

Still streaming with sweat, we move to another African stand and meet Victor Nwosu, a Nigerian in jeans and T-shirt with a square jaw and bright white smile. He's CEO, manager, accountant, cook and sales lead for Wiga Wagaa sauces, also made from his own kitchen. He's extremely friendly and makes plenty of time to talk.

"Nigerians like a salty sweet taste but then bang it up with heat," says Victor. Though he's lived in the UK most of his life, he was born in south-eastern Nigeria and frequently visits his family there to get a dose of his mum's authentic dishes.

The Scotch Bonnet chilli he uses in most of his sauces and meat rubs is a key ingredient for traditional pepper soup from his Nigerian home region. As far as I can glean, a traditional Nigerian soup is essentially just any kind of soup or stew, made from any kind of meat, fish or vegetable, but which is then brewed with Scotch Bonnets to an almost unbearable heat.

He hands me a stick loaded with extract in oil, and I natter to him between scorching coughs about how he extracts the chilli chemicals. I don't know what I'm talking about, of course. I'm just regurgitating Andrew Jukes.

"Oh, you seem to know a lot," says Victor. "Are you a chemist?"

"No, no," I say (cough). "I just…"

"Because I'm a biochemist by training. I studied at Southampton University, then in Sheffield."

"Oh, great." I've bitten off more than I can chew here.

"Yes, then I studied at the European Molecular Biology Laboratory in Heidelberg. It was microbiology, looking at how proteins and DNA interact. Then I was working for pharmaceutical companies."

This is just Victor's fourth week making chilli sauces full time. Previously, he'd been cooking up Nigerian sauces in the evenings and weekends, in between messing around with less important stuff. Stuff like DNA and the basic structure of proteins. The chemical compounds that are the very basis of all life on planet Earth. Do look up his paper on *Over expression of the wild-type gene coding for Escherichiacoli DNA adenine methylase.* It's a real killer.

"The company I was working for was downsizing so I just decided to do something completely different," he says nonchalantly. "I'm really just applying what I know about chemistry to make sauces instead. I'm going to give it a couple of years and see how I get on."

Next to Victor and his Wiga Wagaa stall is Mushemi Fire. It's another African inspired sauce producer, but this time by Zambia. In fact, there seems to be a whole African vibe going on at this chilli festival. That's no mean feat considering we're pretty much dead centre of posh, rural and very white Suffolk.

Steve at Mushemi Fire begins to tell me about his sauces, again labelled with different Zambian names and using traditional Zambian and other southern African produce. He too has a range of mild, medium and hot sauces, as well as chilli oils. I make small talk and let him pitch me, but I'm only half listening because I'd already researched Mushemi Fire before I arrived. He's based in Rugeley in Staffordshire, not too far from Wolverhampton where I'm going to be next week.

"I'm going to make a stab in the dark here," I say, giving

him a brief summary of my Chilli Britain quest. "You don't happen to be around on Thursday to show me how you cook your sauces do you?"

"I don't see why not," he says, handing me his card. "See you Thursday."

Sachio and I head out of the chilli tent and towards the bouncy castles. His wife and mine are just about topped up with chasing our kids around the country fair. Sachio hands over the Red Hot Chilli Fella's chocolate as a placating gift and his wife is just about to distribute it to the children when I stop her.

"Er, I reckon you should try it first. It's made with Naga chillies so if it's strong it could get a bit ugly." The kids are jumping up and down, looking forward to the chocolate.

Michelle takes a square and hands one to me. We savour the lovely rich chocolate as it melts. It's the familiar silky texture from Andrew Rochay's kitchen.

"Oh, it's OK," she says. "In fact it's lovely."

Five more seconds.

"Oh," she says, looking at me a little horrified. "Oh, God."

The Naga heat has hit the back of our throats and suddenly she's floundering around for a bottle of water. She pulls out some artisan biscuits she'd bought as a gift for someone and starts munching them in great gaping mouthfuls to dissipate the burning.

"You want something with lots of fat in it," urges Sachio as she plunges the chocolate in my hands with a wave that says that it's me who has to explain to the little ones why this massive bar of chocolate is only for me. The good thing for the lipid desperate Michelle, and for the disappointed kids, is that there's one thing a country fair always does do well and in large quantities. Ice cream.

So I'm in Wolverhampton for the second time in a month, which is pretty much the same number of visits I've made to my home town in the last year. My brother Darrius picks me up from the station and we head out of town towards Staffordshire. (Yeah, I know, Gideon and Darrius. I won't pretend we had an easy ride at school.)

We're on our way to visit Steve Woodward at Mushemi Fire. His kitchen is on an industrial estate in Rugeley, a small town between Stafford and Lichfield. It's too far north to officially be part of the Black Country, but just about close enough to Birmingham to be part of the Midlands rather than Up North. We Midlanders are very particular about these things, you know.

Like many small towns in this area, Rugeley's past is industrial. It has historically benefitted from the network of canals that criss-cross the whole of the Midlands and which used to be the primary means of transporting coal and iron out to the rest of the country.

On the way there, Darrius and I drive through Cannock Chase. It's 26 square miles of relatively flat shrub and woodlands. It's familiar to both of us as a place of rain, mud, draughty sodden canvas tents and the massive vats of spaghetti bolognese we used to suffer when we came here on Scout camp. I didn't know it then, but Cannock Chase is a Designated Area of Outstanding Natural Beauty and a Site of Special Scientific Interest. It has rare populations of wildflowers, migrant birds and wild deer. But my abiding memory is of being scared witless. Someone had told me once of a boy – about Scout age – who'd fallen down a small hole here and spent three days hanging from a jagged rock by his ears before he was rescued. Night hikes were never much fun with that story buzzing around your head.

Back at the Suffolk chilli festival, I had asked Steve if he would show us around his kitchen, and if he would allow me to watch him in production and perhaps allow me to stick a spoon or two into his chilli sauce during the process. But Steve has other ideas. He's planned for my brother and me to make a batch of fifty bottles of his lead product, Mother's Ruin. Apart from Scotch Bonnets and red peppers, it has gin as its key ingredient.

Gin is known in Britain as mother's ruin because it was so cheap in Victorian times that the poor got so drunk on it that the men became impotent and the women unable to look after any kids they did manage to have. A bit like drinking meths today, I suppose. If you take a look at the skeletal men, wild haired women and kids falling off staircases in the illustration by William Hogarth called *Gin Lane* – drawn in 1751 to support the British Gin Act banning small pubs from selling spirits – you'll get the general idea.

The day's work starts in Steve's office, which is in the corner of a mezzanine floor overlooking an industrial unit rented by a lighting company. Behind lengths of fluorescent tubing and boxes of electrical equipment there's a space overlooked by the Zambian flag. There's a hammock hanging from the metal rafters. Steve sits in an ageing colonial bamboo and leather chair, against a desk piled with chilli sauce bottles, books and papers. He's in his early thirties, with near ginger hair and stubble, and an eager look that says he's spent an awful lot of time behind tables at chilli festivals. He pulls out a well worn leather bound book, with flaking yellow pages and tiny scribbly writing in pencil. It's his Mushemi Bible. Everything he's ever done with chilli sauces has been written in this book. He flicks through the early pages and shows me a set of numbers.

"These are the first sales of my first ever sauce, in a market in Lusaka, the Zambian capital," he says. "I sold three bottles for 15,000 kwacha, that's about three pounds in total."

Steve had been working in Zambia for a renewable energy charity, which had previously also taken him to Latin America. Between business managing the charity's solar projects, he started mixing up chilli sauces as a hobby in a dilapidated house on Mushemi Road in Lusaka. A house where beetles, rats, international volunteers and other assorted wanderers lived together in a kind of uncomfortable harmony.

"Looking back, it was a bit insane," says Steve.

Mother's Ruin was his first sauce product, the making of which was apparently a way to de-stress after working six days a week for the charity. Gin is pretty big in Zambia and neighbouring Malawi, surely a hangover from Europeans sipping G&Ts on the verandas of their colonial houses as they took a break from overseeing the pillaging of Africa's natural resources (and people). Back then, Steve's sauce was a basic mashed-up concoction. But it went down well enough with middle class locals and expats, becoming the springboard to his creating a few other products and also sourcing a honey to sell at market. But it was still a pretty much grind-it-up-and-stick-it-in-a-bottle affair. A shadow of the developed sauces he sells today at UK chilli festivals and foodie markets.

When Steve's placement in Zambia finished, the summation of four years travelling the world, he decided he couldn't face returning to an everyday job here in the UK. Instead, he decided to bring his sauce making efforts home to the rather more ordinary Rugeley, learned better methods for creating chilli products, and Mushemi Fire was reborn. The new, improved Mother's Ruin, the manufacture of which now begins with a three- or four-month fermentation period, is still his flagship product. Last year the sauce won the Hot Sauce Competition at the chilli festival hosted by the Dorothy Clive Gardens, just north of Stafford. It gave Steve the boost he needed to invest in his company and start to take it more seriously.

Steve takes us down past boxes of strip lights to his store room and brew house. In a series of seven-gallon translucent bins there are chunky liquids of red and orange and green, each topped with airlocks, small bubbles pop-pop-popping out of the top. I've done a little home brewing in my time, so I assume the fermentation of chillies using yeast is creating a kind of alcoholic chilli drink and it's that that gives Mother's Ruin its claim to gin soaked fame. But Steve soon puts me right.

The initial mash that is the starting point of many of Mushemi Fire's sauces is fermented with a friendly bacteria, lactobacillus. It turns some of the sugars in the chillies – as well as any other fruit he's using – into a flavoured vinegar. It also generates carbon dioxide – the pop-pop-popping bubbles – which protects the sauce from reacting with oxygen and stops mould from forming. Like brewing beer, it's an ancient process and is used in the pickling of vegetables into many pungent foods like sauerkraut and the Korean side dish staple kimchi.

Steve chops the chillies he tends to use: Scotch Bonnets and Bird's Eye chillies (also known as Piri Piri, or Pilli Pilli, or even Peri Peri chillies, he tells me) and adds other base ingredients. Then they're all fermented in these big tubs. Every couple of weeks he'll do a taste and smell test, just like a sherry brewer takes frequent samples from towers of ageing barrels, to see if his sauce is ready for the next step.

I hover my nostrils over the air trap of a deep orange brew of about a month old and he gently depresses the lid. It forces up a powerful vinegary waft that tingles almost painfully up my nose. I try another barrel, this one four months old, and the waft is more tight and savoury. It's ready to go and Steve has already syphoned off a gallon for us to work with.

Then I take a sniff from one of the deep green bins, the mash for his Green Mamba sauce named after the west African snake. Humans and green mambas don't cross paths too often but when they do the snake almost always comes off better. Unsurprisingly, the waft of Green Mamba mash is eye-wateringly spicy. When it's ready, Green Mamba will be bottled into little phials, the thin green liquid inside offering the appearance of an anti-venom.

Steve pulls out a bucket of Miombo gold honey from wild bees living in forests on the border between Zambia and the Democratic Republic of Congo. The honey is amber-brown, has a stiff buttery texture and a strong and smoky smell. It's nothing like the sickly sweet stuff that we spread on toast. Instead, it's almost savoury and is the base for Mushemi Fire's Honey Hot Sauce.

The bacterial brewing process is really important to Steve; he says anyone can just throw a load of chillies, tomatoes and onions together and pulverise them into a sauce. Brewing creates a distinct flavour that makes the chillies he uses stand out. He's taken time to learn brewing techniques and even paid a biochemist to help him fine tune the processes. Then he's taken more time to perfect them to create chilli sauces with a distinctly African taste. Slight differences in the final product, caused by different brewing times, whether the weather is hot or cold, the natural differences in the pungency and heat of the chillies, are something to be welcomed. Steve feels his products are more honest this way. Boring and absolute consistency is something for the supermarkets.

"Every batch is slightly different. That's the beauty of it," he says. "I can smell it and look at the consistency and just about judge the right time, but this is a living product."

We move to his kitchen, which used to be a large store cupboard full to the top with wood offcuts. Steve and some mates spent a long weekend clearing it out and cleaning, then another weekend painting and finishing. Now it has a corner piled high with steel catering equipment, separate sinks for food and hand washing, utensils, lengths of brushed steel work surfaces, an oven, hob and a bottle steriliser. Much of it is second-hand and his kitchen has been built bit by bit over time. But there's one piece of equipment that has been with Mushemi Fire from the very beginning: an ageing dehumidifier for slow drying the chillies.

Drying concentrates the heat and locks in the freshly picked flavour of chillies. It also prevents them from rotting. Out in Zambia, Steve dried his chillies in the hot sun by laying them out in a disused swimming pool. With importing a swimming pool from Africa being a bit of a chore and the lack of solar heat this side of the Midlands offering an additional problem Steve brought back to Staffordshire his backup dehumidifier as the next best thing.

We get suited up: me in a fresh shirt, plastic gloves and chef's hat; my brother in a BBQ apron from home and a cap offered by Steve from Zambian president Rupiah Banda's 2011 re-election campaign – which he lost. He was then accused of corruption and stripped of presidential immunity. Banda that is, not my brother.

Steve, in his own cap sporting Zambian colours, has laid

out the equipment for today's cooking. First we have to prepare the mash by removing the seeds, skins and other gunk left behind by the brewing process. We're after a thin red liquid as Mother's Ruin will have the consistency of a traditional Tabasco sprinkling sauce rather than a drier, lumpier, side-of-the-plate affair. If it was orange juice they'd call it 'with no bits'.

We have to start by mashing up the mash even further. That can be a messy and, without the proper equipment, a pretty dangerous affair. "You don't want this stuff splashing in your eyes," says Steve as he hands me some goggles. "Nor do you want to breathe it in too deeply," before handing me a gas mask. Masked up I look like I'm about to decontaminate a nuclear plant, not cook up a sauce. Steve pours the mash into a huge pot and presents me with a massive industrial mixer that's about the size, shape and weight of the pneumatic drills they use to dig up the road. Like it's some gigantic whisk I stick the implement into the pot. Steve tells me to hold tight and he switches on the power.

The force of the thing starts to strain my arms as soon as it starts to mash and it's a struggle to keep it straight because the G-force is trying to throw my end round in circles. It's a bit like an unpleasant version of the pulling sensation you get when using a hand mixer to work up double cream into a whip. Only, I don't tend to wear a gas mask and goggles while making Sunday dinner, nor do I have to brace myself against the kitchen cupboards to counteract the sheer force of the whisk.

With the mash duly obliterated, Steve pulls out his second torture device of the afternoon: his triturator. It's a circular instrument with a funnel, massive turning handle, deep blades and what looks like a cheese grater all around the edge. The triturator will separate out all the gunk. In goes the mash and Darrius and I take turns to wind the blades, churning the mix and spinning the liquid out of the sides and into a gigantic cooking pot. When we've both worked up a light sweat, Steve peers into the triturator and tells us it's a good start. So we take turns again, this time working up a sweat wet enough to risk dropping salty beads into the pot. It signals to Steve that he'd better take over. He makes it look easy, of course, until all that's left is a couple of lumps of wet mush. A bit like us after ten minutes of pushing those blades around.

With triturator duly disposed of, Steve points to a sticker on the wall. There he's written the exact measurements of the other ingredients we're to add to the newly mashed, mixed and triturated sauce. I feel the pressure as I'm to go first with sugar. I'm a little overgenerous, but Steve lets it go. I get the lemon juice just about right then Darrius weighs in with the gin and well and truly overdoes it. Force of habit I guess. But we're more or less on the money and Steve moves the pot to the hob, setting the gas to high.

"We're coming up to a tricky stage," says Steve, "as there are lots of steps that have to happen very quickly."

There are 50 small bottles in an oven being brought up to temperature to sterilise them. The aim is to get the bottles hot, the sauce hot, and then get the hot sauce into the hot bottles and the lids on before everything cools down. That'll prevent bacteria – this time bad bacteria – from entering the bottles, allowing mould and spoiling the sauce.

With the sauce simmering and the bottles approaching hot, Steve hauls out a huge bottling machine and attaches it to a compressor. The compressor is the kind of machine scuba dive shops use to fill their tanks with tightly packed air, but in this kitchen the pressured air will push the right amount of sauce into each of the bottles. A bit of an overkill perhaps? But Steve tells me about filling hundreds of hot bottles with hot sauce using a hand funnel and I get the point. Steve hauls out a gargantuan metal cone and attaches it to the top of the bottler. He then fills the funnel with hot sauce. Finally, he pulls out a pedal from beneath the work bench.

"The trick is to have the next bottle lined up, so you can screw on the lid while another bottle is filling," he says. "It's a smooth process. Pedal, fill, screw, pedal, fill, screw. Oh and be careful because the bottles are hot."

Steve then demonstrates, rapidly clicking the pedal, filling bottles with a huge whoosh from the compressor, putting another bottle under the tube, then pushing on caps while his foot clicks the pedal to start the next whoosh. Pedal, fill, screw.

"You ready?"

I'm not ready. Let me see here: left hand lifts the bottle and puts it in place, pedal, then right hand takes bottle, stick a new one under, pull out a plastic cap, screw it on, twist to the right, put the filled bottle down, but somewhere in the process click the pedal again. I try a few dummy runs, then say I'm ready. I stamp down on the pedal and whoosh, my first bottle is filled. I swing round, get a cap then spend an age trying to screw it on.

"You have to push and turn," says Steve as the filled bottle begins to scorch my hand. "Like on a medicine bottle."

I manage to click the top on, lay it on its side next to the others – Steve checks I've screwed it on tight enough – then I'm ready to push the pedal again. Only there's no bottle there. I forgot to line it up and would have whooshed hot sauce all over myself if Steve hadn't stopped me. I try again, but I can't get the rhythm right. Pedal, fill, screw, pedal, fill, screw.

"Maybe you should just do one bottle at a time?"

That's slightly more manageable but I'm still struggling to get the lids on. I can't believe Steve does this by himself, filling 300 bottles in less than twenty minutes. That's four seconds a bottle max. I've only done five or so before my brother yells over, "Come on Bro, let me have a go." That's the thing with him. Better at coordination. My mum and dad always used to say it, between enormous guffaws about the names they'd given us.

Thankfully my brother does just as badly. By the time Steve took over to fill the remaining 35 or so bottles in twenty seconds there was a huge pool of hot red sauce dripping from the bottom of the bottling machine. But the end result is pleasing, a little row of fifty ruby red sauces lying on their sides so the hot liquid inside sterilises those awkward to attach lids.

Steve leads us both back upstairs to his hammock office for the finale of our work of the day: labelling. Mushemi Fire's logo, a black and white oval with a Scotch Bonnet inside, was sketched out on a scrap of paper on the floor of Steve's little house on Mushemi Road. But it felt so right, just an authentic west African feel, that he didn't change it even as the company came back to the UK and became more commercial. No zebra striped vans, *Lion King* sunsets or wooden African masks for him. Though he does give his stand at festivals a subtle southern African feel and says doing so has increased his sales.

He's under no illusions that the marketing image and story behind his sauces is just as important as the sauces themselves when it comes to sales. One of his most important lessons was that selling his bottles in threes at festivals with a bulk discount resulted in more profit than selling one bottle at a time. Likewise, though his chilli jam flew off his stand, it cost him so much to make compared with his other products that he had to prioritise the sauces which offered him a larger margin. He also produces silly hot sauces because he knows he needs to attract hot-heads as well as customers after something milder. It's business and passion in delicate balance.

At the same time, he knows the Zambian connection and his determination to keep it is a key selling point that differentiates him from the competition. Alongside the deep affection for his sauces and the company he's created, Steve clearly has a good business head. He has to make tough but uncomfortable decisions if Mushemi Fire is to survive. But the Zambian and southern African roots of what he does are sacrosanct. Judging by last year's progress, he's budgeted to sell 10,000 bottles this year.

He hands us three stickers each, one front label, one ingredients list, and one best before date. We then get two bottles of the still warm sauce we've just brewed. My labels are wonky and I have to pull them off and re-stick a few times to get them on straight. In the end I'm satisfied I've given the bottles an authentic feel, just the right side of home-made for a small chilli producer. Steve usually powers through the sticking, labelling vast numbers of his bottles in next to no time. But today he's happy just to watch and laugh as my brother and I offer his sauce our fat fingered approach yet again. At least we're consistent.

He boxes up two bottles each and presents them to us, with a few other bottles of sauce as mementos. He's been working on two new recipes: a sweet pepper and tamarind sauce made with papaya, pineapple and green chilli that is sticky and syrupy, a kind of African version of sweet and sour sauce; and a hot sauce called Zwao! which means 'pain' in Cinyanja, one of the seven root languages spoken in southern Africa. Made with nearly fifty percent Ugandan Scotch Bonnets, topped off with a handful of Bird's Eye chillies, it should deserve its name. Both bottles are from his first batch of these new recipes and he sends us on our way asking us to send back our thoughts.

Before we go, I notice Steve diligently marking the number of bottles he's given us in his Mushemi Bible. It occurs to me that for a tiny producer like Mushemi Fire, spending half a day with my brother and me, and then giving us free samples to take away afterwards, is a particularly generous gesture. While I'm sure he marked his time and our freebies on a line labelled 'marketing', those are sauces he could have sold. And his time with us could have been spent manufacturing way more than fifty poxy bottles.

Margins are tight in this game and thousands of pounds of Steve's own savings have gone into building his business. No wonder he keeps detailed records in his little leather book about every bottle he's ever made and sold, at what price, at what festival, how much it's cost him to do so, and what profit, if any, they've created.

On this journey I've not yet met someone who combines such passion, technical knowledge, marketing instinct and sheer business nous as Steve. I've no doubt this commitment to the figures, as well as the quality of his product and its roots, means he'll go far. And if he does, that's all good things for Zambia because Steve is determined to put back as much into the country that inspired him as he's taken out.

"The ultimate aim is to source as much as I can from Zambia, but that will take time. If I can get more money going back to Zambia, I'll feel like I've done a good thing."

Already most of the ingredients he uses in his products are from southern Africa, most often bought through an African wholesale market in Birmingham. He visits at 4 a.m. to get the freshest chillies before spending the rest of the same day processing them into a mash to keep their flavour. This is more than making and selling good quality chilli sauce. It looks like a life calling. He even has visions of setting up a branch of Mushemi Fire back in Lusaka where it all started.

Back at my brother's house, we can't wait to open our samples and get stuck in. Darrius' wife and daughters gather round to join in the action and we all take slow tastes with meaningful looks on our faces. We've watched too many episodes of *Masterchef*.

First, we try our own Mother's Ruin. It's slightly sour, probably thanks to Darrius' over-generosity with the gin. But it's subtle and mild enough to shake over a pasta or fish dish to enrich rather than ruin it. It gets all of our approval, though I usually prefer something a little richer. The tamarind sweet and sour sauce too is good and sticky, welcomed all round the family as an alternative to the Chinese version.

Next comes Mushemi Fire's One Drop. This Ugandan style chilli oil is one for the hot-heads and comes in a tiny bottle with a drop pipette. It's a flavouring, not a sauce, so it's no more designed to be eaten by itself than you'd take a swig of sunflower oil. We take one drop each on our fingers. The rapeseed it's made with comes in first with a pleasant but strong pollen dust flavour. The rapeseed Steve uses is grown not far from his kitchens in Staffordshire. With the African grown Scotch Bonnet chillies, it makes his One Drop an international flavour in the purest sense of the word. The chilli kicks in second and it's a burning that takes your breath away. We're all sweating a little, with the girls also embarrassingly dabbing away a few beads with a sheet of kitchen roll. My brother's hair is soaked. I'm little-of-hair, but my scalp is shining like a wet balloon.

Finally, we go for the Zwao! and it is indeed very hot but exactly up my street. It's thick and bitty and vinegary and lemony, the kind of sauce I like to make a little pool of at the side of my plate and incorporate with each forkful of food. This, Steve had said earlier, is exactly how Zambians like to eat their chilli: a morsel of meat or dried fish, a dab of sauce or slice of chilli, chomp then repeat. There follows a deep negotiation between Darrius and I about how we're going to split our stash. Neither of us wants to let go of any bottle, and we both proudly cling to the bottles of Mother's Ruin we'd made that day. In the end my brother lucks out with the tamarind sauce, while I take the One Drop for its entertainment value when friends come around. My wife and kids would never let me cook a family dish with it. I also take the wonderful Zwao! for personal use only. For weeks after my visit it seems to get more delicious every time I try it, though it's right up there in heat with the hottest sauces I've ever tried. Annoyingly for my wife, it makes me hiccup uncontrollably at the dinner table. She doesn't understand that's exactly what makes it a good hot sauce.

I'm staying at my dad's that night and as the sun goes down I call home to talk to my wife and kids. After kissing my older one goodnight, and trying to understand the blather of my four-year-old who doesn't know how to use a phone, they pass me to mum.

"I miss you," I say.

"I miss you too."

"Can you please bring the chillies in out of the conservatory?"

"Already done it," she says. "Already done it." Now that is true love.

At the Suffolk chilli event I'd been surprised how many African inspired producers there had been. And Mushemi Fire offered a window into how Africans like their chillies. I'd always thought hot food was more of a West Indies/Caribbean thing, alongside the popularity of chilli in south and central America, in China and across the Indian subcontinent. So what's going on?

Let's recap. Christopher Columbus found chillies in the Caribbean at the beginning of the sixteenth century and brought them back to Europe where they spread inland across mainland Europe, particularly the parts hot enough for them to grow outside.

But we also took them via existing trade routes to the west coast of Africa. Then later we took chillies with us when we got into the nasty habit of shipping our iron, cloth, wine and guns out to Africa and swapping them for (or more often just stealing) human beings who we turned into slaves. Chillies moved inland from the west coast of Africa where Africans embraced the capsaicin burn with open arms, accustomed as they were already to food that was highly spiced with black pepper and ginger.

Meanwhile, we exported the slaves – twelve million of them in all – to work coffee, cotton, sugarcane plantations and the like in the West Indies/Caribbean and also in the newly 'discovered' North America. Chillies had gone full circle, via Africa, back to the Americas where we first got them. This, by the way, also explains why much of the population of the West Indies is Black African in origin, rather than Latin American which it had been before the Europeans came along. The former slaves gradually took independent ownership of the West Indies that they'd previously been forced to farm.

What's the lesson from all this? Apart from that we slave-taking resource-exploiting native-people-killing Europeans have an awful lot to answer for, it's that when we think of chillies as native to Africa (or India or China for that matter) we're wrong. Europeans brought chillies from Latin America then sprinkled them across the world. It took just fifty years from when we brought chillies back to Europe for them to be growing in all the territories we'd claimed or were trading with all over the world. And the sheer diversity of species of chilli around the world is down to five root varieties of the plants adapting to the environment and climates they found themselves in.

And that, my friends, is how Africans came to love chillies. And why my old GCSE history, geography and biology teachers are shaking their heads with dismay at my gross oversimplification.

Bird's Eye. Piri Piri. Pilli Pilli. Peri Peri. What's in a name? Well, when it comes to chillies, more than you think. Or should that be chilies? I can't be the only one who gets confused when people talk about capsicum plants and their fruits by all kinds of different titles. Is Paprika a kind of chilli, or another name for it? Is Chile a country, a meat dish served with tacos or just the name of a fruit? What's with the whole Naga/Bhut Jolokia thing?

The answer is not simple. Back when Christopher Columbus brought back chillies from the Caribbean, he called them *pimiento*. It's the Spanish word for pepper because he thought he'd discovered a new kind pepper, of the salt and pepper variety, that were already being shipped over to Europe from India. At the time, the natives of the Caribbean already had their own name for the fruits before Columbus started messing around with it: *aji*, a name they'd brought from mainland Latin America. In the Caribbean, the word is still used. Meanwhile, the native Mexicans called their fiery fruit *chilli*, stemming from their word for red. The Spanish settlers later changed the spelling there to *chile*.

Back in Europe, chillies in Spain are still called *pimiento* (and a smoked ground chilli pepper powder is called *pimienton*), in Italy *pepperon*, in France *piment*, in Portugal *pimenta*, and in the Balkans *paprika*. Somewhere in the mix, we Brits started using Columbus' *pepper* and the Mexican *chilli* together, to create *chilli pepper*. Then more lazily simply *chilli*.

Across the world, the words are added to depending on the type of chilli/pimenta/paprika you're talking about. In Mexico, for example, Tonalchilli is a variety meaning 'chilli of the sun'. Chiltepin means 'flea chilli' (I don't know why) and Chilli Colorado means 'coloured chilli' (I can make a good guess). Essentially, chillies themselves and the type of chilli you're talking about take on various names depending on where you are, where they come from, how they're prepared, what stage of ripeness they're at, and indeed whether you've dried or smoked them. And there's loads of overlap as breeders and chilli hunters hit upon what they think are new strains of chillies that, in fact, already exist elsewhere. (Believe it or not, that's an extremely controversial thing to say in the chilli world.)

So what's the difference between a Naga, a Ghost chilli and a Bhut Jolokia? The chilli-heads might have my guts for breakfast with a pool of Tabasco sauce, but according to my research the answer is nothing. But even then the Naga has its own sub-strains. Should it be Jalapeño or Halapeno, perhaps even Halapeño? Pronounced *khal* or *jal?* With an *n* or an *ny?* You decide. I guess we're just going to have to accept the confusion and muddle along as best we can.

And since you asked, the name of the country Chile has nothing at all to do with chillies. There are a myriad of disputes and theories about that name too, but let's stick to the capsicum debate shall we?

14th April – Habanero, we have a problem. My wife spots me wandering around miserably and finally gets out of me what's wrong. It's not life or death or anything, but a couple of leaves on my Habanero 7 have gone pale. It's the same sun scorching some of my other plants suffered in late March. I thought Habanero 7 had become light hardened by now but the plant is fragile with only a handful of leaves anyway so this is one to watch closely. Like I've said all along, this is a tough plant to grow at home. I'm due to visit a chilli farm soon and I'm going to get the best advice on what to do next. Full sun or no sun, heat or no heat? They say treat chillies mean, but if they wilt or go pale when I do there'll be no plant left to be mean to. And that means no Habanero 7 chillies. Again.

28th April – Habanero 7 seems to be out of the danger zone for now. It's grown new leaves and the scorched ones are now shaded beneath them. It's still pretty squat and taking on none of the height and vitality of most of the other plants around it. Vampire and Friar's Hat are both gloriously strong, with nearly a dozen leaves, a thick stem and are over a foot in height. And Masquerade, just look at you go. Loads of tiny but flamboyant leaves as well as a good stock of sturdier broad ones. There are even a handful of fledgling flower buds hanging down from the higher reaches. Those flowers, properly cared for, are likely to be my first chillies of the season. And it's not even May.

I've started leaving the plants out in the conservatory overnight given we're having a relatively mild spring.

From West India to West Brom

AFTER MY ENLIGHTENING afternoon with Steve in his tiny Mushemi Fire kitchen, the next morning I'm at the other end of the Midlands and this time at the very heart of the Black Country. It could not be more different.

Amidst the urban sprawl and factories of the West Midlands, bumped up against the M5 on one side and West Bromwich Albion's Hawthorns stadium on the other, sits the headquarters and main manufacturing plant of East End Foods.

I've come here because of their Very Hot Green Chilli Sauce. It's a favoured chilli sauce of my kitchen cupboard, but is so strong that it's always a bit of a gamble adding it to the side of your plate. Many a stir-fry, vegetarian chili or indeed egg on toast has been ruined by a slightly too eager pour. Though you just have to eat them anyway, don't you?

It says eat within four weeks on the bottle, but I'd be lucky to get through a bottle in that many months. A small teaspoon of this stuff is more than enough for a meal. In fact, Very Hot Green Chilli Sauce – almost half of which is pure hot green Habaneros, and much of the rest ginger purée – is my challenge sauce. When friends visit and express an interest in my chilli obsession it's always the East End Foods I reach for. There you are, get your gums around that. It tastes good – the ginger gives it an Indian, rather than Mexican or Thai feel – but the heat is mind blowing. I thought it would be fun to discover the source of that wondrous sauce. And to my surprise, it brought me within a few miles of where I grew up.

"I know that place," my dad said when I told him where I was headed. "I've been in there a few times, it's a pretty big Asian supermarket: big barrels of lentils, spices and stuff."

So I'd expected a large Indian food shop with imported sauces and packets laid out, perhaps boxed up in the back. But it turns out that what my dad had visited was one of the three cash-and-carry shops that East End Foods runs. The factory is a whole different affair altogether. A few big barrels of lentils, spices and stuff, as they'd say in West Bromwich, 'it aye'.

The factory reception could fit three or four of Steve's Mushemi Fire operations inside it and still have room spare for the Red Hot Chilli Fella too. There's an ornate staircase, all carved wood in Indian restaurant gold and red, and the reception desk is carved wood too. It has three clocks above it: London, New York, Delhi.

A little research ahead of my visit reveals the company was launched by an Indian Sikh family, the head of which had headed to the Black Country for a better life in the 1960s. In the West Midlands Sikhs have long made up around half of the Asian community, mainly immigrants from India and Pakistan during the seventies.

The West Midlands is still home to the largest number of Sikhs in the UK, so I'm pretty familiar with the laced-up beards and turban wearing Asian sweetshop owners and worshippers at gurdwaras dotted around the city. Roger Wouhra, son of the founder of East End Foods, comes bounding into reception in a blue puffer jacket and jeans, a welcoming grin on his face. No turban and no beard in sight, merely a rough stubble.

He speaks with a softer version of the gritty-but-singsong

Black Country accent my brother and dad have – and I just about managed to ditch at university. Roger's phone keeps buzzing. He's obviously a busy man even though it's a bank holiday. So I thank him effusively for making time for me.

"Oh no, that's fine," he says, grinning again. "I'm selling my car and someone's picking it up from outside the factory. Let me just go and see if I can track him down."

He plonks me in the company boardroom and there's more ornate wood here: a fifteen foot boardroom table, surrounded by carved wooden chairs. It feels so exotic and mysterious, I don't feel worthy enough to sit in the near throne like chair at its head – the one Roger had pointed to as he went off in search of the guy buying his car. Instead I wander around the boardroom taking in the awards, pictures and trinkets sitting on cabinets and small tables around the sides. One table is propped up by four carefully carved wooden swans. It's a little like a shrine and above it all sits a painting of a Sikh man – yes, beard and turban – with a gold garland draped across it. Roger later tells me it's his grandfather, Pritam Singh Wouhra, who is affectionately regarded as the father of East End Foods, even though he had nothing to do with it and passed away before it was formally established.

The photographs below feature Roger, his father, various uncles and his brothers in various meet-and-greets with the great and the good, including David Cameron who visited the factory in 2010. In another frame, next to a globe and ornate golden weighing scales, is a framed clipping from the *Express & Star*. It's the paper I used to browse through to find glass collecting jobs when I was a teenager; the paper which a grizzled old seller would flog outside the Wolverhampton Mander Centre grumbling "ArAyper" at passersby, a bastardisation of "Express and Star Paper" that he'd repeated so many times over the last thirty years that his words had all jumbled together. But we all knew what he meant.

Roger returns: "I'm sad to see it go," he says. "It was a good car, that." He points again to the throne at the head of the table and I sit. I explain my mission and particularly that I'm on a quest today to root out the origins of my favourite Very Hot Green Chilli Sauce.

He smiles with pride. "So you like hot chillies do you?"

"Oh, yeah," I say. "Well, not mad stuff. But I like that sauce."

"You want chillies? I'll show you some chillies today," he says with a proud smile.

Roger's father Tony Deep Wouhra travelled from Delhi to the UK in 1961 with three pounds in his pocket and a determination to find a better life. Here he met his wife who in turn knew a poultry farmer. Tony knew a business opportunity when he saw one and started selling the farmer's eggs door to door. It was the beginning of an interest in food retail that would last a lifetime. Tony moved on to open a butcher's and later a grocer's in Wolverhampton, and his brothers joined him in the early seventies. They were young but committed to hard work, says Roger, and together they launched East End Foods, selling Asian spices and lentils they bought from London wholesalers.

The company rode the waves of Indians, Pakistanis and other Asians coming to work in the car factories and heavy industry in the Midlands during the seventies. South Asians had already come to fill the manual worker gap in the post-war boom of the fifties and sixties, and in the seventies many of their families came to join them. Also in the seventies Asians were expelled from the Commonwealth countries of Uganda, Tanzania and Kenya and they too came to the

West Midlands with British passports looking for work and safety. All in all, it amounted to a huge influx of Asians to the region who each brought with them a desire for a taste of home. That amounted to a big, ready and willing market for Tony Wouhra and his brothers.

By the early eighties the Wouhras were importing foodstuffs from India and investing in semi-automatic processing machinery. Roger says he started at his father and uncle's company while barely out of childhood. He'd work during school holidays and on weekends in the cash-and-carry, stacking shelves and meeting customers. He officially joined the family business eleven years ago and now oversees much of the sales side – and PR, I reckon – of the company. The nineties saw massive expansion including, by the end of the decade, East End Foods' move to the 160,000-square-foot manufacturing plant in West Bromwich. The biggest of its kind in Europe.

Today Tony Wouhra is one of the best known (and richest) Asian businessmen in the UK, and East End Foods one of the best known ethnic food brands. Pretty much every major supermarket stocks East End Foods rice, lentils and sauces in their world foods sections. Back in Essex where I live, that section amounts to a tiny corner next to the gluten free stuff. In the super-Tesco the other side of the M5 in West Bromwich, there are a full eight aisles of world food produce to cater to the local area's immensely diverse population.

"We've seen all the big supermarkets want to attract the Asian customers," says Roger. "They're asking themselves: why are Mr and Mrs Singh going to Asian food shops, when they could be shopping here?" East End Foods helps them to reach that market.

The plant processes nearly 2,000 products, from lentils,

spices, kidney beans and chickpeas, to turmeric, ground ginger, coriander, cumin, basmati rice, pickles, oils and flavourings. And chilli. Lots and lots and lots of chilli. Various chilli powders and flakes, and curry mixes and sauces with chillies as a main ingredient. Chilli makes up a massive chunk of East End Foods' sales.

East End Foods uses Guntur Sannam and the much spicier Guntur Wonder Hot chilli varieties from west India in their millions. But producing and transporting chillies in massive quantities is complex and dangerous. So it's one of the only spices that East End Foods cleans and grinds in India. Most of the rest of their imported lentils, beans, seeds and spices are cleaned and ground right here in West Bromwich. Massive machines remove stones, husks, dust and other impurities before grinding and packaging.

"You can't grind chilli in its raw dried form on this site, or anywhere in the UK," Tony says. "It's a horrible process and the powder in the air would be taking people out on the roundabout down the road."

Instead, various strengths of ready prepared and quality controlled chilli powder come direct from Guntur, the main chilli growing region of Andhra Pradesh, in south-west India. There labour is cheaper, fair enough. Though I can't quite fathom why it's more acceptable for the unfortunate west indians, rather than west midlanders, to do the dirty work of hand removing stems, drying and grinding chillies. Nevertheless, East End Foods imports the chilli powder and flakes ready processed, but blends and packages them on-site in West Bromwich.

It turns out importing and processing chilli on an industrial scale is a complex business. One challenge is providing customers with a chilli powder that is consistent in heat and colour, an earthy matt orange rather than bright red. As I'm learning, chillies can range in colour and heat depending on when they were picked, the soil, the climate and loads of other factors. East End Foods' answer is surprisingly simple: consistently check the heat of chilli powders coming in, then mix them together accordingly to get the heat or colour required.

But that problem is small fry. In India, unscrupulous farmers and middlemen selling in the traditional local chilli markets – called *chilli mundis* – will often bulk up the weight of chilli they sell with all kinds of crud: poor quality and mouldy chillies, fruits grown with illegal amounts and types of pesticide, stalks, dust, salt. Any old junk that will make the crop heavier so they can stack it high and sell it cheap.

Roger showed me a video of his father visiting a mundi in 1990 where in full secret camera style he was shown bogus bartering with traders to get a cheaper price on chillies. He filmed the traders offering to add heavy but clearly knackered chilli cast-offs to the dried crop before processing. Tony was outraged and it led to him completely overhauling every step of East End Foods' supply chain, bringing most processing in-house. Now he works directly with farmers, not middlemen, and East End Foods provides on-site staff to train Indian farmers in good growing techniques, while also keeping an eye on quality.

The revisiting of its supply chain was probably one of the main reasons East End Foods managed to avoid being caught up in a major food scandal in 2005. A bright orange food dye called Sudan I had been banned across Europe because it was thought to be a carcinogen. A number of food companies were unwittingly still using it and Sudan I turned up in all kinds of supermarket sold grub, from curries and sauces, to pizzas and microwave meals. Over 400 products were recalled, amounting to hundreds of millions of pounds of food sales.

Incidentally, the UK ambassador for the African state of Sudan appealed for the name of the dodgy dye to be changed. It had nothing to do with the country and was ruining its reputation. What with their country's human rights violations in Darfur, the PR guys in the Sudanese government probably felt they already had a pretty heavy workload.

I think of the smaller chilli producers I've met so far who are hesitant to grow too big too fast and say they aren't interested in the supermarkets because they worry about being able to maintain quality. Their dismissal of the massive chilli producers as compromising quality and using cheap ingredients doesn't ring true here. It seems East End Foods' investment in quality is exactly why it's been able to grow so big and profitable.

With the – albeit pretty convincing – corporate spiel over and done with, I'm keen to get on with seeing how the factory works and getting right up close to the chilli itself. Roger calls in his colleague Anuj who is going to show me around the factory floor. He's initially sultry and bored as he takes me down past the offices, staff kitchen and general admin side of the business. But as soon as we've both donned our regulation blue hair-nets and white coats, he leads me through to the factory itself and becomes ignited.

We go through some double doors and the plant opens up before us. Its size takes my breath away. And this colossal warehouse is just the first part of the tour. There's a delicious heady fug of spice aroma in the air wherever you turn. We step aside as a chap drives by on a forklift carrying a pallet piled high with packs of green sultanas. On every side there are masses of boxed and wrapped food products stacked three storeys high. There are men in overalls, sporting hair-

and beard-nets, whizzing around on trucks, shifting beans and lentils from one end of the factory to another. This is the shipping area where produce waits to leave the factory. We walk past aisle upon aisle of pallets of black pepper, ground cumin, rice, chickpeas, all ready to be loaded onto trucks and shipped across the country and beyond. More than 180 tonnes of product leaves the factory every day.

Anuj is taking me through the factory process backwards, so the next step is to show me where the processed products are packaged. We amble into a noisy room where rows of conveyor belts have plastic packaging fed into one end and are being filled with ground paprika from massive hoppers above. The machine chugs away and neat little selfseal packets of spice roll off the end of the machine and into giant trolleys ready for bulk wrapping.

We walk into another warehouse, where giant funnels are busy cleaning and then grinding spices. In one of the funnels are millions of cloves, in another a tonne of brown lentils. Inside, Anuj tells me, there is sophisticated equipment for detecting the colour, shape and weight of the spice being processed. Anything that doesn't meet the machine's expectations gets spat out into one of several blue impurity bins.

We peer into one which is full of brown dust and flakes of husk that otherwise would go into the packets with the cloves. Into another there's a gentle putt-putt-putting. Earlier Roger had said his machines remove stones from the raw ingredients they import and I'd assumed he'd meant stones as in the pips of fruits. But no, he meant stones. As in gravel. Gravel from a remote Indian region that has travelled half way across the world embedded in piles of lentils and cloves and is now putt-putt-putting into a blue waste bin in a factory on a West Bromwich industrial estate.

Anuj leads us through the raw materials warehouse which is where raw foodstuffs arrive from across the world in colossal bags like those in which you get sand when you're laying a patio. Each bag is marked with what's inside it. Anuj rolls down the top of a few to show me the contents: 800 kilos of cumin powder, a rich chocolaty brown oozing with a heavy curry smell; 1,200 kilos of deep red paprika, so big you could dive into it, all gathered into a dusty crimson peak. We walk past similarly massive bags of pepper and rice and beans, and Anuj picks up handfuls, holds them up for me to sniff, then lets them run back through his fingers just like they do on TV adverts. Another forklift passes carrying another massive bag of spice. Anuj speaks to the driver in his own language: "Black salt," he nods to me. "From Pakistan."

The deeper we go into the factory the more pungent the smell. We pass through a fridge that is twice as big as my house, where the smell of ground coriander is all around us. It's stored there at exactly six degrees centigrade, the optimum temperature for retaining the flavour and aroma when it is mixed and packaged.

And as we gradually approach the four or five aisles of freshly imported chilli, each aisle about half a kilometre long, the air is so full of hot powder that I can feel it at the back of my throat and tingling in my nostrils. Here the chilli powder is kept in brown paper sacks on palettes wrapped in plastic. They're stacked from the floor, up to five shelves high. The chilli powder can't be shifted around in hessian sacks like the other products because it's so fine it would too easily escape through the cracks and into eyes, under fingernails and generally into where it's not wanted.

A guy seems to be in charge of the whole chilli section – how about that for a job? – and along with the same white coats and hairnets we're sporting, he's also wearing a face mask to stop him inhaling chilli dust all day. Chilli Guy reaches into a sack and fills a little plastic bag with chilli powder for me. I smell it and the pungency is ripe. This is unadulterated powdered chilli. Probably a week or two ago it existed as chillies lying out to dry under a hot Andra Pradesh sun. This is the milder end of the chilli powders East End Foods imports. The label on the 25 kilo sack label says it's 38,500 SHU. Another sack is marked with the very specific 84,969 SHU, but Chilli Guy isn't going to offer me any of that.

"I wouldn't give you that in its raw form," says Anuj. "You can't play with this stuff. And you definitely don't want it in your eyes." Instead Chilli Guy reaches into another sack of 34,000 SHU and bags me up a handful of chilli flakes.

On this site, East End Foods receives all the raw chilli powders and crushed chillies. Some are then shipped across town to nearby Tipton where a partner company, Panesar Foods, manufactures its 'wet goods': sauces and pickles and chutneys, including my Very Hot Green Chilli Sauce. East End Foods supplies eighty percent of all Asian food outlets, pretty much every supermarket and Asian food shop in the land, as well as white labelling their products for other brands.

There are probably no Indian or Bangladeshi restaurants at all that don't use East End Foods products somehow. And every pack of chilli powder and flakes they do use or sell, the chilli in every garam masala or curry blend, the chilli flavouring in every chilli sauce or curry jar, has one way or another passed through these shelves. It feels like the very spot where we're standing, with chilli stacked tonne after tonne, floor to ceiling, is the epicentre of Asian chilli flavour across the whole of the UK. With the chilli powder wafting in the air all around us it's a dizzying thought.

We blink into the sunlight as Anuj leads me to the back of the huge plant and past four enormous steel hoppers. Together they make up the company's new £6 million basmati rice processing mill. The size of the operation here leaves me wide-eyed and when I'm returned to the boardroom Roger Wouhra's smile tells me he knows that I've had great fun. He tells me about his father's latest investment scheme, a partnership with Birmingham City University to build an urban food farming technology centre, complete with hotel, demonstration plantation and vertical algae farm (whatever that is). The development will be built on what used to be Birmingham's former HP Sauce factory. I can imagine Tony Wouhra thumbing his nose at HP with his choice of real estate. Call that a condiment? I'll show you a condiment. Ironically, Heinz left the site to move production abroad.

"You can tell my dad is a bit of a character," says Roger, in a 'parents, what can you do with them?' kind of way. His ambitious entrepreneurial zeal hasn't done Tony Wouhra any harm. He's now worth over £80 million. Not bad for three quid in your pocket and selling eggs door to door.

Today chillies are the most widely used spice in the world and there's no mistaking that chillies are a significant part of Indian cuisine. Indeed chillies are so cheap and easy to produce across much of the Indian subcontinent that they're the only spice millions of poor Indians can afford to eat regularly. They actually have a higher content of vitamin C than oranges, though probably wouldn't go down quite so well in a juice carton in your kid's lunchbox.

Despite being such a key ingredient of Indian foods, and India being the biggest exporter of chillies in the world, no Indians had even heard of hot chillies, let alone grown them, until about 500 years ago. The Portuguese got hold of chillies after Christopher Columbus and other explorers had brought them back to Europe at the beginning of the sixteenth century. Much of the evidence suggests that it was they who took them to India, probably starting out in Goa, the original home of the Vindaloo. From there chillies spread like wildfire. It's all a bit political, with Spanish historians claiming their ancestors were the chilli spreaders in India and China. Whatever. The steaming hot curry had been born and thankfully is still with us today.

As he sends me on my way Roger hands over a presentation box of swag to take with me, proudly pulling each product out to show me. There's a garlic chilli sauce, a jar of minced red chilli, a catering sized pack of hot curry powder and another of chilli flakes. And then with a jokey smile he pulls out a bottle of Very Hot Green Chilli Sauce. He presents it to me across his forearm like a posh waiter presents a fine wine. "A little gift from all of us," he says. He seems pleased I've shown an interest in what his family does and has achieved.

It's with regret that I leave the Black Country that day – and let's be honest, that's not something I've said very often in the thirty odd years I've been trying to escape it. But today I've peered through a bright window on a region that is best known for heavy industry and even named after its reputation for filthy work, dirt, grime and smog. In search of chillies I've once again seen entrepreneurs at work. But this time on an enormous scale. East End Foods has picked up the mantle of the industrialists and entrepreneurs who worked on these same sites years before. And it's showing their same commitment and passion for the local community, and indeed the country at the heart of which the region sits. The West Midlands often gets a bad rap because of its mixed race population and its supposedly dumb accent. But I say those things are some of what makes the West Midlands so special.

It is a diverse community that has – infamous Wolverhampton MP Enoch Powell and a few BNP lunatics aside – mostly lived and worked in harmony for nearly three generations. It's a diverse little melting pot, a little… hold on… what's that strange feeling in the pit of my stomach? It can't be, can it? I think it is. It's pride in my home region, the place of my upbringing.

Wolverhampton Wanderers are playing a crunch match against Rotherham on the same day as my visit to East End Foods, which is situated right next door to their – our? – derby rivals West Brom. It's a match that will confirm Wolves' place in the Championship. For the first time since the early 1990s, back when Steve Bull lit up Molineux and was selected to play in the England squad for the Italian World Cup, I feel an almost irresistible urge to check the football results.

We won, 6-4.

1st May – I've noticed many of the taller chilli plants are slightly leaning towards the sun. My chilli advice book says I should rotate the pots frequently, particularly if this happens, so that the leaves search for the best sunlight. It generates a strong central stem instead of one that permanently leans. I'm also advised to leave the windows open occasionally, particularly when it's windy, because that too will strengthen the plants.

If there is no wind, one YouTube video suggests, I should gently run a sheet of paper over the plants to gently flex them instead. So a couple of other things to monitor and remember. And one thing to do when no-one else is looking. Who'd have thought growing chillies could be so complex? But I'm still determined to get this right so I'll do what it takes.

6th May – The weather has turned and it's rainy, windy and cold outside. Everything in the conservatory seems to have stopped. The plants aren't in danger but aren't going anywhere fast. My Scorpion and Bhut Jolokia seedlings still only have their immature leaves and aren't doing much else. But it's much too much effort to be bringing it all in and out of the conservatory every day. And I'm too tight to put the radiator on in there.

A burning business

I'M BARELY OUT of my cycling shoes before Jamie Sythes is showing me Wiltshire Chillies' latest product. It's my first stop on a long weekend of chilli visits that will also involve lots of cycling. What I hadn't planned was abruptly ending 25 years of vegetarianism.

I've just ridden ten miles from Chippenham station through the gloriously green Wiltshire countryside and arrived at a little village called Whitley, near Melksham, where Jamie has his farm. I'm still sweating when he leads me into his kitchen where he's just taken a delivery of a batch of chilli chorizo. He'd sent some of his home-grown Habaneros down to a meat curer in Cornwall. After three weeks of hanging, they've sent back some smoky hot sausages to add to the Wiltshire Chillies range.

He wants me to share this first try with him and before I've had time to protest, he's cut me a thick chunk and taken one for himself. It seems rude to refuse so I take a bite and actually enjoy the rough piquant taste and even the dry, slightly fatty meat flavour. There's not much chilli fruit to it but it has a spiciness you're apparently supposed to expect from a Spanish sausage. Jamie seems a little under impressed but we both take another slice and these ones are much hotter.

"Looks like they didn't quite mix the meat up with the seasoning properly," says Jamie, "which means the chorizo is inconsistent in its heat."

It's no surprise that Jamie is testing out another new product to add to his almost 100-strong range of chilli based sauces, jams, nuts and chocolate. Like Kellogg's has to continually re-invent its cornflakes – now with a sugar coating, now with honey, now with dried strawberry, now with chocolate, now with yoghurt flakes – Jamie knows he has to continually innovate to stay on top of the chilli industry.

The idea of the 'chilli industry' is why I've come to Melksham. Is there really a chilli industry in Britain, or is it just a bunch of amateurs and home kitchen producers struggling to survive? Are a few National Trust and English Heritage properties just laying on chilli festivals to bring new people to their castles and country homes, or is there really a demand for them? Jamie Sythes has been recommended by a number of people in the chilli world as someone who can talk facts and figures with me, the business end of the small scale chilli market in Britain.

A first glance at his set-up – a few untidy outbuildings nestled behind his parents' farmhouse and a stretch of five empty polytunnels in the field behind them – almost answers the question for me. There are tyres and bits of plastic scattered about the place. There are boxes stacked up, dismantled tractors and piles of old tarpaulin. This is no industrial chilli sauce plant. It's a home producer making do. But looks can be deceiving. To start with, this is only part of Jamie's operation. As well as the polytunnels, he has a massive greenhouse near Chippenham. And I've come at a quiet time.

"In about a month, everything here will look totally different," he says. "We'll have a few frantic weeks putting in the watering systems, transplanting and getting everything ready for the summer growing. The farm will be packed with helpers; we need to get many thousands of plants in the ground as quickly as possible."

He shows me a polytunnel full of seedlings which are already far larger than my shameful efforts at home. They're all closely packed on wooden benches, sitting on heated mats. There's another full germination tunnel sitting next door, adding up to 3,000 plants on this site alone. At the greenhouse there are another 4,000 poised for replanting. Each of those plants will produce masses of chilli fruits.

The scale of Jamie's operation begins to become apparent. This isn't a hobbyist, it's a professional farmer just getting prepared for the season. The polytunnels and lengths of rubber pipe take on a new meaning. It may look shabby now but this is the calm before the storm.

He leads me into his stockroom where there are 3,000 full jars, bottles and packets stacked high. And this is only half of his current stock; the rest is out there around the country. Wiltshire Chillies is at 26 festivals, events and markets this weekend alone. In the late summer, when the harvesting season is at its height, Jamie says the farm will produce 4,000 units of produce a day, supplying more festivals and events. He'll also be stocking up for the winter when his products fly off the shelves at Christmas markets as stocking fillers and gifts.

"We do sell a few chilli plants, but to be honest we need every chilli we can get to go into our own products."

Next to the storeroom is the labelling and boxing room. It's dotted with nifty machinery for sealing bottles with foil tops and quickly processing labels. This used to be Jamie's kitchen, until his production outgrew it and he had to clear another outbuilding on the farm to build a new one.

Jamie is as keen as I'd hoped to talk about business plans as well as chilli plants. With not too much to see before replanting begins he leads me to the frantic family kitchen, where his mum and dad, a selection of toddlers, kids' toys and dogs vie for floor space. It's a proper farmhouse kitchen, with lots of wooden panels and cupboards, teapots and other trinkets. An Aga is tucked into the corner. We sit down at the kitchen table with mugs of tea and Jamie tells me his story of corporate high-flyer turned chilli farmer. He was a business analyst with a busy but ultimately dissatisfying life and a three-hour round trip commute to Gloucester every day.

"Me and some friends were having a conversation in a pub and it came round to what we wanted to do when we grew up," says Jamie. "Mine was to be a chilli farmer though I don't really know where that came from."

The financial crisis saw Jamie end up working in a local pub and growing chillies as a hobby. In 2009 he made up some sauces with his chillies, sold them across the bar and people seemed to like them. By the beginning of 2010 he'd produced what he called his first 'proper' product and started selling it at a market stall. By 2011 he was selling 1,000 sauces a year. By 2012 he was working full time on the farm selling 2,000 a year. By 2013 he was growing many tens of thousands of chillies a year, and producing a broad range of products with them. Crucially other chilli sauce makers were buying chillies from him for their own products.

That's what gives Jamie the edge. Many of his chilli plants are on his family farm, just metres away from his kitchen. He's also grown big enough to be able to buy ingredients, bottles, packaging and labels in bulk. It means his costs are low compared with other chilli producers. And that means more profit per product sold. Not that – whatever impression other chilli businesses like to give – the chilli industry is particularly profitable. Jamie seems to do alright exactly because of his cost savings. But he estimates based on his own experience that other producers, and even chilli farms, may just about scrape by.

The other advantage Wiltshire Chillies has is that Jamie has come up with a business model that shares some of his risk. Those who sell his sauces at markets and festivals across the land most weekends don't work directly for him. They buy the sauces, chutneys and chocolate at a knock down price, cover their own costs for transport and stalls, and everyone benefits from the strength of the Wiltshire Chillies brand.

But that doesn't mean just anyone can sell Wiltshire Chillies products, nor that Jamie is disconnected from the sellers he works with. Everyone is expected to work on the farm and in production. They have to get to know how the company works and what's coming up in production and to offer feedback. It's like a big Wiltshire Chillies family. And Jamie puts in the hours just like everyone else. He works five days on his farm producing, then another two every weekend selling.

However, he reckons that the chilli industry may be reaching its peak. In the first years of his farming, Jamie did extensive research on the size of the market. He believes there's one or two years left before there will be too many producers doing too many of the same kinds of things. It's something I observed at the Suffolk Chilli Festival: when your sauces are relatively similar, and each stall has the same general line-up of mild to hot sauces, then slight differences in flavour and marketing can only go so far.

Jamie is also worried about the ever-present shadow of the supermarkets and super-growers. Like almost everyone else I've met so far, he wants to keep the large supermarkets at arm's length. He's too often heard the story that a large multiple will buy up your stock and ask you to produce more in large quantities, making you reliant on them. Then the next year they demand all-or-nothing discounts that leave growers and suppliers in a comply-or-fail position. He's also seen the huge growers starting to get in on the chilli action. There are colossal operations of greenhouses in the UK, Spain and Holland that are seeing the upward sales curve in chillies, and can easily switch from growing tomatoes and sweet peppers to something hotter in just one season.

The result is a thoughtful, though not worried man. But one who appears to be nearing decision time with his business. In one breath he talks of funding a new house, even a swimming pool, with what he's doing. But at others he wonders whether his business – and others' – is a very long term prospect.

"My big question in the next few years is: is it sustainable? Should I really push the boat out this year or will chilli fall in on itself? I wanted a small family business but what I've ended up with is a complete life changer. Do I want to grow massive or have an exit strategy?"

We consumers may currently be welcoming the return of local and artisan producers, and be buying from them at markets and events both because of their quality goods but also because it offers a nice shopping experience. Wiltshire Chillies alone has 600 days of markets and stalls lined up for this year. But shopping is a fashion and fashions can be fickle.

It's a sad thought, but almost everything I've seen so far – the fun and keen small producers, the festivals, the websites and special sauces – may be short-lived as hot sauces and foods become normalised rather than special. Any trip to the snack shelves of any large Tesco, Sainsbury's or Morrisons and their growing ranges – from chilli sauces, to crisps, to chocolate – is testament to a depressing but possibly inevitable march of progress. Heinz has just launched a Tangy Jalapeño Hot and Zesty sauce to add to its growing spicier selection. Asda has just released packs of hot Pork and Three Chillies sausages as part of its Extra Special range, and is now stocking Hot-Headz Insane 2nd Assault hot sauce. Consumer research company Mintel has recently launched its own Heat Index.

"If you went into a supermarket in 2010, you'd get simple 'chilli flavoured' crisps. Go in now and you get chipotle crisps, and Thai chilli crisps, all kinds of varieties," Jamie says. In an increasingly tough market, it strikes me that those who will survive will be people like Jamie. He has the business background to be continually looking at his figures, assessing his progress, projecting forward and making tough decisions.

He takes me to his office to show me graphs and spreadsheets and business plans, and he talks animatedly about some of the other larger chilli growers and producers that he works with. There's no hint of competition or arrogance. In fact, there's an underlying implication that they actually work together more than they'd like to admit. Perhaps – though I have no certainty on this – they share buying power, equipment and processes, even fruits and growing space. At the very least, Jamie says, he has an attitude of helping and supporting others doing what he's doing. He doesn't want the supermarket approach of crushing the competition. Unite and survive.

And no wonder. Because Jamie is a chilli-head in the purest sense of the word. He loves the plant and its fruit. He shows me endless pictures of chillies he's grown, all neatly cut up and presented against a measuring scale as if they were butterflies neatly pinned for a display. He shows me a dissected picture of one of his favourite specimens, the

Condor's Beak. The chilli changes colours at different stages of ripeness, and he has examples laid out in a pleasing row.

He's also spent long hours thinking deeply about his chilli products' names, their labels, the message of his brand and working on flavours. He has a personal collection of very special chillies and says he is always collecting new seeds, creating new seedlings and looking at new plants for his own interest. It's all about tasting and testing and if he finds something new, unusual or interesting to look at, he'll grow a larger sample to see if it scales up. Then the next year bring it on to a commercial level. A breakthrough like that is rare but it helps to be continually innovating.

It's like the chilli chorizo that broke my almost lifelong vegetarianism. He's putting something small scale out there to see if it works. He'll learn from sales and customer feedback then make a tough decision about whether to scale up for Christmas or next summer – regardless of how much he likes the product himself. And Wiltshire Chillies have had some real hits: a series of sauces linked with comic book characters; an annual festive gift box of three sauces; Hell Mouth, a sauce playing on the popularity of Buffy the Vampire Slayer (I had to look it up); a sauce called God Slayer that – surprisingly or perhaps not so surprisingly – is a huge hit at Christmas. This last one was Jamie's response to the sheer number of sauces out there that use devil, evil, fire and brimstone connotations in their names: Satan's Shit and the Dartmoor Devil, etcetera.

With Jamie in real chilli love territory it seems a good moment to ask a question that's been on my mind since I started looking into the very hottest chillies. Why do the hottest ones always seem to be so wrinkled and decrepit? Take a look at the Carolina Reaper or the Maruga Scorpion, currently the hottest two chillies, and you'll see a shrivelled, pitted, heavily veined thing that may be incredibly hot, but certainly is no Duchess of Cambridge. Perhaps, I wonder, because they've been continually bred for heat, the other things that go into making a chilli appealing to birds like colour, plumpness and smell have fallen by the wayside. After all, crazy hot chilli plants are not naturally selected in the wild. They're specially bred.

But this connoisseur of the chilli plant doesn't think so. He shows me pictures of wonderfully plump fruits with thick and full skins. He says these will knock your head off just as much as the shrivelled numbers. He pulls up a picture of a White Fatalii chilli from his own collection.

"It's an unusual white chilli that's particularly hot. We're planning to do something this year with it. It's a good looking product, it has a high heat and it's really collectible."

But the days of going down the route of creating mentally hot sauces and extracts, says Jamie, echoing many others I've met, have long gone. In the industry that's become a necessary business decision. There's a small but steady market for that kind of stuff, but supplying it alone isn't a long term growth strategy.

"As you get to this heat level, you'll find that people can't really tell the difference between them," he says. "I've tried all of them and the flavour difference at that heat is minute."

In fact, there's another underlying theme – though again I feel it's only implied – that the continual race to produce the very hottest chilli might be a bit bogus. It's something I've considered on my journey so far too: how come slightly hotter chillies seem to be produced every year? Each August or September there are a wave of news stories about this or that fruit being hotter than last year's: the hottest in the world. There's then a renewed interest in chillies for a week or so, perhaps some increased sales to the chilli sauce collectors – yes, there are people who collect bottles of sauce just like stamps or fossils – but soon everything dies down until next year's announcement.

In fact, other chilli producers have told me behind the scenes – I can't believe I have collected 'Deep Throats' who want to talk off the record in the chilli world – that they question whether the new hottest fruits are really any different from those already produced. Are they just fruits that happen to have come out particularly hot that year? It's claimed there are 8,000 or more strains of chillies. But the University of New Mexico has started a systematic DNA cataloguing of fruits and early indications are that there are far fewer, maybe as few as 2,000. They're just being renamed – sometimes intentionally, most often accidentally – time and again. It reminds me again about what Andrew Jukes said about heat in chillies. Environment, soil, sunlight and even picking time are at least as important to Scoville results as the fruit or its genetics. In other words, while the latest Ghost chilli or Scorpion or Carolina Reaper might be officially recognised this year as the world's hottest chilli by the *Guinness Book of Records*, exactly the same plant in next year's crop may be nowhere near as hot. It could be luck, not judgement or expertise.

To the everyday consumer, it's a little PR race that makes no concrete difference. After all, once you've tasted last year's hottest chilli, the only thing you can do with this year's is to taste it too, maybe buy a sauce, then wait for the following year. Most mainstream consumers just don't like it that hot, and it's the mainstream consumption of chillies that is the growth market.

The ChilliFoundry website lists over 260 chilli growers and seed-sellers, producers, hot sauce and other chilli product makers. The number of chilli festivals in the UK continues to grow, with dozens listed by information website SuperHotChilli.com. Chilli FestUK hosts its own eight town-centre weekend festivals, and loads of garden centres and country houses put on their own too. That means many tens of thousands of chilli enthusiasts, not-quite-sures, their friends and families will visit a chilli festival each year. The biggest of the bunch is West Dean Chilli Fiesta with capacity for 21,000 visitors, with 500 camping. The North East Chilli Festival had 12,000 visitors last year. The Great Dorset Chilli Festival celebrates its 25th year in operation in 2014.

The consumer research group IRI says that while table sauce sales were down in 2013, sales of chilli sauce bucked the trend and grew by 1.7 percent. Sweet chilli sauce enjoyed a 6.6 percent growth. It says in 2013 we spent £21 million on chilli sauces, but that probably doesn't include sauces, pastes and chutneys bought directly from smaller artisan producers, the real heart of Chilli Britain.

Salvatore Genovese runs the biggest chilli farm in Britain, in Blunham, Bedfordshire. He is by far the biggest producer and seller of chillies. He says he started messing around with chillies 'for a bit of fun', but now sells to four of the biggest supermarkets, shifting up to a million chillies a week at peak harvest time from his seven acres of greenhouses. He's been supplying Tesco with the Dorset Naga for four years, clearly illustrating that even day-to-day shoppers have been looking for something far hotter to add to their cooking. Today's British diners are eating food 400 times hotter than our parents could handle, according to research appearing in the *The Guardian* newspaper.

Just walk into any garden centre in the UK, and you'll notice a distinct difference in the plants they've been selling. Five years ago you could get seedlings marked 'chilli' or 'hot chilli' at best. Now, each garden centre offers a range of five or six ready grown plugs for everyday kitchen growers to take home. The huge Garden Centre Group recently shifted from selling generic chilli plants to a whole range, including the Bhut Jolokia, Jalapeño, Cayenne, Nasu and Medina varieties. In the US, where chilli sauce is a daily ritual, another market research company, IBISWorld, predicts chilli sauce revenue growing 4.1 percent every year until 2017. Incredibly, it rates chilli sauce alongside 3D printing and online glasses in the world's top ten future growth products.

Nevertheless I leave Jamie, his farm and his annoyingly delicious chorizo in a pensive mood. For the first time I'm a little worried about the fragility of the artisan, home produced and small scale chilli industry – just as I'm beginning to have a real affection for it, and the effusively friendly, passionate and committed people I've met. Clearly it's far from over. But like any industry the small producer's exciting Devil-may-care growth may soon need to take a long hard look at itself and its future. After all, most of us decry yet another Tesco or Starbucks on our high street or in out of town shopping complexes. But we still shop there, don't we?

From Melksham, I head back into the beautifully green countryside, up a slight rise on the A365 through Atwood then down a terrifyingly speedy drop through Kingsdown about eight miles out of Bath. I'm on my way to Clifton but searching for a cycle route between Bath and Bristol which I'm told will take me the fifteen miles between the two without my tyres sharing an inch of road with a car.

A rambling gent on a steel bike ambles up as I wait at a roundabout at Bathford looking lost. I've just shot by him down the hill at about 35 miles an hour and am now a little embarrassed to be standing there like a lemon as he approaches. But we strike up conversation as cyclists do and he says he's happy to lead me through Bath and plonk me right onto the cycle route.

Philip is a local guy and he's soon snaking up little rises, around roundabouts and through a complex of designated cycle paths with me in his wake. We chat about my project and he tells me he worked for twenty years for a spice company which in its time was probably the biggest importer of chilli and other aromatics from India to the UK. He now works for Pieminster, a gourmet pie producer that was born in Bristol, grown at festivals including Glastonbury and is now taking on the rest of the UK with shops in Covent Garden and in the Midlands, as well as stalls, at pop-up shops and markets elsewhere.

We split just as the cycle path leaves the Avon and turns into the disused Midland railway track that reaches all the way to Bristol. It has been closed to trains since the 1960s when it was converted into a cycle path and amounts to some of the most relaxed and carefree cycling I've ever encountered. The countryside opens up just out of Bath and the hills either side continue to impress while there's barely a rise or drop in the path itself. Nevertheless, by the time I reach my hotel I'm out of puff and so hungry the paltry three gingernut cookies left by the side of the miniature kettle in my room don't touch the sides. Luckily, it'll be just half an hour until I join the Clifton Chilli Club and get a chance to gulp down a dish of hot tasty curry. It's just what I need to top off the day. With about thirty miles of cycling I've just about earned the calories.

Chilli nuts

THE HILLS IN Clifton just seem to go up and up and it's seemingly right at the top that I find the Coach and Horses, the spiritual home of the Clifton Chilli Club. There's a plaque on the wall and everything. I've been invited to the club for their first big get-together of the year with a promise of chat, chillies and curry. The Wurzels will be on the stereo and the cider will be flowing.

For those who don't know the Wurzels, and I'd only barely heard of them before my Clifton visit, they're a bunch of old-timers famous around these parts for playing light humoured Somerset folk and have a combined age of about a million and three. You may well have heard their hit 'I've Got a Brand New Combine Harvester' and probably watched them on *Crackerjack* in the 1980s. Though they're no longer appearing on TV, no West Country festival – or it seems chilli event south-west of Swindon – is complete without their twingy-twangy banjos and gurning voices playing in the background.

Inside the Coach and Horses I meet Chilli Dave, Jim Booth and Dave MacDonald. They're propping up the bar and welcoming other members and friends of the club as they arrive. Dave Mac asks if I want a drink and I ask for a pint of lime and soda.

"I'm not ordering that," says he, harrumphing in a friendly but resolute way from his bar stool. "I don't drink with teetotallers."

Chilli Dave steps in with a "You'll get used to him," and orders my drink, as well as a pint of Thatchers cider for himself. Jim Booth says he too is having a quiet one tonight. Most of the club are off to the chilli festival at Eastnor Castle tomorrow, but Jim is ducking out.

"My missus already says she's a chilli widow so I'm taking it easy," he says. Then he orders himself another pint. Chilli Dave invites me outside so he can have a smoke and, between hacking coughs, gives me a short history of the club.

"Let's start with your name," I ask, pen poised to paper.

"Chilli Dave," says Chilli Dave.

"Yes, but your real name."

"Is this for publication?"

"Well, it might just be." *I am writing a book.*

"Then it's just Chilli Dave," he says with an 'I could tell you, but then I'd have to kill you' look.

I'm not going to write about how the Clifton Chilli Club got started, because you already know how the Clifton Chilli Club got started. Everything chilli related seems to be born over a few pints. Suffice to say, they were a bunch of mates who lived locally who weren't interested in football so started talking about hot food and chillies instead. The three had looked around for other chilli clubs but found none and so set up their own.

With a Facebook page, a website and simple logo of two crossed fat red chillies, hot-heads and chilli enthusiasts from around Britain flocked to them. The Clifton Chilli Club soon outgrew Clifton, then outgrew Bristol, then became UK and then (more or less) world famous. Every now and again, you'll see them on mainstream cookery programmes. BBC, ITV, Channel 4 – they've done the lot. They have their own YouTube chilli tasting channel topping 3,000 subscribers and more than 260 videos. They're even paid to run chilli eating competitions at chilli festivals.

These guys are not just about jerking around with hot sauces. They're serious about the fruits and have clear aims and objectives on their website. Learning about new chillies and chilli products, and educating people about chillies, is at the heart of what they're trying to do. They're capsaicin evangelists. Like Darth Naga's, their weekly chilli and chilli sauce reviews are well regarded in the chilli community.

"My taste is a bit shot," says Chilli Dave, waving his cigarette around. "But Dave Mac, Jim, Jay, they have very refined palates."

The Clifton Chilli Club has some lovely merchandise: hooded tops, some pretty stylish darts type polo shirts and even jewellery. I notice later the three founding members have matching leather necklaces with little ceramic chillies hanging from them. Each of the members grow their own chillies, collections that again put my conservatory effort to shame. The club also has its own polytunnel on the Upton Cheyney Chilli Farm up the road.

"We're all about attracting and then educating people about chillies," says Dave. "You can't do that by waving the hottest things in their face and saying eat that. They'll never come back. You have to bring them in with flavours they do normally eat like Jalapeños and take it from there. It gives them a scale so they know what to expect.

"In reality," he says without embarrassment, "we're into spreading the chilli love."

Chilli Dave is in an excited mood tonight and people are keen to pull him aside and hear about his latest exploits. He and another member, Jay 'Chillihead' Webley, have just returned from the United States where they attended the New York City Hot Sauce Expo. Since their visit they've been posting videos from the expo, as well as their own chilli tasting at iconic Manhattan sites like the Empire State Building, the Statue of Liberty and Times Square. The series of videos, which Chilli Dave calls the club's *US Documentary*, starts with the pair testing Cajohns Calivera sauce at 36,000 feet on their way to New York.

"The air hostess was really keen to be on the video, so we offered her a walk-on part offering us some milk."

The videos are fun to watch and show the club is known well in the US, where the chilli sauce world borders on fanatical. Over there, salsa picante has outsold ketchup since 1992. The funniest part of the documentary is towards the end where an American chilli lover tries to take off Darth Naga, but in a terrible British accent that comes out South African.

"If I was doing this video as Darth Naga, I would be sitting here puking on the table and crying like a little girl, like I always do in every video," he tells the camera. At least it confirms Darth Naga's fame in the chilli world. The sheer amount of chilli sauce Chilli Dave and Jay must have consumed out there beggars belief. There's more than one or two references in the videos to time spent in the men's room as a result.

Chilli Dave and I head back indoors and the thirty or so club members and friends are starting to take over the pub. A table has been set out with chilli patterned tablecloth, a range of chilli sauces from Upton Cheyney, some chilli plants, a gigantic cuddly chilli and a load of other Clifton Chilli Club merchandise. There's an enormous jar of not-very-appetising-looking peeled eggs. They sit in a murky vinegar of chillies and other flotsam. Locals are tasting the sauces; a few have bought plants. I don't see anyone trying an egg.

I look around the pub to assess those who've shown up. You'll excuse me if I throw out a few stereotypes here but I only describe what I see. There's something about chilli fanaticism that attracts a *larger* gentleman. Ones with goatee or full beards are far from rare. Judging by the pint glasses in everyone's hand, those bearded gentleman either like a cloudy traditionally brewed cider or a real ale of some sort. Each is squeezed into a fun T-shirt of some kind: something geeky, superhero or chilli related. The exception is Chilli Dave, who apart from the cider drinking, is none of these things. I could describe what he looks like but then he'd have to kill you.

Dave Mac has decided he is going to buy me a drink after all, and I choose a bottle of non-alcoholic beer. It at least looks like a real beer and seems like a reasonable compromise that will spare him the blushes of talking to someone with a pint of lime and soda in his hand.

I'm soon chatting with other members of the club. Pete Frisby, aka Mr Friz, is super friendly. He's recently started Mr Friz and Friends, another YouTube chilli and hot foods review channel based out of Derby. He's short, has a huge grin on his goatee bearded face, an alien T-shirt pulled over his slightly round belly, and he's drinking... OK, you know what he's drinking. He tells me of an international scheme he's set up among chilli nuts from different countries. Like penpals, they send boxes of a variety of their local chilli sauces for their counterparts to try, in exchange for receiving a 'global care package' of their own.

"There's been a revolution over the last ten years in the UK with all these chilli festivals," says Mr Friz. "People are just realising the range of sauces out there and once they're attracted and know what they like, they know what to look for in future." He's into spreading the chilli love too. It's almost political. "You have to put chilli festivals in the centre of towns," he says, "at least for the first year. The people need to be educated and organisers need a big footfall, so everyone wins."

James Read is taller, equally broad, but he has no beard this time. He's founder of the ChilliJunkies website, a kind of Waitrose Online only a lot hotter. His T-shirt says: 'I'm the chilli sauce in your kebab'. He's from Wigan and like most people from Wigan he's pretty proud of the North and thinks the South gets all the good stuff. He's on a mission to bring chillies further up, perhaps to open the first chilli shop outside of the southern chilli ghetto. He wants to change what he says is the Northerner's mindset of thinking super hot curry is as good as it gets.

"There's definitely a North-South divide. We're still at the foothills, where we're buying chilli from the supermarket and that's a far cry from what a real chilli can be. When you get past vindaloo, the only place to go is to start getting interested in flavour and heat together. It's an education that's not just about blowing your head off."

Between the two of them, we chat for half an hour and I buy a round of drinks. Then someone calls food time. Jim, who used to be a chef, has been in the pub's kitchen and emerges with big metal trays of curry and rice. As I approach the front of the queue it becomes apparent that there are two curries on offer at £3 a pop. They're both made with Naga Masala sauces, the ones I'll be selling in Merthyr Tydfil. There's a mild chicken curry and a very hot beef one.

I look up from my empty plate and notice it's Dave Mac serving up. I now have a dilemma. Tell the bloke who wouldn't buy me a drink because it didn't have alcohol in it that I don't want any of his curry either because it's got meat in it? Or just suck it up? I decide eating is the best approach, but now have another challenge. I probably ought to go for the chicken because, as meat goes, it's probably the least meaty. But I want hot, because after all I'm with the Clifton Chilli Club and so I ought to go hot. I don't want club members thinking I'm some sort of chilli fraud, pretending to like chilli so I can be in their gang. So should I go for the beef? In the end Dave Mac piles my plate high with equal amounts of both and tells me my dish is on the club.

And do you know what? It's delicious. The chicken is light and full of texture. The beef pulls apart and the deep red curry sauce it sits in has a fruity, manageable heat that is really tasty rather than overpowering. It occurs to me that this kind of curry is made for this kind of meat. When I've finished my plate I'm back in the sweat zone. But it's good, like a guilty pleasure.

Over the grub I meet Jay Webley. He wears a black chilli patterned bandana over long dark hair. He has a goatee, of course, and wouldn't look far from home behind the drums in a heavy metal band. Under the sleeve of his shirt you could imagine a tattoo of a naked woman encircled by a snake or something. Only there isn't. Because under his sleeve is a tattoo of a great big, bright red Bhut Jolokia chilli. With Chilli Dave, Jay has just returned from the New York Hot Sauce Expo. In one of the videos he can be observed curled up in a ball on the floor, reeling from the intense heat after tasting a chilli extract.

But the bandana wearing Jay is just one of his personas. At chilli festivals he goes by the name of The Chilli Alchemist. Holding a gnarled wooden staff, he walks around in a long grey cloak, tied at the waist with a thick rope, his hood pulled darkly over his head. He stands in a dark cave-like tent, among bubbling cauldrons, wax seals, dozens of tea lights and signs written in old Latin script.

"Alchemy was a precursor of science and played with the idea that we could do more with things than we first thought we could," he says. His range takes that attitude as its foundation. Jay is into inventing new chilli based products, mixing sauces in unusual ways and presenting what he produces in distinctive alchemy style packaging. He created a chilli popping candy for a bit of fun but it became one of his signature products, shifting fifteen to twenty kilograms a month. He does chilli nuts where the Habaneros have been smoked for fourteen hours over wood from oak whisky barrels. He does a spiced banana ketchup, just one of his range of sauces that come in olde worlde apothecary bottles. Each is individually sealed with dripping wax so no bottle is the same. His range has made the podium in the Good Food Awards best condiment of the year, where flavour, originality and presentation were the deciding factors.

"We give it all a bit of theatre to stand out. At festivals there are a lot of people doing a lot of the same thing. I want to give myself an edge by doing something that people remember."

I buy another alcoholic cider for Jay and one more non-alcoholic beer for me. I'm beginning to get very gassy and in other circumstances I'd be well on my way to pissed by now. When I look up from my empty plate of meat – reflecting that I've now broken my vegetarianism twice in as many days – I notice that everyone else *is* pretty hammered. So, of course, someone announces a hot chicken wings eating competition. Because that's what you do if you're a chilli club with members who are full of cider and, despite the curry, look like they could still eat a horse.

The twelve or so contestants who sit around the table – like the top table at a wedding, I can't help but think – are a mix of members, locals and the pub landlord. Only one contestant is a woman. I excuse myself saying I'm full (which is a lie) and that I want to watch anyway (which is not). Jim, along with a teenager called Sebastian who works in the kitchen – and who everyone keeps taking the piss out of for, essentially, being a teenager – brings out a plate of chicken wings per person. Jim reminds the contestants they'll be instantly disqualified if they touch them before he says go.

Here are the rules of a hot chicken wings competition. Eat chicken wings that are dripping in hot chilli sauce. As quickly as possible. The gorger who finishes their four wings first, indicating that fact by holding up the bones duly stripped of flesh, is the winner. Jim says go.

What follows only just bears description. If you've seen that bit in *Jurassic Park* where the velociraptors tear into a crowd of dinosaur hunters you're only halfway there. People are plucking, sucking, gnawing and pulling. The whole pub is cheering as the hot wings go down. Mr Friz is holding them up to the light, gnawing at little flaps of skin, sucking on bone after bone. Pub Landlord is just tearing at the chicken on the plate, like a grizzly bear tears fish on a stone. Chilli Woman has her head down, her blonde hair modestly shadowing the gnashing below. A few locals, a guy with tattoos and a bald head, another in a smart shirt who looks like he's just stepped into the competition by accident on his way home from work, are gamely struggling through.

There are faces covered in bright red sauce. Beards dripping with grease, fingers plastered with flecks of meat and caramelised chicken skin. The cheers and shouts ramp up as the eating reaches a climax. Finally Pub Landlord leaps up with stripped bones in one hand and a clenched fist in the other. Jim does a quick check just as others are beginning too to hold aloft their stripped carcasses. But it's

Pub Landlord who emerges victorious, to cheers and boos and jeers of 'fix!' He is awarded a cheap T-shirt with *Winner Hot Chicken Wings Competition* printed on the front. Later I see the same T-shirt on Chilli Woman with *the hottest* scrawled above the print in marker pen.

There's much finger licking and mopping of chins, cheeks and brows as the competition rounds up. There are no second places in a hot chicken wings contest. Dave and Sebastian – stupid GCSE teenager, go wash some pots – hand round the remaining wings which I can't help but try. The meat is tender, but still requires embarrassing gnashing and gnawing from the bone. It's a messy affair and the sauce marinade is a little painful and a lot sticky. But it's satisfying, salty and caramelised. Just like a barbecue grilled Linda McCartney vegetarian sausage never *ever* gets. In short, it's really good.

We go back to our drinks and Mr Friz's cheeks are glowing. "The problem with chicken wings is not just the heat in the mouth, but it's the sauce. It gets all around your lips and chin, over your fingers, so it feels like your face is on fire. But when you try to wipe it off, you're only wiping more on." He says it like it's a good thing.

I stand at the bar and reflect on the men and women around me. They're not leery or aggressive. There's no machismo and not *too much* swearing. These are passionate people having fun, meeting up to discuss and – dare I say it – celebrate the wonderful thing that they have in common. Just like I might hang out with cyclists and talk new wheels or chainsets, or a book club might sit around and blather about Hilary Mantel, there's an affection for their subject matter and for each other.

The Wurzels on the sound system are doing modern numbers now and I shake my head at their banjo rendition of Oasis' 'Wonderwall' and can barely stand it when they murder 'Common People' by Pulp. Their Britney Spears, I have to admit, is better than the real thing – though, I imagine, not so nice to watch live. The cider has flowed so freely by this part of the evening that it's only fair that I no longer identify people by name.

One person less than gently persuades me that what I really need is a Clifton Chilli Club hooded top in British racing green. Just £15, and exactly what I'm going to need for my already hot cycle ride back to Bath tomorrow morning. A couple of members are singing 'I've Got a Brand New Combine Harvester' at the tops of their voices, though I don't think that's what the Wurzels are actually singing. There are secret handshakes and hugs between members. We try to do a group photo but no-one is sober enough to take a good picture. By the end, we're all holding on to each other to prevent ourselves falling down. I'm pulled aside by another and told how the Clifton Chilli Club has changed people's lives.

"That guy over there," he says between hiccups. "He first came to us with no confidence, a stutter, all kinds of issues *(hic)*. Now look at him. He's a different person. Do you know what's done that? *(hic)* Well, do you?"

"Er…"

"Yeah," he says. "Chillies have done that."

Without a word of a lie I then hear someone say in an authentic Bristolian scarecrow drawl: "Aye they make that there cider pretty strong in these parts, don't aye?"

Jim – the one who was going to take it easy due to chilli widowing his wife – is absolutely rolling. I can write that, because it's a matter of public record. And if there's one thing we all know about drunken evenings it's that he who is most drunk is he who is most likely to be taken advantage of.

One chap – let's call him Geoff to protect the guilty – pulls out a tiny red canister marked with a label all done up in fire: Texas Creek Pure Evil 9.7 Capsaicin Drops. There's only one reason Geoff has brought that little package of mischief to this event and he's about to get his chance to execute it. He waits until Jim has turned his back and pipettes a few drops into the remaining third of his cider. Those in the know sit back and wait for the magic to happen. Jim turns back to his pint, takes a good sup and swivels back to the person he's shouting at. But his face slowly drops and then contorts into a look of horror.

"Oh you bastards, oh shit," and he looks around in resigned knowledge that he's been spiked. He begins shaking his head as if to throw off the heat. It's no good and amidst riotous laughter he heads for the toilets. Another member follows and returns to tell us Jim is chucking up in one of the cubicles. Now let me be clear, spiking drinks isn't funny, particularly if the spiked is in a position of vulnerability. But come on: Jim may make some pretty awesome chicken wings but someone had to get it and, chilli widow or no, tonight it was his turn.

Jim returns a little pale from the toilets and I examine the 9.7 drops, taking the drop pipette from its little red case. There's absolutely no smell, just off-pink liquid. 'Use with extreme caution' says the bottle, which to Jim's disadvantage we just didn't. I take a swig of my Bitburger Drive and my mouth starts to tingle a little. The left side of my lips and the area around it start to feel hot. I try to wipe the heat away with my fingers but the heat is spreading.

"Did you spike my drink?" I ask another guy. Me being, apart from Jim, probably the strongest candidate for being spiked that night, what with being a new innocent face, all trussed up with my intrusive questions, pen and notepad.

"No, mate, we'd never do that," says he. "We only do it to Jim because we've known him a long time, it's a trust thing really." And I instinctively know he's telling the truth. It's only what Jim would have done, so fair's fair. I conclude that by handling the bottle of 9.7 I must have got a bit on my fingers and transferred it to my lips and then, when I tried to wipe it off, smeared it even further. It's a painful pain rather than a chilli heat. Later at my hotel I rub my eye with the same fingers. Even though I must have washed my hands three times since handling the bottle I have to spend fifteen minutes blinking to wash the sting from my eyeball.

Suddenly it's nearly midnight and the pub is beginning to empty. I do the rounds to say goodbye and every club member still standing is friendly, hand shaking and back patting. And it's not just the booze talking. They're excited about my project, promise to send me photos and samples and to keep in touch. They can't wait to see me again at some festivals over the summer and I feel the same way. Many of these guys will be up early in the morning to run a chilli eating competition at Eastnor Castle in the Malvern Hills. But not Jim. He's probably pushed the chilli widowing as far as it's going to go this weekend. "It looks like you came off pretty badly tonight," I say before I depart. He rocks before me, like tall grass swaying in the wind.

"Nah," he says taking a swig of a brand new pint. "We've all had much worse."

When I get back to my hotel I check Facebook and discover the shenanigans have continued back at someone's house and one member is posting photos. One is pictured in T-shirt and boxer shorts in a suggestive pose with an enormous bottle of chilli sauce. There's the obligatory – fully clothed thank goodness – nipple licking photo. That kind of stuff. I think I left at the right time.

Pushing peppers

NO REST FOR the knackered. I'm up first thing the next day and make a quick visit to one of Clifton's many independent cafes for an expensive, though delicious (over here they'd call it 'lush') breakfast of porridge, scrambled eggs and toast. I'm fuelling up for another ride along the cycle way back to Bath, where I've been invited to sell chilli sauces on one of Wiltshire Chillies' many town centre market stands.

It's a gorgeous day and Bath is packed with locals and tourists. First stop is Green Park Station, a former railway terminal that closed in the 1960s. It was formerly a staging post for the Bristol to Bath railway line that I'd cycled along that morning. The space has been converted into incubator business units and there's a regular market in the middle aimed at supporting growing local and artisan companies.

Despite the gargantuan Sainsbury's towering over it, the market is full of shoppers sampling goods from the dozens of market stands. There are local butchers selling enormous loins of beef, cheese stalls, fresh bread and cakes, home-grown fruit and veg stalls, mushroom and lentil soup for a pound a cup, freshly ground coffee, one company selling nothing but enormous scotch eggs and the ubiquitous pushy olive stand.

This is the middle class at play and you can hardly move for swinging hessian bags bursting with organic leeks. There's even a string quartet in the centre, playing as shoppers and their kids weave in and out of each other with their wares.

After fifteen miles at speed, I reckon I've just about worked off my breakfast and chomp on an enormous and scrumptious chunky fruit laden flapjack before I go off in search of the Chilli Hut. It's a joint venture between Jamie at Wiltshire Chillies and a business partner. The Chilli Hut – which as you can imagine is a wooden shack that is stacked to the rafters with chilli produce – is one of only three permanent dedicated chilli shops in Britain. The others are a tiny cubbyhole in St Nicholas' market in Bristol, Dr Burnorium's Hot Sauce Emporium, and Brighton's Chilli Pepper Pete shop. The fact that three dedicated chilli shops even exist – with James from last night trying to set one up in Wigan – is ample demonstration of our increasing interest in hot foods.

I ask Holly who is staffing the hut to show me around. That's not really asking much given we're in a three sided shed. There are the necessaries to the front: a tasting table with little pots of Jamie's sauces and wooden spatulas; baskets of dried Chipotle chillies, each a luscious glowing earthy colour, and bars of chilli chocolate. And in pride of place there is a basket of Jamie's brand new chilli chorizo.

The Chilli Hut doesn't just stock Wiltshire Chillies products. On the back wall there's just about every brand that I've come across – Mr Vikkis, Hot-Headz, Grim Reaper Foods – and a load more I haven't. There are jams and sauces, flakes, shakers, chilli rubs and powders, crisps, chocolates, boiled sweets and lollipops. There are bottles with wax. Bottles with pictures of the Devil. One range topped off with a skull shaped cork stopper. On the right-hand wall, stocked ground to roof, are sauces from outside the UK, mainly from the United States: Tabasco sauces, barbecue jellies and jams, bags of dried chillies and chilli coffee.

It's by far the widest selection of chilli stuff I've ever seen; but Holly shows me more. To the left-hand side there are chilli shaped strings of lights, earrings and cufflinks, chilli shaped pens, ice cube trays and books. And there's a brightly lit glass cabinet that is locked like in a jewellery shop. It contains a range of glass phials and packages, with requisite nuclear warning signs, skulls and crossbones, and health advisory stickers. A tiny drop pipette bottle of 13 million Scoville extract Hand Grenade will set you back £20, a phial of 6.5 million Toxic Waste another tenner. On the centre shelf is a limited edition Blair's Zam, the bottle dressed up with red and black melted wax and headed by a screaming skull. It's just £35.

This is certainly a shop for the hot-heads – Holly tells me there's a steady stream of familiar faces each week coming to get their fix. But mainly the shop attracts a passing trade which is why the milder sauces, shakers and chilli chocolate are pushed to the front. Get them hooked first, then move them on to the hard stuff.

I'd like to stay because Green Station has a friendly vibe as well as some wonderful offerings for lunch. But I'm already late for my market stall. In the centre of Bath, Union Street offers a thoroughfare to the Roman thermal baths and a constant stream of visitors to the city are heading in that direction. With the sun shining it'll be a busy day for the pop-up market stalls, human statues and street performers looking to extract a little cash from the tourists. Jamie's parents, Mike and Kay, have set up a stall at the top of the street and have invited me to spend a few hours promoting Wiltshire Chillies' produce with them. There's a big green gazebo behind which I park my bike and change out of my cycling gear. We're opposite the cosmetics shop Lush which billows into the air its distinctly overpowering smell of soap that makes me feel sick most of the day.

Mike and Kay have neatly laid out a selection of the sauces, along with cylinders full of tasting sticks and little jars of each sauce. At the mild end are the sweet-and-sour and the fruit sauces, each with only a hint of heat. In the middle are jams and chutneys with Wiltshire Chillies' biggest sellers: the Mango Hot Chilli Sauce and the salt and chilli flakes grinder. At the hot end sits the more head banging stuff, though as I listen in to Mike and Kay's sales patter, they're described as 'very full of flavour, but with a slowly building heat at the end that keeps you coming back for more'. Behind the counter, I learn, is a special bottle of very concentrated chilli sauce that's only to be brought out for those who find the 7-pot Habanero Septenary sauce still doesn't satiate their burning desire.

As I listen in, and start to observe passing trade versus the customers who come to the stall, I recognise a distinct pattern. There are those who look over and read the word chilli, then recoil with horror and scuttle off before we get a chance to offer them a taste. Then there are those who stride up to confidently ask what we've got. I guess in these circumstances you can't persuade people to like chilli or even try to like it. You just have to cater to those who don't run a mile. When men come to the stall they tend to make a beeline for the hot end. Women more gingerly approach the milder stuff. After a while, I've picked up a few choice phrases and feel confident to start selling myself.

"Do you like chilli at all?"

"Feel free to try them."

"Everything is grown just six miles up the road. We go from greenhouse to kitchen over just, ha ha, 200 metres."

"We go from mild to hot, here's a tasting stick."

"This one's just like a brown sauce really, but the fruit is chilli with a slight heat. It's lovely."

"The Fireside sauce just won an award last week. We only produced it for Christmas but it was so popular we just kept on producing it."

"You like it hot do you? Well I've a little something special behind the counter if this one isn't hot enough for you."

"Oh, too hot? OK, you just need some fats. There's an ice cream seller a few stalls down. We should get commission, ha ha ha."

"This one is very full of flavour, but with a slowly building heat at the end that keeps you coming back for more."

I had a picture in my mind of burly blokes approaching the stall and challenging us to give them everything with both barrels. But it's nothing like that at all. There's an international crowd with lots of Americans, South Africans, a smattering of Latin Americans and some Japanese too. My first sale, a £5 bottle of the Hellish Hot Sauce, is to a German and I'm quite proud of myself. Lots of the visitors to the stand are shopping for their dad or brother or friend. One petite Mancunian twentysomething claims to be buying for her boyfriend, but proceeds from mild to hot very quickly. By the end of it she's tasting even the scorching sauces on the table without blinking. She buys five bottles. Two Columbian teenage girls bet each other to try the hottest sauce, eventually settling on £2.75 for whoever tries the Septenary. One does, but – duly paid – races up the road to spend it on an ice cream.

I listen to Mike's sales patter which is far more refined than mine. He can tell who's a serious chilli shopper and notes from a mile off whether they're of the cooking or hot-head type. Kay and I overhear his chat about the salt and chilli flakes grinder as he speaks to a middle aged woman he's clearly pinned as a kitchen cook.

"It's great on steak or on roast potatoes, maybe char-grilled vegetables straight out of the oven," he effuses. "Just pull them out from under a hot grill still bubbling, grind a little of this on top and serve straight away. It's a truly delicious experience, would you like to try?"

Kay turns to me, raises her eyebrows and whispers in her soft Scottish accent, "He goes on all about food and how to cook this and that. He's never cooked a thing in his life."

They're a friendly middle aged couple who've travelled the world together and in between busy periods I chat with Mike about cycling (he used to ride and race for Bath cycling club), vintage cars (of which I know nothing, but pretend I do) and travel. They talk over each other, and drink black coffee from a flask and eat sandwiches from a packed lunch they've brought with them.

"We've tramped around Africa, China, Asia," says Kay taking a seat behind the stall with a 'but we're much too old for that caboodle' sigh. "And look at us now, selling sauces at market. We don't even particularly like chilli sauce."

I won't pretend the stall was busy all the time. A lot of the visitors were hell-bent on visiting the baths and weren't looking to be distracted. But the day offered some satisfying sales and a few pockets of amusement. One woman turns up with her daughters, shopping for her husband who likes it hot. She doesn't want to taste anything but the mildest sweet-and-sour, but asks for the hottest thing we've got. I offer her the 7-pot, but say I've a little something under the counter if her husband really is into the hard stuff. I show her the little bottle of the £8 God Is Dead chilli concentrate.

"Oh, I don't like that," she says, "I don't like that all. God Is Alive. Jesus Is Alive Today!" and she storms off with her children before she's even had time to read the sauce's subtitle, Fucking Hot Sauce.

Another couple pitch up and I begin to give the big bloke with the broad shoulders and beer belly my spiel. "I can tell by looking at you that you like a hot chilli," I say. "Would you care to try something from the hotter end?"

"Don't talk to me, I can't stand the stuff," he replies then points to his rather smaller partner. "She's the one you need to talk to. She'd eat it on her cornflakes if she could." Despite my slip-up I manage to sell them a three bottle set.

Another Asian lady with short purple hair comes over and says she doesn't like hot sauce at all but, egged on by her friends, wants to try some anyway. She's immediately coughing and spluttering and I tell her sympathetically about the ice cream bloke down the road.

"No no," she says, "it's hot, it's so hot. But it's so gooooood," and proceeds to take another spatula full with a wicked grin. Another sale.

Kay tells me it costs just £18 for a stall on Union Street on a Saturday and they normally expect to shift 150 bottles or so. By the time I have to leave to catch my train I calculate the sales I can claim, including one bottle of God Is Dead. It's just over £50 which more than pays for the stall and is probably not too bad for a first timer.

But whether I'd want to sell chilli sauce on the streets of Bath every weekend, particularly when it's cold and wet and you have to practically beg the punters to come near you? Well, that's another matter. For all the fun making chilli sauce and other products might be, you still have to sell the stuff and that means long hours on stalls and at festivals. Delis take some, but sometimes don't push them hard enough, Jamie had told me. So you're on your feet every weekend, saying the same things over and over again. I'm lucky to have got away with three hours and no pressure to sell in order to pay my bills.

My trip to the Wiltshire Chillies farm and working on a stand in Bath town centre has offered an insight into what risks and sacrifices some chilli producers take and make. And how those who gave up a career in banking or media to pursue what they think will be an easier life may just have accidentally found themselves in a career even more unforgiving.

13th May – Masquerade still leads the pack in the growing stakes and has three fully open flowers now. I haven't seen many bugs around but it'll soon be time to open the windows and see if we can't get some pollination going. Pollination can also be done by the wind, I'm advised, so that'll help. And if you're really desperate, by a soft paintbrush brushing pollen onto the flower stamens.

Prairie Fire also has some infant flowers. I'm starting to see a real difference in the various plants. Red Missile is squat with its flower buds pointing up, all gathered together at the top. Prairie Fire is taller but also gathers together what will be chillies in a little peak. Friar's Hat, Lemon Drop and Vampire are much taller and more flamboyant. They have wide leaves sprouting sideways to create a lovely pyramid shape. Purple Tiger is beautiful. It has widely spread branches at the end of which droop deep green leaves mottled with light yellow stripes, obviously the way the plant got its name.

Habanero 7 has wide green leaves but sits low in the pot. This is about as far as I've ever got with that plant before so I'm considering myself lucky. But I'm starting to get impatient to see some actual chillies growing. There's at least a month to go yet.

Hydroponic dreams

ON AVERY ISLAND in Louisiana (it's not really an island) sitting on the southern and hottest coast of the United States is the manufacturing plant of one of the world's best selling chilli products: the iconic McIlhenny's Tabasco sauce. Nearly 700,000 bottles are made every day and shipped to over 160 countries. That's a whole lot of Tabasco chillies. It calls for thousands of acres of fertile land and more than a little automation when it comes to planting.

This is how the planting works: on some of the vast farms McIlhenny uses in southern America a huge tractor is hooked up with machinery at front, middle and back. The driver sits back in the cabin but doesn't have to worry so much about driving. The whole set-up is controlled by GPS. Satellites control the tractor's direction, ensuring it moves in near perfect lines, up and down acre upon acre of fields. At the front of the set-up are lines of sharp curved blades, which dig into the soil, churning it into dead straight neatly ploughed furrows. Towards the back of the tractor another machine punches three or four inch holes into the ground every foot or so, four or five rows across. At the back, there's a platform where a row of farm workers sit leaning over, neatly plonking Tabasco chilli seedlings into each of the newly punched holes. Row after row after row, furrow after furrow, field after field. The scale and speed is awesome.

At the Suffolk Chilli Farm, planting Jalapeño seedlings with the knowledgeable and ambitious Adrian Nuttall is nothing like this. His wife Denise ambles along with a wheelbarrow full of seedlings they've germinated in a bathtub sized propagator then raised in a greenhouse on heated mats. She plonks piles of them in the gravel by the side of raised beds. Adrian lays out the plants along the furrows he made the day before with a rake. And there am I, squatting over the furrows in trainers and jeans with a trowel, shuffling along to scrape back the dry earth, stuff in a Jalapeño plant and scratch up some earth around it, before moving forward a foot or two for the next one.

The immature plants tickle my backside as I balance over them ungraciously to plant their sisters. My trainers dig into the furrows on either side, threatening to dislodge the plants I've already put into the ground. It takes me about three minutes a plant and I'm sweating so much my shirt is dripping wet and after about, I don't know, three or four plantings my lower back is aching from the crouching position I'm in. My bald head is glistening in the sun, making me wish I'd plastered myself with sunblock and worn shades. But I have to keep moving. Denise is watering the seedlings behind me and she's rapidly catching up. If she and Adrian didn't bicker lightheartedly about how best to water the plants, and whether this is the best weather to be planting the seedlings into the beds at all, I'd have a wet arse by now.

Adrian and Denise Nuttall are farmers, entrepreneurs and dreamers. They set up the Suffolk Chilli Farm and restaurant in December 2005, appearing on Channel 5's *Build a New Life in the Country* programme. As those fly-on-the-wall shows do, it didn't take long for the narrator to stick the boot in: "With no building expertise, no restaurant experience and big plans to do all the renovation work themselves, it's going to be a roller coaster."

But it was. The farm has undergone a couple of transformations over nearly a decade. Gone is the restaurant, replaced by a smart deli and coffee shop. But that's rented to someone else to bring in some cash.

"Chillies on their own are not a big income. We do a bit of growing for restaurants and a few suppliers," Adrian says with a resigned sigh, as if it's been an awful long tough journey to find out. "We've had to look at it all again."

So the pair host events, chilli planting and raising classes, school visits and taking paying guests to view their hundred strong chilli plant display. They also have their own range of chilli sauces – made from their own chilli plants – and they run a little shop on site, Smoke and Spice, where they sell them and other chilli related products. It's only with this diversification that the couple have managed to keep the farm in the black.

It was the Suffolk Chilli Farm's chilli display that originally gave me the idea to set up my own edible exhibition in the conservatory. Two years ago, my wife had bought me a tour of the display for my birthday and I was amazed by the diversity there. Huge plants, tiny bonsai-like ones. Long red, pink, yellow, purple, orange and green fruits. Wrinkled, tiny, cherry shaped, elephant's trunk shaped, ornamentals. Chillies with names like Fish, Wrecking Ball, Bulgarian Carrot and Firecracker. In their sweltering hot greenhouse we took in the display with awe. And I decided to try to do the same, albeit on a far smaller scale. I stole a piece of paper and a crayon from their children's education centre – now, I note, a little run down and being used as storage – and I wrote the names of the most interesting, colourful and stunning twelve plants from their vast collection. The next day I ordered my seeds from their seed supplier. Overnight, my chilli eating hobby had been joined by a keenness to grow the plants too, maybe even harvest my own crop.

I call Adrian and Denise entrepreneurs and dreamers because their farm does always seem to be changing, the pair never quite settling on what the farm is supposed to do. Let's be honest – and it's something Adrian would admit too – it's really him that's the dreamer.

"I'd be very surprised if any of these plants produce many, if any fruits," he says as we both look over the 100 or so Jalapeños I've just sweated to plant. In our climate, chilli plants don't grow so well outside. So the work I've just done is an Adrian Nuttall experiment. If he can take the seeds from the chilli fruits that do grow out here, get those hardy ones to grow again outside next year, then take the strongest ones of those new plants and sow them again for the following season, and then again and again for just a mere seven years – the time it takes to get a plant strain officially recognised – then Adrian will have created something new: a hardy outdoor plant that could revolutionise chilli growing in Britain. No more greenhouses and polytunnels, no more heated mats, no more expensive chilli food. That's the dream.

"Growing under glass is extremely expensive. The golden chalice would be finding a variety that can grow outside in the UK. I've got eleven acres here, and if I can plant even one acre with chillies, it'll generate a fair profit." He reckons he can get the farmer next door to rent him more land if his experiment works. "It'll be a lot more profitable than the rapeseed he's currently planting. And the best part is this: other chilli farmers will have to pay me for seeds of the new hardy outdoor strain."

Adrian's eyes flash with the potential. Mine are interested but sceptical. But already Adrian has something else to show me. Inside his display greenhouse he's set up 100 plastic tubs, each filled with water and chilli feed with seedlings popping out of the top. This is chilli growing without soil at all. It's called hydroponics and it's the way Adrian has grown chillies almost since he began.

Chillies don't actually need to grow in soil, he tells me, they just need a substrate – in this case a kind of clay gravel – to prop them up. Each of the plants sits in the gravel on top of its tub, its roots drooping into the water below. The trick is to get the right amount of water and chilli feed, and leave enough air at the top so the roots can also take up oxygen. The plants will then take up as much water and oxygen as they need. It goes against what I thought I knew about chillies: that they don't like much water. In normal weather, they should be watered only once a week at best. Treat them mean, keep them keen. But here Adrian is bathing his chillies constantly, leaving them to their own devices. And it works.

This is so much cheaper and easier than planting in fresh compost each year then having to constantly water them and feed them. With hydroponics, you put them into the tubs and let them go. Adrian is animated now and is demonstrating his extremely deep knowledge of chillies. This is a man who's done his research, spent hour after hour reading and researching on the internet. He's been all around the world – Australia, Spain, California, New Mexico – looking at how chillies are grown. Eating not a little more into the farm's bank account, I think. But he's brought the techniques he's learned back to Suffolk and is trying his own versions to adapt them to British climates. In the corner there's a melon plant growing out of a water-filled dustbin.

The problem with his current hydroponics set-up, he tells

me, is efficiency and space. You can only grow one plant in the pots each season. You still have to use expensive chilli food and you have to use a whole greenhouse for 100 plants. If you want to do that on a commercial scale, you still need acres and acres of land and a hell of a lot of greenhouse. So Adrian has another experiment to show me.

He leads me over to a ladder of three-metre cylindrical gutter tubes on a wooden frame. The tubes are stacked six or seven high, and each tilts at a slight angle with an end pipe leading them down to the tube below. The result is a huge version of the marble run my kids got for Christmas last year. Along each of the tubes three-inch holes have been drilled, each about half a foot apart. Into these will be planted chilli seedlings. It's hydroponics taken one step further; vertical rather than horizontal. Water, with chilli feed mixed in, runs down from the top of the ladder, through all the plant roots and into a large tub at the bottom. Then a pump sends the water back to the top.

"In about five metres square, I can grow 300 plants. Show me any system that can do that. Imagine this greenhouse stacked end to end with these; imagine the efficiency savings."

I can't help but be impressed because he has a very good point. Who says plants have to be laid out side by side? And the best thing is, he says, that the same equipment can be used to grow salads, lettuce and strawberries when it's not chilli season. You couldn't do that with soil based plants. You'd have to start all over again each time.

"I could keep the whole of Wimbledon supplied with strawberries." His eyes light up. "I could set up one of these outside Wimbledon and serve strawberries and cream right off the plant. Pick, squirt cream and there you go."

But for Adrian Nuttall, the great chilli inventor and

dreamer, even this isn't enough. There's even a problem with *this* system. You still have to use expensive chilli feed if you want to produce the best crops. He wants to show me yet another experiment and he needs my help. I'm delighted because I'm starting to melt in the greenhouse.

"My wife criticises me because I always have so many ideas," he says with a grin. "I'll wake up in the night with an idea, and by the next day I'm out here putting something together to try it out."

When I arranged to visit the Suffolk Chilli Farm I didn't really expect to be talking about selling strawberries at Wimbledon. And the last thing I expected to see was a tank full of fish. Adrian shows me a giant plastic tub in which are swimming a handful of small trout. It's the first stage in a long row of contraptions and baths that lead into the greenhouse, then up into chilli growing beds. This is Adrian's small scale trial of aquaponics.

"Aquaculture is the breeding of fish. Hydroponics is growing plants in water. Why not put the two together? Aquaponics," he says.

Here's how aquaponics works: the trout eat traditional fish food which is far cheaper than chilli feed. The water in which they swim, with all its fish faeces and urine, is sieved then piped down into a sump. There, naturally occurring bacteria and a series of other natural processes turn the waste into nitrate rich water. That plant food filled water is pumped into the greenhouse where it fills a vat of clay balls, in which dozens of chilli plants will be grown.

But there's more: the clay is full of tiger worms too. They process the fish waste the chillies don't want, producing their own plant food in the process. Then the water falls into another huge vat which Adrian is busy filling with Styrofoam slabs floating on the water. He'll drill holes in the slabs and grow more chillies in them. At the bottom of this vat will grow oysters, which will clean and filter the water. It'll then be pumped back into the fish tank where the whole process will start again. It's a little mini environment mimicking what happens on a massive scale in any natural ecosystem. And once it's set up, it'll just keep going with only the cost of cheap fish food and electricity to run the pump. That's the theory.

And here's the very best bit, says Adrian. You can eat the fish, the oysters and the chillies. Once again, his reasoning is entirely sound. And he's making me feel inadequate about my own edible display.

There's loads of tweaking to be done, which is why this is a pilot project. There are just a few fish and the aim is to balance the right numbers of chillies with them. If chillies and tiger worms don't take out enough waste, the fish will die. If there aren't enough fish or the right kinds of fish, the chillies won't grow. Carp would be better, says Adrian, and he's convinced – not entirely convincingly – that the eastern European appetite for carp will catch on in Britain eventually. But once he's got it right he'd love to scale up the project: hundreds of fish and many thousands of chilli plants at minimal cost. He says a farm in Australia has already upscaled the principles successfully.

I make a tiny token gesture towards the future of his project. He gets me to cut a bit of tubing and feed it into the vat of clay balls while he goes to switch on the pump. Only the pump doesn't work, so I end up drilling holes in a cylindrical piece of guttering instead to at least contribute something.

"No pressure, but that's the only piece I have left," he says. I make not a bad job of it, despite the drill continually slipping and the fear of cracking the plastic.

I come away from the Suffolk Chilli Farm enthralled. But though his pilots seem sound in theory, I wonder whether Adrian has too many things going on at once and whether he really has the attention span to juggle all the balls without trying to add yet more. At the end of the day, he and Denise need to keep the farm profitable and Adrian says he has to work on paid IT projects during the week to fund his latest scheme.

Adrian sends me packing with pages and pages of notes about what I may be doing wrong with my chilli crop as well as loads of advice for later when they start fruiting. First problem is that there's no guarantee that my Scorpion and Bhut Jolokia will fruit at all. I know my dad got them via eBay from Germany. If the seeds had to pass through an x-ray machine they may have been rendered infertile.

Secondly, I may have planted my chillies into too-small pots. Those that are squat may stay that way unless I repot them again because the roots would be restricted. Most chilli plants can grow quite large but small pots mean small plants. No wonder Masquerade, Friar's Hat and Vampire are doing so well. They're in the biggest pots. Meanwhile, Adrian says, don't make the pots too big. The plants will have to put too much energy into growing long roots to seek water, weakening what's above the soil. Also, I've made a mistake potting into clay and ceramic containers. They'll absorb the water themselves, reducing the amount going to the chillies. A look at the soil confirms his suspicion; the soil is permanently dry and water tends to run through them rather than getting absorbed by the plant. If I want my display to really bloom, there's a whole load of repotting to do. Plastic pots may look rubbish, but they work the best. To be honest, I'm not sure I'm up for the job.

Adrian also offered a few other snippets of advice. The

pots should be sitting in little trays, so I can water the plants from the bottom up. That'll send the roots downwards, strengthening the plants, instead of gathering everything at the top. And Habanero 7, he had added like a little knife in the gut, I've been overfeeding. Before it fruits it should only get a small dose of plant food. Only when chillies grow fruits should I step up their mealtime, and still I should only feed them once a week. I've been adding feed every time I've watered and he can tell by how green Habanero 7's leaves are − I showed him a picture on my phone − that it's been overkill. It wouldn't hurt to introduce some marigold plants to the conservatory too. Not only do they look good, but they're classic insect attractors. They'll bring in pollinators, as well as ladybirds who may help to keep in check the aphid attacks my chillies will inevitably experience.

It feels like I've been dressed down by teacher, but it's all taken with respect. The only question remaining is what of his advice I can get away with avoiding and what is a must-do. Some things are easier to fix than others. When I get home I take a look at what I now feel is my paltry rather old-fashioned display, with its compost and bulkiness and only occasional watering and need for expensive chilli food. To be fair, it already looks better than last year. But Adrian's enthusiasm is infectious, and I have to at least try something. I find a small barrel, fill it with water and pour in a cup of chilli food. I cut some extra holes in the bottom of a small plastic plant pot and stuff it into the barrel spout. I then take a Prairie Fire, one left over and suffering from claustrophobia in its original germination tray, and shake the compost off its roots.

I plant it with a handful of gravel from our driveway in the top of the barrel. When I come back that night I expect to see the plant drooping, the leaves half dead with dehydration. But they're not. The plant is sitting upright, stiff and smart. The leaves are stout and green. The next day tiny flower buds begin to appear on the previously barren plant. I have gone hydroponic. That night I wake up in the middle of the night with the inkling of an idea. My dad has a fishpond…

20th May – It continues to be sunny and that can mean only one thing: continued glorious growth of my plants. Vampire, Joe's Long Cayenne and Friar's Hat are huge, each about two foot high. Though I think they could reach three or even four feet by maturity. Etna is kinda spindly, but has lots of leaves and a good head of flowers at the top. Sweet Pepper Sunshine is small but also putting out flowers. And Habanero 7 is sitting green and luscious in its pot, making up for its still rather small size.

But there's a problem. My wife was doing some potting of other plants and I asked if she'd please pot-on my Scorpion and Bhut Jolokias, the ones my dad had given me. She was happy to do so but when I came to inspect her handiwork I asked the obvious question: so which one's which? She didn't know, she hadn't kept track. So now I have a few pots of each of them but no way of knowing which plant is Bhut Jolokia and which is Scorpion. I also know the fruits – if indeed they do fruit – don't look too different from each other. That's what happens when you just don't care enough, I don't tell her. I may have to call in the experts at a later stage.

28th May – Ding dong, ring the bell: I have fruits! I've been checking out the small flowers that have started to bloom on about half of my plants. Prairie Fire has a whole bunch but as far as I can see only one or two have attempted to open. The rest are flowers in waiting. Same for Red Missile and Sweet Pepper Sunshine. Vampire has a few *hanging stalks but no flowers yet. I'm watching it eagerly. The plant is so tall and beautiful. It has a thick purple stem and wide dark leaves with purple veins. I just know the flowers that do come, when those hanging stalks eventually blossom, are going to be stunners too. I'm expecting bright pink blooms, tinged with a deep purple at the edges. This is what I'm doing all this for. It'll be worth it without even a taste of chillies. All the rest are biding their time, still putting on leaf weight rather than flowers. But even Habanero 7 continues to look eager.*

But Masquerade you continue to do me proud. It has dozens of flowers. Some have been and gone already and there are another dozen stalks yet to blossom. And if I look closely, right in the centre where dried out petals have dropped away, I can see tiny pale yellow pods. They're just the nose of the fruits but they definitely are fruits. This is the end of the beginning. The chilli fruiting season has begun!

The UK's hottest curry

I'M IN EDINBURGH at around half past four in the afternoon and Abdul breaks off our interview to unlock the doors of the Kismot curry house to let in a very pregnant woman.

"Abdul, you have to help me," she says. "I need something hot, really hot."

"Oh my gosh," he says in a slightly confusing mixed south Asian and Scottish accent. He bows at the woman and her partner, putting his hands together in an endearing gesture of welcome.

"Come in, come in. When? When?"

"The due date is tomorrow," the woman says. "But I tell you, Abdul, I've really had enough now. I'm ready to go."

He sits her and her partner in a corner and returns to our table, continuing to speak to me at a thousand miles an hour. His head is shaven on both sides, with highlights of gold in the curls on top. There's a sparkle in his eyes and I'm certain he has the whitest teeth I have ever seen.

"We've got one in tonight," he says. "Tried the Naga curry last time and called to ask us to prepare the Kismot Killer this time." He definitely doesn't mean the pregnant woman.

This curry house serves what is reputedly the hottest curry in the UK. Other Indian restaurants may make the same claim, but it's the Kismot Killer that has landed people in hospital. That's A&E, not the maternity ward. And it's what has brought me to Scotland this weekend.

In 2011, the Kismot restaurant hit the national press after hosting a curry eating contest during which two of the contestants were taken to Edinburgh Royal Infirmary. Some of the rest ended up vomiting so violently outside that Abdul and his brothers had to create a cordon to prevent passers by from slipping in sick. "We should have had buckets," says Abdul. "It was our first time and it was a bit all over the place."

An older woman emerges from the kitchen wearing a blue and gold sari. She's tiny, a little toothless, with red hair underneath a scarf lightly draped over her head.

"This is my mother, Jahanara Ali," says Abdul. She bows and extends a hand.

"You eat," she says. She makes a gesture as if she's picking up food with her fingers then brings it to her lips two or three times. "You eat."

Her son waves her away, speaking in Bengali. Jahanara is the centre of the Ali family and Abdul is keen to emphasise that it's down to his parents' strictness and hard work that the Kismot has become one of the most famous Indian restaurants in Britain. "When people look up to her, it feels like they're looking up to us," he says.

Jahanara did a paper round when the family first moved to Edinburgh while Abdul's father Ibrahim worked in Indian restaurants – most of the 8,000 'Indian' restaurants in Britain are actually run by Bangladeshis like Abdul and his family. She demanded her sons and daughters gave her every single penny they earned in their teens, so she could dish it out and they wouldn't spend it on fripperies. He mentions a story in the Koran where seven brothers were fed with a single grain of rice.

"She always said save, save, save," says Abdul. "I'd have

gone out and bought a car, but my parents would never allow it. My mother still shops at the Poundstretcher down the road."

Ibrahim Ali comes over in a curry stained apron pulled around a generous stomach, a fake grump on his face. You could just imagine him running his hand along the radiator accusing his sons of turning up the heat.

Ibrahim's family comes from Sylhet in Bangladesh, a region of lakes and mountains in the east of the country. He came over to Britain when he was twelve with his own father who worked in restaurants trying to find somewhere to settle. Ibrahim returned to Bangladesh to marry, then came back to live in Wolverhampton – yeah, that place again – to bring up his family. After not too long he left Wolves for brighter horizons, and headed north to Scotland: Glasgow, Dunfermline, then eventually Edinburgh.

Ibrahim was working as a chef in an Edinburgh Indian, soon joined by Abdul's older brother Aftab, then Abdul joined them as a dish washer. Over a shared meal one day they'd sat around wondering how they'd all ended up working in the same restaurant.

"We were pretty much running the place. We'd come home together and look at each other and say: surely we could do this for ourselves as a family business?"

Two white girls walk into the restaurant wearing Kismot uniforms, one Scottish, the other Polish. They're here to start their shifts. I look at Abdul, puzzled.

"My sisters are part of the business but they're still in their early twenties," explains Abdul. "We can't often get them to come and work in the restaurant. You know, boys and stuff."

The family set up their own takeaway in one of the rougher outskirts of Edinburgh where Abdul – still just a teenager – would work between his studies. But there were a number of racist incidents and then one evening two very drunk Scots had kicked off. Ibrahim had had to push his wife and kids into the kitchen, then lock himself in too before calling the police. The family returned to central Edinburgh where Jahanara had done her paper round. One day she'd returned excitedly to their house after seeing a shop to let.

"You sell, you sell," Abdul says, putting on his mum's broken English. "She'd asked the builders in there if the place was for sale. By the time she got home she'd already made plans."

And then the shop next door came up for rent too. Everything came into place. "It just felt so right," says Abdul excitedly. "It was like fate or something." The Ali family named their new restaurant Kismot. It means 'destiny' in Bengali.

That was in 2006. But in an area of Edinburgh that was becoming increasingly crowded with restaurants, particularly Indian ones, making it work would be a challenge. The family had brought their previous takeaway customers with them, and families from Jahanara's paper round could be relied on to come into the restaurant too. But there was little else to set Kismot apart from being just another Indian. Even being wholly family run wasn't going to be enough.

"We got to a stage where we realised we had to do something different. I watched a YouTube video of this guy eating a home-made chilli curry and I became inspired by some Americans eating very hot foods. I'd watch TV shows like *Man Versus Food* and other mad challenges where people were eating hot chillies."

Every other restaurant around had its signature dish, Abdul had thought, so why not make the Kismot's signature dish super hot? It would certainly set them apart from the rest. But Ibrahim was sceptical. He was too conservative even to change prices unless the other restaurants did it, let alone take on the risk of veering from the everyday Indian menu. Abdul's brother was equally against it, thinking it too outlandish.

But Abdul waited until Aftab was away for a couple of weeks, then rewrote the menu – which was in English and his folks couldn't read. He wrote that the Kismot was offering Scotland's hottest curry. Anyone who finished it would get it for free. "It existed on the menu, but we didn't actually serve it," says Abdul. "It was just a draw into the restaurant. I wrote 'limited availability' on the menu, meaning we could always say it wasn't being served tonight."

When his brother returned and saw what he'd done, he went ballistic and told his father. "What you trying to do?" Abdul puts on his dad's voice. "You trying kill people? You want us lose money?"

Trust me, Abdul had said. And he was right. Customers came knocking in search of this killer curry. A local paper arrived wanting to cover the story. The only problem was that the restaurant would now have to follow through on the promise. They'd actually have to make the dish. Ibrahim cooked something up and the brothers tried it, but it was no stronger than the family would eat at home. Dad, we've got to really hit them hard, Abdul had told him.

"OK, you want a curry, I show how to make curry," says Abdul in his father's broken Bengali-Scottish accent. He cooked up the restaurant's hottest vindaloo, then added Naga Morich chillies from their home region. It was mind blowingly hot.

That was the first edition of the Kismot Killer. People started coming in from all over Edinburgh, then elsewhere in Scotland, then from further afield wanting to take on the challenge. But too many people came in and finished the curry, says Abdul. With the expensive Bangladeshi Naga Morich chillies they were buying from a local supplier, the marketing ploy risked backfiring.

"These people were animals. We used to joke around the kitchen that we needed to kill them. But my father didn't want to spend the money on more chillies."

Then on holiday in Bangladesh, the family ran into a distant relative who had his own chilli farm in the foothills of the mountains in Sylhet. He promised to send them as many Naga Morich pods as the restaurant could handle. So handfuls more Bangladeshi Nagas went into the New Kismot Killer, along with other chillies including Bhut Jolokias for good measure. Customers began to struggle to eat it; and the more people who failed, the more people came to try.

You can tell Abdul has a sharp marketing sense. Instead of sitting on the success the New Kismot Killer had brought, he thought of another idea: a curry contest for charity where contestants would eat three curries of increasing heat – the Kismot Killer, the New Kismot Killer and then something even hotter. The New Improved Kismot Killer.

This is the curry that someone is coming into the restaurant tonight to take on. It starts with a handful each of Naga Morich chillies, Bhut Nagas and Bhut Jolokias. They're all blended until there's about a litre of base mixture. The base is then slow cooked (sending hot and sharp fumes around the kitchen and – if someone forgets to close the door – into the restaurant and customers' lungs). Then Ibrahim adds more chillies: Bird's Eyes, Scotch Bonnets, green chillies, then chilli oil and chilli powder.

"Anything else?" I ask.

"Onions."

The chilli mix is then added to whatever cooked meats or vegetables the customer has ordered and, if they don't eat it, that'll be £30 please. "Let me show you," says Abdul, leading me for a tour of the kitchen.

It's a tiny affair, hazy with a warm smell of naan bread and curry powder. Ibrahim and Jahanara are crowded around the cooker with assorted other bodies moving in and out. The cooking is Abdul's parents' domain and Ibrahim seems to scowl at anyone who gets too close. The only exception seems to be a guy in the back who is sitting on a bucket chopping a tower of onions without a tear in his eyes.

There's a huge pot of gravy bubbling away on the stove, the base for Kismot's more regular curries, and an assortment of frying pans and skillets lined up next to it. Ibrahim is ladling in gravy, pulling huge tubs of spices off the shelves and throwing handfuls into the pans. Abdul leads me past the hobs to the tandoor, a deep clay oven where the naan breads are cooked.

"Watch your hands," Abdul says as I peer into its depths. "My mother can put her hands in there but for everyone else it's too hot." I turn round to see the tiny Jahanara still wrapped in her sari despite the stuffy heat of the kitchen. She's uncovering a tray of shiny wet buns. They're the dough that will be flattened then pressed up against the inside of the tandoor to cook into naans. She hauls out a huge bathtub of a bowl from underneath the counter.

"Fifteen year," she squeaks and nods her head, moving her hands in a massaging motion.

"She's had this tub for fifteen years," explains Abdul. "She insists on making the naan dough herself. She squats here on the floor twice a week and kneads it all by hand. Enough for the whole restaurant. I bought her an industrial mixer but she won't use it. Show us your muscles," he says, holding up his mother's arms as if she were a wrestler flexing their biceps.

"I like it hard work," she says, offering another grin. His dad grabs my arm and pulls me back to his end of the kitchen. He has a tub of bright red bitty mixture to show me. It's the Kismot Killer base. I take a sniff and am surprised that it smells only of oil.

"No smell, but when cook," Ibrahim motions with his arms in big circles. He makes a 'boom' sound. "Very hot, very hot."

He leads me to a row of bowls where he's lined up some of the chillies that go into the Killer. At one end there's a bowl of yellow-green pods about thumb size. They're the Naga Morich chillies. Then there are dried Bhut Jolokias, a bowl of Bird's Eyes, two or three yellow Scotch Bonnets and then a bowl of the base sauce. He looks on with pride as Abdul uses my phone to take a picture of me with the chillies and he insists I wear a Kismot chef's hat for the shot. Abdul's mother steps over again.

"Eat," she says shaking my arm and making that same motion with her hand. "You eat. You eat." It's not a question. Abdul guides me out of the kitchen and plonks me onto a table while he goes off to welcome customers who are now arriving in a steady stream.

In about twenty seconds my table has been filled with an empty plate, a deep bowl of curry and a mountain of pilau rice. It is, of course, chicken. I'm kinda getting used to this. There's no heat to the curry – perhaps they're taking it easy on me, knowing what's to come later – but it's delicious. Am I allowed to say that the subtly spiced chicken just falls off the bone, then doesn't even need chewing as it breaks apart when it's in the mouth? That the gravy is rich, the pilau slightly sweet and coloured with yellow and pink strands?

The Kismot is far from your traditional Indian. There's not a red carpet, gold tassel, tea light warmer or turmeric stained tablecloth in sight. Nor are there the telltale signs of the more upmarket Indian: all sparse walls, overdone uniforms, waterfalls and tiny portions. There's pumping Asian music on the stereo, not whining or overenthusiastic Bollywood numbers. This place has more of a street cantina feel to it. The tables are wooden and unfussy, the cutlery steel and the crockery is plain, off-white and has seen better days. There are TVs in the corners showing a highlights reel from Kismot's TV appearances: a game show with James Cordon trying the Kismot Killer, a curry competition at a Brighton chilli festival, stuttering footage from a local BBC news package. It reminds me I have to ask Abdul about the hospital incident.

There's a resigned look of guilt on his face. He knows the fallout from their first curry contest could have been disastrous for the restaurant, even though he thought they'd planned for every eventuality.

"By the second round, people were starting to pull out. But some others didn't know when to stop and wanted to go all the way. When people eat the Killer here they usually go outside to cool down or to the toilet. But the restaurant was packed with spectators and they had nowhere to go. They got claustrophobic, couldn't move and got very upset tummies."

The Red Cross, which had agreed to attend the event simply because so many spectators were expected, got more than it had bargained for. Some of the contestants were getting such bad stomach cramps that they couldn't deal with it. The Red Cross advised Abdul to call an ambulance. The next day journalists were queuing up outside the restaurant wanting an interview; not because it was a scandal that a restaurant had put people in hospital, but because of the hot curry angle. *The Sun*, the *Daily Mail* and the BBC all wanted to run stories, says Abdul, but they were all taking the funny side.

"The nurses who come in here said that every Friday and Saturday night they have to deal with a hospital packed with injuries from drink, drugs and fights. But one person comes in with a bad stomach from a hot curry and it hits the headlines." In the end no-one had really got hurt. I suspect the publicity didn't do the Kismot too much harm either.

These days, anyone who enters the curry contest or orders the Kismot Killer is vetted by phone or is asked to come into the restaurant first to try just a little bit. They're asked about their health and their experience of eating hot foods. You can't just walk in off the street and have it. "We've got to a stage where we often advise customers *not* to eat it," says Abdul. He says the curry competition is much better planned now.

There are shouts from the kitchen – Abdul's parents – and it sounds like they're arguing. I glance through the food serving area and realise that's just how they communicate. They're lined up again behind their ovens: Jahanara is slapping naans into the tandoor, Ibrahim is creating flames from the hob as he pours and shakes, throwing pans this way and that.

I've gobbled my food in what feels like no time. Abdul goes off to welcome a group of women who lurch into the restaurant in a twenty-strong line and head for a long table laid up at the back. The sashes they're all wearing inform me it's Deb'z fiftieth birthday – yes, it's spelled with a 'z'. By the look of it, Deb and her pals have been in and out of Edinburgh pubs all afternoon. They're up from London for the weekend, bringing with them a mishmash of accents and sizes. There's a whole pink theme going on, lots of makeup and a couple of pairs of improbably tall pink heels. There's not a small quantity of animal print.

I watch the fun for a while but then Abdul's pulling me to the other side of the restaurant. He hauls up a chair and sits me next to a bunch of student types. He presents one of them to me. I look the guy up and down. He has brown skin, a tuft of beard and a wiry frame. He's awkward looking, wearing a rock band T-shirt and fiddling with his knife and fork. Every moment or two he takes sips from a can of Guinness.

"This is Amit," says Abdul. "He's the one having the Kismot Killer tonight. I'll leave you two to talk." I glance at the student type again. *You're kidding?*

Amit seems a bit unfazed by it all and doesn't quite understand why I want to talk to him. He tells me his heritage is Indian, but he's been in Britain for seven years. He read about the restaurant on the internet and he'd been in a month before for the second hottest thing on the menu.

"I wanted to try the Kismot Killer, so I've come back today to have it."

"So, you must like hot food?"

"Yes."

He's a talkative guy, this one. I try again. "How often do you, say, have a hot curry?"

"I have a curry hotter than a vindaloo three times a week," he says very precisely. "I like a phall." That'll be the hottest thing on most Indian restaurants' menu. A vindaloo plus some. He speaks as if he regularly puts one away for breakfast, then goes for a vindaloo for lunch.

"And how did you find the Naga curry?"

"I couldn't finish it," he says.

"Oh?"

"It was the portion size. They put the rest in a takeaway box and I had it the next morning."

"For breakfast?"

"For breakfast."

If Amit is a little wooden with me his friends are a lot more forthcoming. They're all bushy beards and baggy jeans. A petite and pale girl with bobbed hair seems slightly out of place. They're a band, explains one of them. Amit is a fan and friend. They've come here to watch him eat the legendary curry.

"What's the band name?" I ask.

"AlbaRoma," says one of them and I nod. *Isn't that a car?*

"What kind of stuff do you do?"

"We play a kind of Balkan Plasma Punk."

Oh, that's nice, I think. I like a bit of Balkan Plasma Punk, me. It's all I can do to resist asking them if they happen to have a CD. After all, my collection of Balkan Plasma Punk is a bit sparse these days. (By the time you read this, they'll probably be massive. Then I'll look like a tit.)

There's a cheer and then applause from the other side of the room. It's Deb'z table. A woman is standing at the end holding an empty plate high above her head. They've been having a curry eating competition. The victor hasn't just finished first, she's *licked* the plate clean. You can still see thin streaks of the sauce left by her tongue. The women start up in song but it's so slurred I can't make out the words.

AlbaRoma's food has now arrived, a selection of the usual curry, rice, naan breads, bajees and papadoms. The band begin to tuck in but all Amit gets is a little slip of paper. It's the Kismot Killer legal disclaimer form.

"You are totally aware that you are having probably the world's hottest curry… If you die whilst eating, members of the table with you will share the cost of your Kismot

Killer... If you find you are experiencing any problems with your lover then under no circumstances are you entitled to blame Kismot Restaurant... For your own well-being we highly recommend that you immediately put your toilet roll in the freezer when you get home."

It's all pure theatre of course but it's nothing compared with what comes next. When AlbaRoma are just about finishing their curries, the space in front of Amit is still empty. He keeps taking furtive glances in the direction of the kitchen. He's a little shy anyway but now he's started to look like he doesn't want to be there at all. He's definitely on his third can of Guinness.

Abdul winks at me and it's his signal for me to step aside. One of the girls flicks a switch on the stereo and the *Jaws* theme creeps up in volume from the speakers. Across the restaurant conversations come to a stop. The kitchen doors open and Abdul strides through just as *Jaws* fades out and the theme from *Rocky* kicks in. Abdul's wearing a gas mask and holding aloft a bowl of deep crimson curry. He begins wandering round the restaurant, pointing at guests in this direction and that. *You, it's for you!* He goes over to Deb'z lot and a look of genuine terror appears on the face of one of the women who thinks – just for a moment – that her friends have stitched her up.

Abdul eventually arrives at Amit's table. With a flourish he places the curry and a pile of naans in front of him. A couple of the other diners go back to their conversations but most eyes are on Amit. Obviously feeling the pressure he takes a small forkful and looks up with neither a smile nor horror.

"It's good. Hot and good," he says to AlbaRoma and he begins to heap spoonfuls onto a naan. I return to my position close to the bar where Abdul's cousin Mirage (yes,

Mirage) is standing. He tells me in a thick Manchester accent that he's just popped in to say 'hi' after returning from holiday but had been roped in to help. I suspect no-one in the family comes through the door without having to do at least some work. But nor do they leave without being properly fed. Mirage tells me he used to do the whole *Jaws-Rocky*-gas mask routine but has now retired.

"He seems to be taking it in his stride," I say.

He shakes his head, reaches under the counter for a pile of serviettes, and his eyes move back in the direction of Amit's table. "You'll see," he says and ambles over. Uninvited, he places the serviettes in the centre.

By this point AlbaRoma have tried the curry, just the tiniest bit on the tip of a fork. They're all coughing and no-one is smiling. The petite girl with the bob has gone bright pink. I notice one of the beards put his hand on Amit's shoulder: are you OK buddy?

Amit is not OK. He's stopped eating and is staring into dead space, breathing deeply. He picks up Mirage's pile of serviettes and starts dabbing his forehead and mouth. He grabs another can of Guinness and opens it. It fizzes all over the table but Amit barely notices. He doesn't say a word. A definite yellow tinge has descended on his skin. He half-heartedly picks up a sliver of naan and, with reluctance, dips the smallest corner into the sauce. He blows out deeply before putting it in his mouth. He's wrapped an arm across his stomach. An almost full bowl of curry still sits in front of him. This is a man who is suffering.

And do you know what you want when you're really suffering? That's right, a bald headed guy with a notebook getting right up there in your face. I edge over to the table, trying to be as nonchalant as I can. "So, how are you finding it?"

"Hot in the mouth," Amit says. He's trying to catch his breath like you do when you've jumped into a freezing cold swimming pool. "But when it goes to the stomach, it's creasing me." He shakes his head again. Abdul has come over to ask how he's doing too.

"Can you please bring me some," deep breath. "I need some ice cream." He's begging.

"Of course, right away." Abdul runs to the kitchen and returns with a mammoth bowl of the cold stuff. He's obviously done this a hundred times. Then Deb'z group launch into a drawled rendition of Happy Birthday. I wince, imagining exactly how welcome the screeching is in Amit's head. Abdul is suddenly over at Deb'z table with trays of cupcakes with lighted candles on top of each one. He sure knows how to work his restaurant.

I turn back to Amit, but he's disappeared outside. Through the window I can see that he's doubled over. The girl has followed and is trying to reassure him. She gives up and comes back in.

"What did he say?" asks one of the band.

"'I'm feeling faint. Just don't touch me.'"

One of them pushes the curry towards me. "Time for a bit of gonzo journalism," he says. In other words, my participation is expected. I lever a small forkful from the curry bowl and drop it onto a side plate, then I grab a corner of naan and dip it in about a centimetre. Abdul dashes over with a disclaimer form for me but he's only joking.

It's not unpleasant but it's not delicious like my earlier curry. It's more like a paste than a sauce: gritty and seedy, and the flavour only brings to mind a very deeply seasoned lumpy gravy. There's a chilli taste coming from the fresh fruits and none of the bitter aftertaste that comes with chilli extract, but otherwise I can't detect much by way of flavour.

I make that raised eyebrow and turned-down-mouth face in the band's direction that says: 'mmm, not bad'.

And then the heat kicks in. It's hot. God, it is so incredibly hot. It is incredibly, astonishingly, unbearably hot. My mouth begins to flame. My lips to sting. I realise I haven't even swallowed yet and now I have no choice. It's like red hot swords lined with razor blades going down my throat. And not in a good way.

It's not like some of the hottest sauces and chillies I've tasted. It doesn't make me cough or hiccup. It's just pure unadulterated heat. It's so hot that there's now a strange numb feeling in my mouth but it hasn't taken away the burn. Yet despite the incredible pain of heat, it's also ridiculously moreish. I take a few more dips, this time lumping a fair amount more onto the bread, and start to munch. I start to sweat profusely and notice a fresh pile of napkins has arrived from somewhere.

I then take a moment to consider. Aren't I doing exactly what Amit was doing not five minutes ago? He got a taste for it and now look at him: squatting outside and holding his stomach looking like he's going to chuck. He's from Calcutta. I'm from Wolverhampton. You do the maths.

There begins a deep churning in my stomach. The same incredible feeling of heat I have in my mouth and throat now spreads across my belly. I know where this is going and the heat concentrates exactly where my ulcer is. I can't help but think of Darth Naga and his *poke and puke* mantra.

Amit returns to the table releasing me to observe again from a distance. He's still breathing heavily, but gamely takes another few corners of naan-soaked Killer, interspersed with large spoons of ice cream. But he's soon clenching his stomach again and shaking his head. I look down and notice I too am holding my stomach which has gone into cramps.

But here's the thing. I reckon I've had the maximum of a forkful of the curry. With lots of naan bread. Sweat is streaming off me. But I truly desperately want some more. It's like a drug and I'm considering going back to the table. I'm having an endorphin rush.

But Amit's friends have taken his curry away. He's grabbing for it with not too much effort and they're passing it between each other to prevent him eating any more. One of the beards passes it to Abdul who whisks the curry to the kitchen.

"I think that's sensible," says Mirage. "Usually you see friends urging them to eat more and more, giving them no choice, but I think these guys must truly love him."

"Mmmm, hmmm," I say. It's the most I can manage and he laughs at me.

By the bar stands a glass case with a trophy inside for the Curry King. Neither I nor Amit are in any danger of getting this tonight. Underneath there's a newspaper clipping from *The Sun* about last year's competition: Hot Stuff Paul Is Curry Champ.

Paul Rafferty shovelled up Abdul Ali's mouth melting curry in three minutes, says the clipping. The refrigeration engineer – is it only me who finds that funny? – narrowly beat Hibernian Ladies goalkeeper Dani Downs to the title. "I decided to just wolf it down," said Paul, 33.

Dani tells *Sun* readers: "It's lethal."

Abdul goes to Amit's table with a certificate and a paper crown. A deep look of relief spreads across Amit's face. The restaurant applauds him and it's photos all round. The band invite me in for a shot too.

The waiting staff then bring out little bowls of Amit's unfinished curry and offer it to some of the longer and rowdier tables in the restaurant. At one table Steven is goaded into taking the dipped end of a fork, while his friends take just a toothpick. One at a time their faces go red, except Stephen who goes completely pale. He heads outside. Fraiser, an enormous Scot, is shaking his head vigorously. Peter takes himself off to the toilet.

A woman is crying out, but with a smile: "When does it stop?"

"Ha, ha," says her friend. "Tomorrow!"

"No," she says again, any amusement gone. "Really, when does it stop?"

Another table sees me loitering and drags me over to meet Richie Ramsay, a pro-golfer who works the European Tour. His caddy tells me he's playing an Aberdeen Pro-Am tomorrow. Richie takes the end of a fork's worth and within thirty seconds he's hurting, holding his head in his hands.

"Aye, ye dunnae look good lad," laughs the caddy. I imagine exactly where Richie Ramsay plans to shove his nine iron once he's recovered. All around the restaurant people are ordering mango lassi, glasses of milk and ice cream.

"Well, it's a side benefit," says Abdul.

There's an atmosphere of fun and excitement across the whole restaurant. A dour Indian eating house this is not. Whether the Kismot Killer really is the hottest curry in the world, in Britain, or even in Scotland I really don't know. I really don't care. It is cripplingly hot and the vibe and theatrical atmosphere here is catching. But eventually, the show is over and the restaurant slowly empties.

"Ah, man, we're so grateful you've come all the way up here to see what we're doing," says Abdul. "I worry about my mum and dad but, God willing, we'll continue to be OK."

I pop into the kitchen to say thanks for the food where

Jahanara is − of course − still working. She's moved to the sink and is washing up. She bows at me. "Thank you, thank you," she says as if it's me that's done all the hard grind that night.

Abdul's dad comes over and offers a firm hand. "You come back, yes? You try more?"

Abdul leads me out of the kitchen. Instinctively we hug rather than shake hands. Then he pulls out Kizmot T-shirts in children's sizes, one in pink, one in light blue. There's a heart shape made out of chillies on the front.

"I hope you don't mind, but… well, I saw the pictures of your children on your phone…" He hands over the T-shirts with an embarrassed look.

And I don't mind at all. It's just about the sweetest thing in the whole world.

1st June − As well as a few small chillies on Masquerade I'm now starting to get decent sprays of flowers on half a dozen of my plants with Red Missile, Prairie Fire and Vampire also leading the charge. My little hydroponic Prairie Fire is notably the most prolific of the whole bunch. The rest are recalcitrant, but I'm imagining it'll be any time now. Which raises the important prospect of pollination. For chillies to grow, the flowers need to be pollinated. The pods then grow from where the impregnated flowers were.

Chilli plants − the naughty things − are able to self pollinate. That means there are no boy and girl flowers. All that's needed is the pollen to be transferred from the stamen (which appear in a bulbous ring around the inside of the flower) to the stigma (the single rod in the middle).

Adrian Nuttall at Suffolk Chilli Farm told me there's generally four ways this can take place. First is by insects: bees, hoverflies, in fact any hungry winged critter who visits the flowers will help transfer the pollen.

Second, the wind. A slight breeze over the plants will shake the flowers and transfer pollen that way. If there's no wind, then a gentle hand shake of plant can do the same thing. Finally, there's the paintbrush technique. Take a small soft paintbrush and gently tease the pollen from the stamen to the stigma in the same flower, or a different flower on the same plant. This final technique is only for the desperate. Or the crazy.

I'm going to let nature take its course because I'm not crazy. OK, maybe I am a bit. I've been found a couple of times gently probing away at flowers with a brush from my daughter's painting set. I've also now introduced a marigold plant and placed it dead centre of my chilli collection. I'm hoping the scent will bring my winged friends racing to the nectar within. I haven't spied any bees yet but I'm looking forward to a veritable swarm once those marigolds are fully open.

While we're on pollination, it's worth noting that, like tomatoes, chillies cross-pollinate very easily. I've now got thirteen varieties of chillies in my conservatory and if a bee is on a nectar collection spree it's very likely to visit Vampire, Friar's Hat, Lemon Drop and any number of their flowers, exchanging pollen between them. If you're already a keen gardener you'll be rolling your eyes right now. But I was puzzled about the effect that would have: would growing my chilli plants together end up with a Frankenstein mix and match of fruits on each of them? There's no shame in looking things up and what I discovered was that a Vampire plant would still produce Vampire fruit this year, but the seeds inside might grow into a cross-bred chilli variety when they are planted next year.

This is why some chilli enthusiasts purposely cross-breed chillies. They're trying to produce seeds which may grow into hotter or more hardy strains the following year. It's also why purists will grow only one variety of chilli or make sure different varieties are well separated so cross-pollination is avoided. And it's also why if you're buying seeds you need to go to a reputable supplier every year – one who will have protected the heritage of the variety – and not just replant your own seeds or those from a friend's crop. That's unless you welcome the chance to breed a new strain of Frankenstein fruit, and good luck to you. I'm certainly going to try it.

The Kankun Luchador

"AMIGO GIDEON! THANK you for your interest in KANKUN, I think what you are doing is awesome!!! I invite you for a dining experience in one of the most authentic Mexican restaurants in London, I promise you will have a KANKUNFANTASTIC time with me.

"Warm regards amigo! Rolando, aka 'KANKUN LUCHADOR'."

As email replies go, it certainly beats Andrew Jukes' "I'm talking at a carrot meeting."

No book on chilli flavours and characters could be complete without bumping – rather like Christopher Columbus did – into Latin America; or more specifically into Mexico. In popular imagination Mexico is the very home of the chilli. It is chilli's country of origin, has food that is eye wateringly spicy and salsas that are burning hot. When you see little cartoon figures of chillies they are often wearing a sombrero and shaking maracas, probably with a cactus in the background.

I was surprised that on the British chilli scene Mexico wasn't as well represented as African, Asian and Caribbean flavours, presumably because there hasn't been a particularly large Latin American immigration to the UK compared with those other places. To begin with I couldn't even find a Mexican influenced chilli enthusiast to speak to. But then Rolando Cardenas stepped into the ring. If he's one of the only Mexican sauce producers in Britain I wouldn't be surprised. He's certainly the only one who sells his products wearing a cape and bright red underpants over a lycra superhero suit.

For Rolando is not just a purveyor of hot and smoky chilli sauces; he's a Mexican wrestler. And that's not just a marketing gimmick. Wrestling is Mexico's national sport and back in Mexico City where he comes from Rolando was a keen amateur. Now living in London, he's a member of Lucha Britannia – he's actually the only Mexican member – and goes by the fighting name of the Kankun Luchador (Kankun is a Mexican beach resort, luchador means *fighter* or *wrestler*).

Rolando has invited me to join him to talk Mexican food, chillies and wrestling at his favourite Mexican cantina in London. I know just who to take with me. My friend Dan is adventurous. He's travelled the world and he drinks in culture like the English drink tea. He loves trying new things, especially food, and he's so laid back he can barely stand up straight. He'll talk to anyone and I know he'll ask intelligent and interesting questions while I'm busy scribbling answers in my notebook.

He also happens to be a purple belt in jiu jitsu. If the tequila flows a little too readily tonight and this thing comes to the crunch, well, I'm just a little intrigued to know whether it will be Dan or the Kankun Luchador who will hit the canvas first.

We arrive twenty minutes early for our dinner appointment giving Dan and me time to wander around Dalston Kingsland, an area of London I lived in ten years ago. Back then, it was all chicken friers, betting offices and cornershops that couldn't quite decide if they should sell overseas phone cards, mobile phone covers, £1 bowls of fruit and veg, high alcohol booze or internet access, so kind of sold the lot at the same time. Let's be honest, the area was rough and I'd only venture onto the high street if I had to catch the train. Now, however, the area is on the edge of painfully trendy. Late-teens stride confidently around wearing drainpipe turn-ups, sporting beards and flatcaps while they head to a converted warehouse art gallery or a bar where all the 'distressed' wooden furniture looks like it was nicked from a skip.

Dalston did always have a smattering of excellent Turkish and West Indian restaurants if you were willing to brave the street drinkers to get to them. But now it has a whole row of independent eateries replacing what were once cheap shoe and hair extension shops. One of those restaurants is Mezcal Cantina, against the bar of which Rolando is leaning, wearing a smart pink striped shirt. Not, I'm disappointed to see, his wrestling outfit. The place is all inflatable cacti, Mexicans riding horses and shooting guns, waitresses in sombreros and Mariachi singers going from table to table.

OK, it's not really like that at all. Except for the guns. We'll get to the guns later. Mezcal is dark but has subtle tea light candles and bright paper decorations hanging from the roof like piñatas. On the walls are giant painted skulls but they're traditionally decorated with luminous pink and yellow paint to take away any of the scariness. The seats are wooden and the tables are covered with plastic tablecloths onto which tins of knives and forks as well as a selection of hot sauces have been plonked. The bar is plastered with Mexican bingo cards which offer illustrations of wrestlers, baseball players, fruit, fish, skulls, dancers, musical instruments and religious icons. On the TV on the wall a vigorous Latin American dance competition is taking place: the general idea seems to be to swing and spin your partner around so forcefully that their head, arms and legs almost drop off. Dan tells me it's cumbia: a violent style of dancing popular all over Latin America. He points out that though the dancers sport huge grins, their body language shows their moves are really quite uncomfortable.

The restaurant owner, Cesar Garibay Reyes, pops over to greet Rolando and my host explains that I've come to try Mexican food and to talk chillies. Cesar immediately pulls up a chair and begins talking about Mexican cookery and what he's trying to do with Mezcal. Within a minute he's been joined by his head chef. The three talk over each other, practically tugging Dan and me to their respective corners to tell us about this or that regional dish.

"What do you want to drink my friend?" Cesar looks a little how you imagine a Mexican mafia boss might look: round, thick necked, informal white shirt and jacket, with a swinging gold necklace. All that's missing is the cigar. I tell him we're here for the authentic Mexican dining experience and to give us to drink and eat exactly what a Mexican would expect if he came in here.

The chef, Daniel Sanchez, is smaller and is wearing a flat cap. But unlike the hipsters outside, it looks like it belongs on his head. He has excited eyes and yet more excited hand gestures. He keeps pulling up images on his phone of Mexican dishes, chillies, beans and plants to illustrate his latest point. It's as if no-one has ever shown an interest in their cooking before. We've become the cantina's centre of attention.

The drinks arrive: Cesar has chosen for me a non-alcoholic cocktail of tamarind and sweet agave syrup. Dan lucks out with a Jaritto Empedador, a cocktail of the Mexican spirit mezcal (after which the cantina is named), passion fruit, mango, ginger beer and lime. It comes in a clay tankard with a passion fruit floating on the top and the rim is lined with chilli powder. Mine tastes like a non-alcoholic cocktail (i.e. fruit juice). His tastes amazing, a smooth alcoholic warmth with the chilli pulling out the various flavours of fruit inside. A waiter brings over a plate of thin orange slices, these too with chilli powder sprinkled over the top. I'm amazed by how the smoky heat of the chilli really emphasises the orange citrus. The effect is cleansing and refreshing.

"This is what would be on sale on street corners in Mexico, especially outside schools," says Rolando. "Parents would buy this while waiting for their children and sprinkle on chilli to bring out the flavour. It's very traditional."

Before we've even finished our cocktails, Cesar returns from the bar with small shots of mezcal all round. It's a clear spirit originating from the Oaxaca district of Mexico, but now made all over the country by tiny family brewers. Each one only produces a thousand or so bottles a year. Tequila is actually a specific type of mezcal, and both are brewed from the agave plant.

Like Bordeaux wine has to come from Bordeaux in order to be officially called Bordeaux, tequila the spirit has to come from a specific region of Mexico: in this case the northwest of Guadalajara and in the highlands of north-western Mexico. Outside that, it's mezcal you'd generally drink. The one litre bottle Cesar brings to the table has a label featuring a skeleton in a suit and jaunty hat and is numbered 1945/2000. Even in Mexico it would be expensive, but with import costs and duties it tops off at more than £80 a bottle over here. No wonder Cesar is slightly stingy in the amount he's given us.

Rather more disturbingly Daniel dashes off and then returns with two glass bottles of Tequila, each of which is shaped like an enormous gun. He then holds one of them to his head, makes a suicide gesture then jokes about 'Tequila shots', earning a groan from all around the table.

Aloe moisturiser comes from the agave plant too and Daniel urges us to dip our fingers into the spirit and rub it on our skin: it really does feel soft and silky. And it's the same when it goes down the throat: soothing like a good whisky, without overpowering alcohol. I'm no big fan of Tequila; I find it harsh and rusty. But then again, my only real experience of it has been doing shots on top of a belly full of beer so I'm hardly a connoisseur.

Traditionally mezcal is sipped, often with a side of salt, orange or lemon, and chilli powder. Yes, Mexicans really do wipe salt on their hand before drinking. Rolando has a tiny worm in his more generous glass of mezcal (though I think his is from one of the cheaper bottles). I ask whether the worm is hallucinogenic. He gives me a shrug that either says he's got no idea what I'm talking about or that he couldn't possibly comment. But when he's finished his mezcal, he chews the worm meaningfully.

Cesar talks about how chilli is central to Mexican eating and drinking, and most often in Mexican cookery the chillies used are smoked rather than fresh. He takes me down to the basement where he has boxes and bags of various deep brown dried chillies. He's stuffing them under my nose as he reels off the ones most traditionally used in Mexican dishes: dried Morita, Mulato, Pasilla, Guajillo, Poblano and Ancho. The chillies are much bigger than I'd expected – almost a hand's width in some cases – and have a chocolatey sheen to them, as well as a smoky smell that lingers in the throat. They're leathery and flexible rather than crinkly and wrinkled. The Arbols, the name for dried Poblanos, are long and a finger's width; a lovely brown-crimson colour. The

Pasillas have the shape, size and deep purple colour of a flattened aubergine. The Anchos look like long oversized prunes. All of them have that delicious aroma of a white-smoking barbecue that has just been doused with water.

Cesar uses only Mexican chillies from a Mexican importer. As well as the dried chillies, he shows me huge tins of sliced Jalapeños, Poblanos and Chipotles marinated in oil. There's stack upon stack of soft corn tortillas on the shelves waiting to be filled, and packets of Chihuahua – it's a traditional Mexican cheese, as well as a yappy little handbag dog.

"Each Mexican dish must use very specific chillies for it to taste like it should. You can't mix them. When you go to another place that claims to serve Mexican food, if they're not using the right chilli then that's not the dish because it doesn't taste right."

As we head back upstairs, Cesar tells me that lots of Mexicans come to eat in his restaurant. He knows if a mole sauce was made with the wrong smoked chillies, they'd be at the bar demanding their money back. Chillies are not just for heat, they're the very foundation of a variety of Mexican flavours. Mole sauce, generally cooked with Ancho, Pasilla, Mulato or Chipotle chillies depending on the region where it's made, is very Mexican and has nothing to do with the small black insectivore hated by owners of manicured lawns. Though dishes served with it do tend to look like one has been cooked up and then doused in the sauce.

All three seem so excited about Mexican cookery and chillies that I wonder whether it's all a bit of a show put on for our benefit. But I have a basic understanding of Spanish and catch them talking, arguing and joking among themselves about Mexican flavours, their family traditions, food regions and favourite dishes too. This is the real deal.

A starter plate of mixed tacos arrives as well as some prawns glazed with a brown caramelised chilli marmalade. The tacos are soft and made with the corn tortillas I'd seen downstairs. They're about the size of a beer mat and piled high in the middle with various meats: chicken, beef, lamb and pork with a token vegetarian one in the middle. Dan takes one look at all the meat and the prawns and licks his lips. Then leans over to me and says: "Looks like you're going to have to suck it up."

"Yeah, I know." For the first time I'm not quite sure if I'm beginning to enjoy the meat emphasis of my chilli journey because the dishes have always been so well prepared or because, well, because meat turns out to be really quite nice.

Dan takes a prawn, removes the head, and plonks the prawn into his mouth tail and all and begins to crunch. I take his lead and the caramelised chilli marmalade is incredible. It's sticky and hot, not unlike the marinade I tasted after the Clifton Chilli Club chicken wings contest. I'm surprised by how tasty the prawn is and how the crispy crunch of the tail is an enjoyable rather than distasteful part of the eating.

Dan looks down at the tacos and can't wait to get started on those too. But he asks first how are we supposed to eat them. On the rare occasions I use tortillas at home we load up huge flour discs with various stuff: refried beans, avocado and then an indistinct vegetable or meaty tomato gunk, sprinkle on a bit of cheddar and fold it into a wrap. But these far smaller discs are already stacked high with filling so no rolling is possible and ten different tiny plates of sides have arrived too. There's a green tomatillo salsa and a red tomato one too. Daniel tells us that the tomatillo used for the green edition grows in cute little paper lanterns but English growers mistakenly wait for them to turn red which they never do. There are refried black beans, a few finely chopped onion salads, a plate of limes and some grated Chihuahua. There's also a line of Rolando's own Kankun brand hot sauces.

One good thing about Mexican cooking is that it is virtually illegal to eat alone. Traditionally all the food goes into the centre of the table and the emphasis is on sharing. Rolando and Cesar and Daniel are tucking in, so we quickly follow suit. Cesar explains that you take a taco and fold it into a half-boat between your fingers, before sprinkling any extras you'd like – chilli sauce, or Mexican cheese, or salsa – onto the bit you're about to eat. This is how a lot of Mexican food is eaten: it's mildly hot to begin with, then it's spiced, flavoured and seasoned to your taste. It reminds me of how Steve Woodward at Mushemi Fire told me the Zambians eat chilli.

Rolando takes up a taco, half rolls it, adds a squeeze of lime and his own chilli sauce and puts it to his mouth. Cesar and Daniel point and laugh. Rolando has stuck out his little finger, as if he's drinking afternoon tea from a china cup.

"That's very Mexican," they say. I'm not sure if it's a joke or not.

I take a chicken tinga, a mountain of spice-seasoned, finely shredded chicken in a sauce with dried chilli, onion, tomato and oregano. I add a little red salsa and take a bite (half-extending my little finger, just in case). The chicken is light and tasty, but the mix spills out of my mouth, over my fingers and onto the plate below.

"Ah, now you're eating like a Mexican," says Rolando. I get the impression that 'like a Mexican' means the messier the better and shows I'm enjoying the food. Dan and I swap tacos. He's working on the pork one and this time I add some of Rolando's Kankun Habanero hot sauce. The pork is in small pieces and pleasingly chewy. Then the sauce comes with a very sharp taste and a soft burn. In no time our table has polished off the prawns and the tacos, except for one that remains in the centre of the plate. Dan can't help but point out that it's the vegetarian one.

We're still licking our fingers when the main course arrives: a mix of dishes that can only be described as a hot Mexican meat filled food fest. There's a rack of glistening sticky ribs that have been cooked in the chilli marmalade. There's a lamb shank, deep brown and dotted with sesame seeds sitting like an iceberg in a thick gravy made with dried chillies and Mexican beer. And there's a huge bowl of what appears to be a Mexican stew which Cesar tells us is pozole. Each dish comes with a pile of rice cooked in a light tomato and chilli sauce, sprinkled with oregano.

The ribs have the same smoky caramel sauce as the prawns from earlier, and I try them tentatively – and then with more gusto, spreading the sauce all over my face just like a Mexican is supposed to. Dan and I are so impressed by the lamb shank we insist on having our photo taken with it. Cesar shows us how to eat it: use a deep spoon to pull away some of the meat, scoop up some of the Chipotle and beer gravy and then pile on any one or more of the condiments from the small bowls. I don't remember the last time I tasted lamb and it's hard to describe – I can only think it's like a nice tasting soil – but it's very tender and Daniel says it takes five hours to cook. The sauce is not particularly hot but I add salsa and chilli sauce and it brings out the smokiness in the dish.

Cesar says: "We tone down the heat just a little bit here because people don't like so much chilli, but if people like it hotter we can make them hotter or they can make them hotter themselves using the salsas and sauces."

The ribs and the lamb shank may be impressive to look at, but it's the pozole that gets all the attention. This, the three tell us – all at the same time, talking over each other of course – is the most traditional of Mexican family dishes. It's made with Jalapeño Chipotle chillies which are rehydrated before being slow cooked in the stew. Each family has their own version and it's the kind of thing you'd serve for a big get-together, rather like our own Sunday lunch.

The dish is nearly four thousand years old and like everything we've been eating tonight is pre-New World discovery by the Spanish and Portuguese. Dan and I agree that there's nothing Spanish about the flavours here. There's no clean or sharp spiciness. Instead, it's all deep and smoky like it's been cooked in a big pot over a campfire.

The pozole, says Rolando, is an amazing hangover cure. It's essentially Mexican comfort food and his eyes go a bit glossy at the thought of home. Dan and I are about to dive into the stew when Cesar stops us. There's a very specific way of eating this dish too. Once again, we're supposed to sprinkle on the condiments we want: some salsa, some onion salad, oregano, a dash or two of the sauces. He then tells Dan to mix it up with a huge spoon. As he does so, enormous lumps of white corn rise to the top, along with chunks of pork. Rather than a gloopy stew, it's slightly thinner like a soup with lots of little bits of different things. It's like Mexico in a bowl and once again it's supposed to be shared. Everyone is dipping their own spoons in, eating the pozole between mouthfuls of deep fried tortilla.

"If you weren't here, I'd have just sat by myself and eaten this as it comes," Dan says to Cesar. "I wonder how many times we go into restaurants and just eat food in exactly the opposite way to how it's supposed to be eaten. It makes a real difference to learn how things are cooked, then to be shown how to eat them properly."

He's clearly enjoying everything about this evening. I'm having a great time too and the food is nothing like I've ever tasted in a Mexican restaurant before. There's a Mexican place close to where my in-laws live. The vegetables clearly come out of a plastic bag from Iceland, the cheese is cheddar and the corn chips may well be straight out of a bag of Doritos. Now I think about it, it's run by Asians and there's a huge neon sign of a cactus and sombrero outside. But there's a question I've been resisting but I know I have to ask: "So, where does chilli con carne come into all this?"

The three throw their hands up in horror and I almost feel like Daniel is going to shoot me with his tequila gun. "That's Tex Mex," says Cesar – not the same thing at all. "There are 148 Mexican restaurants in London" – this man has done his research – "and I've only found four or five that are run by Mexicans, and one of those is this one."

Apparently, there's nothing Mexican about burritos, or chilli con carne or those hard shelled tacos piled with mush you get at festivals. "I won't serve a burrito in this restaurant," says Daniel with disgust. "You can't buy this here; it's not for sale."

Cesar tells stories of people coming in asking for burritos or chimichangas and being disappointed that a supposedly Mexican restaurant didn't serve them. They then have one of his dishes and complain that they're expensive. "'This is the most expensive enchilada I've had in my life,'" he mimics. That's because they're used to having cheap meat in huge deep fried flour tortillas from food stalls that are made with the wrong ingredients and the wrong chillies, or just have Tabasco sauce or Jalapeños sprinkled over the top.

"My mission is to bring Mexico to the UK," says Cesar.

"Right now British people are getting used to different flavours; they're liking chillies and good Mexican food is starting to become more popular. But before that..." He shakes his head.

"I get it," says Dan. "It's like how a pizza place will put a few Jalapeños and chunks of pineapple on a Margarita and call it the Mexican Special." He's in his stride now: "Imagine an English Special: it would be covered with broccoli and cauliflower, with a little tub of English mustard on the side."

It's Rolando's mission to bring a little taste of Mexico to the UK too and he doesn't just mean his hot sauces. After the food is cleared away, he pulls out his Mexican wrestling mask. This is not like one of those cloth Spiderman masks my son wears when it's dressing-up day at school. It looks like red leather, has intricate seams and is embroidered with gold, silver and red sequins. There are terrifying holes for the mouth, nose and eyes. It covers the whole head and laces up at the back with thick leather cord.

It's the same mask that adorns the front of his Kankun sauces and is inspired by ancient masks that the Mayans used before going into battle. The style of Rolando's wrestling mask is from the 1940s when wrestling started to take off in Mexico. Daniel and Rolando talk animatedly of legendary wrestlers – El Santo, Blue Demon, Mil Mascaras – that are still revered in Mexico today, just like we revere Nobby Stiles, Bobby Moore and Jackie Stewart. I daren't mention Big Daddy.

"I'll go and get changed," says Rolando.

He goes off to the toilets while Dan returns from his own tour of the chillies with Cesar. "I'm never eating a burrito again," he says. He's impressed by how welcoming the three have been and how keen they are to really show us about chillies, cooking and Mexican traditions. It's a window on a world we know nothing about and it's right here on our doorstep.

It's exactly the same welcome I've encountered across my whole Chilli Britain journey. Everyone seems flattered to be even asked about what they do. They're only too happy to talk and give up their time to show and even to allow me to participate. I remember what Chilli Dave said when I met him at the Clifton Chilli Club. He wanted to educate people and 'spread the chilli love'.

"I feel like tonight we've been let in on a secret," says Dan. "There's a world of amazing food and tradition there just below the surface. They're proud of it and want to share."

Rolando returns in his wrestling costume, only it's not Rolando anymore. It's the Kankun Luchador and he seems to have taken on a more confident persona. People in the restaurant are looking around and he visits a few tables handing out sample sachets of his sauces and having pictures taken with some of the diners.

He's wearing the mask which completely covers his head and you can just about see his eyes. You can only see his mouth when he opens it to speak and the effect is truly scary rather than comical. He's wearing black lycra leggings and a matching short sleeved top. There's a long, flowing and sequinned red cape over his shoulders and it matches long boots that are laced up with leather cord like the back of his mask. He's wearing those patent red wrestling pants and the word Kankun is written across his chest with red lightning bolts springing from it.

After doing the rounds of the other diners he returns to our table and I ask if he usually gets that reaction. "Oh, yes," the Luchador says with a giggle that doesn't match his costume. "Whenever I'm at a festival or a show, or if I'm on the tube" – *the tube?* – "people always want their photo taken with me. It's good for the marketing. At places where there are celebrities, they come over to me and want to have their photos taken."

He shows me paper masks and sample sachets he gives out then pulls up a picture of how he organises his trade stand with samples offered around a tiny wrestling ring, with the corn chips in the middle. There are even little wrestling figures standing in each corner.

But here's the thing. There's not a shred of embarrassment about what Rolando is wearing. He strolls around the restaurant perfectly comfortably. This isn't a costume, it's a sports kit. This is who he is.

His interest in wrestling and its connection with chillies grew from an early age. He and his brother used to dress up in wrestling gear all through his childhood and they'd steal Habanero chillies from their grandmother's kitchen. Before they went into battle they'd eat a Habanero and pretend it gave them super strength. It unleashes the power beneath, he says. In Mexico City, Rolando wrestled in amateur tournaments and has tried to keep up his fitness in England. He dreams of organising a wrestling tournament over here to promote his sauces, perhaps pitching famous Mexican wrestlers against British ones. Dan asks him what the difference is.

"British wrestling is a lot more about grabbing and testing strength," he says. "Mexican wrestling is a lot more acrobatic and theatrical; it's showmanship, you can see the moves and it's about joking and being cheeky. But if there is a rivalry, then it can be very serious."

Daniel does a quick search on his mobile and pulls up a newspaper clipping showing a man covered almost head to toe in blood. The headline next to the picture reads: *Morir en el ring.* Death in the ring.

Rolando tells us how Mexican wrestling works, at least in traditional matches called *lucha libre* – free wrestling. First the contestants wrestle in their particular colours: their costumes which most often include masks. The winner of that match – putting the shoulders of your opponent down for the count of ten – gets to remove their opponent's mask, humiliating them by showing their face. A mask-to-face fight then continues and if the same guy loses he has his head shaved right there in the ring, with the audience jeering around them. More humiliation. Then the fight continues.

"Is it judged after three minutes or something?" asks Dan. He's obviously thinking about jiu jitsu which has a referee and a points system based on successful moves executed.

"No, there is no time limit."

"So, how does it finish?"

"When someone gives in," says Rolando simply.

I ask Rolando about his sauces. He does three using smoked Chipotle chillies – a mild and a medium sauce, and a medium marinade. And then a hot sauce made from fresh Habaneros. When Rolando came to Britain he fell in love with the country, but struggled to find anywhere that served good Mexican food. Instead, he'd lay on big Mexican banquets at home and cook up his own sauces to complement them. Then he started making bigger batches, selling them to Mexican friends and friends of friends until he was producing a thousand bottles at a time.

As the sauce making took off he started manufacturing at a kitchen on an industrial estate in west London. But he could neither keep up with the growing demand nor make any profit because the costs of production were so high. Instead, he moved the manufacturing to Medellín in

Colombia where his brother-in-law already had a food production factory. They worked together to perfect the recipes. Now smoked chillies are imported from Mexico to Colombia where the sauces are mixed and bottled, then shipped over to the UK for sale. He started by bringing over a few boxes, but now receives pallets of his sauces every six months.

Despite his marketing, which I know would go down well there, Rolando has tended to stay away from chilli festivals. Customers there don't find his sauces hot enough and he quickly realised that producing a very hot one would be both inauthentic and a bad business move.

"You see, people buy a bottle of very hot sauce and three months later they've still got most of the bottle left. So they only buy one bottle from you." Mexicans take lots of sauce with everything they eat, not a tiny dab. Rolando tells us he had scrambled eggs for breakfast this morning and polished off about a third of a bottle of his Habanero hot sauce alongside it. Eating too much of your own product, I think, could also be a bad business move.

Rolando says his sauces go down well at larger food festivals where he can sit in the Mexican corner, alongside sellers of Tequila, corn chips and salsa, as well as at catering trade shows where he can promote his sauces directly to delis and restaurants. He works closely with the Mexican Embassy and Mexican Tourist Board and will join them whenever they have a promotional exhibition or event.

"It's like having my childhood in a bottle because I still remember my granny making exactly the same sauces as I do."

We ask for some corn chips and set about tasting his sauces. The mild Chipotle has a very easy heat, which only has a slight burn at the back of the throat. The medium marinade is a tiny bit hotter with more tomato. When we get to the hot Chipotle sauce there's a definite smoky and snappy heat smell, and a longer burn on the tip of the tongue. It's a very Mexican flavour, Dan and I agree – because we're now apparently the experts. The Habanero Extra Hot is bright red and comes in a dotting bottle rather than a pourer. There's a lot happening in this sauce, it's subtly sugary and very fresh with the fruity flavour holding its own against a heat that's intense enough to create that familiar moreish endorphin rush. We all sit there for a few minutes munching on corn chips and enjoying the sauces.

Then Dan and I realise it at the same time. We've been sitting with Rolando for about 25 minutes since Dan came back from his chilli hunt with Cesar. That means for the best part of half-an-hour we've been talking to a man in full wrestling costume, mask and all.

"I've just realised you're still in your costume," says Dan a little tickled. "For you it must feel so natural. But I can't believe we're here in a restaurant on Dalston High Street and people are walking past and looking inside, and we're interviewing you wearing that."

It is indeed surreal and not something I'm willing to pass up the opportunity to photograph. It starts quite tame, with Rolando and I behind the bar at Mezcal striking muscly poses. But all of a sudden Cesar has pushed a bottle of mezcal in my hand and Rolando is brandishing a bottle of his own chilli sauce. Then Cesar is in on the action too, holding up one of the tequila guns as if he's shooting up at the sky. Then the barman takes up the theme with the other tequila gun and is pointing it towards the camera like a Mexican James Bond.

I'm wearing brown cords and a cycling T-shirt. Among this lot, I can't help but feel it's me who looks the fool.

It's actually a myth that chillies originated in Mexico. True, Mexicans had been farming and eating chillies with abandon for thousands of years by the time Columbus turned up at the start of the sixteenth century. The myth probably stuck because the chillies the Mexicans grew were more suited to growing in European climates.

In fact, the capsicum family was being farmed about a thousand years before the Mexicans embraced them. The original species come from far further south. It is thought that the first chillies appeared in the wet forests of the Amazon in Peru, Colombia and Venezuela, as well as other drier areas of Brazil. People there apparently liked chomping on chillies – and probably farming them – so much they painted pictures of them on their cooking pots as early as 7,000 years ago. Some archaeologists put chilli cultivation many thousands of years before that, but the evidence all gets a bit hazy.

Birds probably did most of the early movement of chilli plants around Latin America, and about 3,000 years ago Latin Americans from the north started migrating to the Caribbean in little boats and took chillies with them to farm.

The fastest spread of chillies around Latin America, though, probably came along with the growth of the Incan empire along the western edge. The Incas' conquest of South America started out from the Cusco region of Peru (think the tourist destination Machu Picchu which they built in 1450) and then gradually spread out over the next eighty or so years into Ecuador, Bolivia and Argentina. Then the Spanish reached the west of Latin America in 1529 and – with their own brand of pillage and conquer subtlety – put a firm stop to that kind of caper. But it did lead to the Europeans spreading chillies elsewhere around the world.

8th June – It's hot. It's so unbelievably hot today and I've been stuck all day about fifty miles away from my chillies. When I return, the conservatory is once again like a sauna. And the chillies are as dry and forlorn as I've ever seen them. I sling the windows open to get some of the still but slightly cooler air from outside, then inspect the damage.

Sweet Pepper Sunshine has crinkled up crusts of leaves that look like they belong in a cigarette. The usually robust Prairie Fire is in deep trouble, with the leaves curled in on themselves and drooping. Masquerade and Vampire, usually the brightest of the bunch, don't look good. Just when Masquerade was putting some weight on its chillies and Vampire was developing a great spray of purple tinted leaves too. And Habanero 7, is this the end for you? The plant is curled up and is almost bending in the middle. It looks like a teenager who has slunk off in a mood.

I decide drastic action is in order. I know pouring water from the top isn't going to work: it'll just run through, soaking the conservatory floor. Instead I head to the shed and find my kids' purple and green plastic sledges – hardly needed by my kids in this weather, are they? – and fill them almost to the brim with water. Then one by one I place the patients into their bath and urge them to drink.

A few hours later I return and they do seem to have perked up. In fact, they've perked up a lot. Habanero 7 is upright, its broad leaves uncurled and is reaching them out in forgiveness. They say treat chillies mean, but today the National Society for the Prevention of Cruelty to Chillies ought to have been knocking on my door.

The problem is that I just can't get the hydration of my chillies right. Everyone tells me that more chillies are killed by overwatering than leaving them dry. But I don't seem to be able to get them to retain water at all. It just runs straight through the parched soil and out the other side of the pot. In hindsight some hydration gel or peat should have been mixed into the soil, but it's too late now.

But the other problem is heat regulation. I now know it's good to keep chillies at just over room temperature – at about 21 to 24 degrees – whether day or night. That's OK if you have a heated greenhouse, but without one in Britain it's almost impossible to maintain enough heat during the night and prevent absolute scorching during the day when the weather is like this. It's the same reason that chilli plants, except for the extremely hardy varieties, are just not likely to fruit – or at least fruit abundantly – if you keep them outside.

The only option is to sit there watching a thermometer, continually adjusting the windows and heating accordingly. That isn't just an investment in your home-grown chilli plants. It's the kind of thing that could get you detained under the Mental Health Act.

9th June – After yesterday's shock there's work to do to put my chilli collection back on an even keel. Those Scorpion and Bhut Jolokia chillies my dad gave me are now too big for their pots, so I follow Adrian Nuttall's advice and go out and buy some deep, ugly plastic pots. I know these will be hard plants to get to flower and then to fruit so it's worth the investment. Each of them will sit in its own ugly plastic tray and, I promise, I shall only water them from the bottom up. And I definitely won't leave them to melt in a baking hot conservatory while I'm out enjoying an early summer cycle ride.

11th June – It's that time, I can wait no longer. Masquerade has been leading the charge, of course, and growing flowers and, after them, sprouting healthy purple chillies. There's one that's a good inch or so long, and the general rule is that if you keep picking chillies then more will grow to take their place. And anyway, I'm just desperate to taste my first crop of the season. Whether it's ripe or not, I don't really know. But Andrew Jukes told me chillies are at their hottest just before they *reach full ripeness, so now is probably as good a time as any.*

I cut the chilli off with a pair of scissors, stalk and all. I take a quick selfie — just me and my first chilli — then munch away. The tapered end of the chilli is a little bitter. I think it's just this side of unripe. Further down the fruit I can detect mild heat but only on the tip of the tongue. Masquerade is only about 60,000 on the SHU scale so I wasn't expecting something mind-blowing. It's also a colourful and ornamental chilli. You can eat them, but they don't have much flavour and so are rarely used in cooking.

A little let down? Maybe, but I had to start somewhere. I'm feeling that the now thoroughly blooming Prairie Fire is going to be next on my list. Another ornamental but this time slightly hotter at 70,000 SHU. I also want to revisit Masquerade to see if a more ripe chilli packs a bigger punch.

15ᵗʰ June — OK, a slightly more ripe Masquerade chilli packs a bigger punch. There are lots of fruits so I couldn't resist another munch. My mouth is on fire. If that's what 60,000 SHU can do, what will the rest be like?

Peppers to the people

ALEXANDER MUSTANG IS a man on a mission. And with a name like that he ought to be. He's a deep believer in the power of chillies to bring people together, create communities, give a lift up to dilapidated towns and generally make the sun shine bright in the darkest recesses of Britain.

This is hot chilli peppers for the people and for one day in the middle of June, buried deep in the valleys of south Wales, I am to be at the heart of the mission.

Alex is a Brit of Punjabi descent, a jolly and passionate man with a winning smile and a knack for sucking you into his idea that chilli is the world's social lubricator, equaliser and economic driver all at the same time. Since 2010, Alex has been organising small scale chilli festivals, a business that started by accident in the worn down seaside town of Shoreham in West Sussex. That year had been the worst for weather for decades: a wet winter had turned into a wet summer, with so few days of sunshine even the *Daily Mail* failed to come up with a front page picture of half-naked white flesh on Brighton beach.

The country was struggling and, thanks to the weather, Shoreham was struggling too. The council was looking for new ideas to bring people to their coast that wasn't the beach, the arcades or an economy dependent on ice cream. Another year of wet weather might have been calamitous for the town. Alex got talking to a friend who was the town's events organiser over a drink. It may be apocryphal but it's a good story nevertheless. The town planner had said the town needed to find something 'to spice things up over here' and Alex jokingly suggested a chilli festival. The town planner told Alex: well, go and do it then.

The sleepless nights began and a few months later he'd created a business plan and presented it to the local council. What Alex really presented to the bigwigs at Shoreham was a few figures and a funny logo (a mischievous chilli wearing a turban) and the name ChilliFest UK. But by the time he met with them, he'd already launched a website, Facebook and Twitter accounts and without too much effort was pulling in Likes and Retweets and whatever else social media does that local councils get excited about. It was enough. The Great Shoreham Chilli Festival was on for the summer of the next year.

"We only had twelve stands at that first event and a few bands. I would have called it a success and been happy with a thousand visitors," he said. "We got nearly 3,000 on the day."

Alex discovered a winning formula: put people at the heart of your chilli festival, host it in run-down towns, get local councils to support it and advertise it for you, and use social media to bring in the punters. Alex prefers to call them 'fans'. Desperate towns across Britain heard about what ChilliFest had done in Shoreham, says Alex, and began queuing up at his door to host their own small chilli event.

He didn't realise it at the time, but Alex's events became part of a few small towns' regeneration strategies. With dwindling tourist trades and hard-hit local businesses, Britain's growing love of all things hot could bring thousands of people to an area. The event would not only create trade for chilli product makers in the region, and perhaps inspire others to launch their own chilli or other food businesses, but for the day itself it would also generate business for local hotels, shops, cafes and pubs.

"In 2014, we'll have ten events. Next year, we're hoping that will double," says Alex. Not bad for someone who was persuaded to organise his first ever event over a drink and a packet of crisps.

The Arriva Trains Wales carriage out of Cardiff and into the deep valleys of South Wales is from a bygone era. Unfortunately it's not the golden age of steam or luxury Pullman coaches. It's the less romantic bygone era of the 1980s when the tiny tram-like trains were like cattle trucks held together with masking tape, the seats were all ripped to shreds and for the smaller stations you had to ask the conductor to stop the train so you could get off.

Merthyr Tydfil is the end of the line in more ways than one. My late afternoon Friday train pulls into the town next to an enormous Tesco Extra Super Size Megastore. It's packed with shoppers and offers everything you could possibly need: not just your groceries and food, but shoes, clothes, a pharmacy, bakery, fish counter, beauty area, furniture and a gardening section. Behind the superstore opens up Merthyr itself and it's dead. Those shops that aren't boarded up for good have already closed for the night and their metal grates are pulled down. There is no Costa Coffee or Marks & Spencer or BHS here. Only a small handful of brands – the Co-op, Thomas Cook and Superdrug – dot the high street, side by side with a few charity shops and credit unions, greasy spoons and pound shops.

Tesco seems to have sucked up everything the other shops used to do and spat it into a huge tin shed next to the train station; along with all the shoppers. I'm told there's a regenerated out-of-town complex, all cinemas and superstores, which has contributed to the customer drift from the town centre. At just past tea time, the pedestrianised high street doesn't have a soul on it. Only the Wetherspoon's shows any sign of life, a beacon of noise and light in an otherwise deserted town. The grandly entitled Imperial Hotel at which I'm staying has nothing grand or even imperial about it. It's a pub with rooms upstairs and I can only get to mine by going through a back door in the darts room. I'm staying, it seems, in the attic. My room is at the end of a corridor decorated with pub knicknacks, pictures of boats and landscapes and a rather sinister looking terrier dog in full military uniform. The overall effect is as aged and depressing as outside. So I head to Wetherspoon's and plonk myself on the corner of a table of Welsh girls out for a night of bright luminous frocks and even brighter luminous alcopops.

The pub looks out on Penderyn Square, newly created as part of Merthyr's regeneration strategy. And it is indeed a large square of brightly polished concrete slabs, benches as yet unsullied by skateboards and a manicured lawn behind low fencing. As I watch the sun go down behind the hills over the valley in which Merthyr sits, there's an air of unspoilt potential about the square. And tomorrow we'll put it to the test. The Merthyr Chilli Festival will be the first public event the square has seen since the new tiles were laid.

Dic Penderyn had stood – or rather had hanged – on exactly this spot, trussed up by the authorities for crimes against the state. Specifically for stabbing a soldier with a bayonet during the Merthyr uprising in 1831, where thousands of Welshmen and Welshwomen marched on the town demanding higher wages and cheaper bread. Penderyn was pretty obviously innocent but framed as a way of warning the Welsh working class to stop being so uppity – I don't think they got the message. Thus he is regarded as something of a local hero here and the naming of the square after him is regarded as righting the wrong of an innocent man put to death. The Prince of Wales opened the square just for good measure.

As I look out over the regenerated space, a young and solid looking guy who had rocked drunkenly alongside me at the bar – and with whom I avoided eye contact just in case – staggers out onto the square and promptly drops a full pint of lager which smashes in the corner. It's what Dic would have wanted. If ever there's a town that needs a dose of Alex Mustang's chilli magic, Merthyr Tydfil is certainly it.

For all his chilli pepper for the people values, Alex is a hard taskmaster and runs a tight ship.

"You'll be at the square at 6 a.m. ready for the stallholders to arrive an hour later," he tells me sternly on the phone before the festival. "You'll start by helping to set up the festival stalls in the square, then greet the companies as they come to set up and allocate them their space. You need to spend ten minutes with each of them, ask them how they are, how was their journey, whether they need anything, and if they need any help. Then you'll work on my stand for the rest of the day, selling our sauces. Then it'll be time to pack up again at 5 p.m.

"I want you to really know what hard work putting on a festival like this is."

Back-breaking erecting of stalls wasn't exactly what I had in mind when signing up for this project but I'm game. But what will Alex be doing while I'm hard at work pushing his sauce mixes to his punters, sorry, 'fans'?

"I'll be mingling," he says. "Mingling with local councillors, other dignitaries." In a town as small and isolated as Merthyr I can easily imagine that will take all day. He offers another instruction. The festival has a strict chilli only policy. Traders have already been warned, but there's to be no sale of non-chilli goods. No baked potatoes, no chips, no doughnuts. Nothing that people can get from a normal shop.

"If people want even a cup of tea or coffee, they won't be able to get it at the festival. It's all about chillies. People come here to suffer." Which seems a bit full-on but you can see his point. The more non-chilli food on offer, the less fans are likely to buy from the chilli product makers themselves. It'll dilute their takings, they won't come again and Merthyr will end up with a failed event that won't be repeated. Besides, part of the point is to create footfall for local shops and cafes. Alex is clearly serious about supporting local traders and the chilli community. He even tries to keep his festivals relatively small because too many traders means less business for each of them. Thus fired up by ChilliFest's central value of chilli inspired communism, I decide to call it a night. It's an early start and there's a lot of work to do tomorrow.

I'm up at 5.45 a.m., but as Alex doesn't offer a minute's grace there's no time for breakfast. By 5.58 a.m. he's already texted me twice telling me he's arrived at the square and is setting up. Better get there quick, the festival opens in just a short four hours' time.

To be fair to him, I had asked to see what it takes to run a chilli festival. Many times I've been to food events and chilli festivals, but it's always been as a punter. I turn up at my own convenience, sniff some cheeses, dip some nachos, trundle unimpressed or simply uninterested past dozens of stalls, buy the kids an ice cream and if I really can't avoid it, I may try a few olives from the usual guy. I've never got underneath the skin of an event. I've never seen the beginning, middle and end. I've never watched it unfold from the inside looking out.

Alex has given me my own curry sauce stand and is expecting me to be completely involved in every aspect of the job. It starts with a Meccano-like gazebo which I have to pull here, push there, stick a pin in, lift and then separate, until it finally unfolds like a swan's wings awaiting the side panels I need to hang underneath. I set up my table – another Meccano affair – and then go back to the van to collect a mountain of produce.

There are three sauces: mild, wild and hot. They're cook-in sauces made with fresh Naga chillies and none of the sugars, preservatives and other gunk supermarkets often stick in curry jars. As I discovered with the Clifton Chilli Club where Dave Mac served them up with chicken or beef, they're delicious. I unload dozens of rectangular buckets with fresh tubs of sauce stacked inside. Each bucket then has to be unpacked, and the sauces built into appealing pyramids with the spare produce stacked underneath. I then fill a hundred or so clear plastic bags with leaflets and cut up twenty huge flour tortillas into exactly the right sized tiny bits.

"Don't make them so small they don't pick up any sauce," Alex instructs. "But not so big someone can come and have their lunch here."

As I stuff and chop, I try to work out what my system will be today: How will I keep the towers stacked? Where will I keep the cash? Will the sauces my customers buy come from the table or from my stash below? What's going to be my sales patter? And who the hell is going to be convinced that this near bald white guy is the man behind a range of home-made authentic Punjabi curry sauces anyway? (Alex comes up with the idea that I'm an albino-Indian, but I don't think it's going to work.)

I pour out samples of the three curries into little bronze bowls and put brand new tea lights into the warmers they'll sit on. All I need is a match and I'm ready for my first chilli hungry punter. I hope they like curry for breakfast. It's only 7.30 a.m.

Over the next two hours the shiny square gradually unfolds into our own little chilli village. Cars and vans come in and out, dropping off produce, pop-up stands and trestle tables. There are negotiations about whose stand is going where: the chilli olive guy wants more prominence than he's been allocated; we realise trying to squeeze too many stalls in too tight a space will mean we'll all just about get in – but the customers will have nowhere to enter the square. A barbecue guy arrives in an ex-Ocado refrigeration truck, pulling what looks like a mini railway diesel engine behind it. This, it appears, is his barbecue. Alex's folks, as well as various arms of his extended family, are running what is essentially a full curry house and bar. Their complex network of electric wires, gas pipes, fridges, cookers and pans of boiling oil is a colossal but well drilled affair. At its centre will sit the famous Auntie Jee – Alex's mum, it turns out – on a little stool chopping onions and deep frying bajees and lentil balls in a humongous vat.

I'm delighted to see Steve Woodward from Mushemi Fire, who greets me like an old friend. He says he's developed two new sauces since my brother and I visited him in Rugeley. I tell him his Zwao! has become my favourite table sauce and he says he's tweaked the recipe to make it even tastier (yay!) but slightly less hot (boo!). Across the square is Jay Webley, who I met in Clifton, wearing his trademark chilli bandana and setting up his Chilli Alchemist store. He hands over a tube of his best selling chilli popping candy. It offers a startlingly good, if strange, mix of Naga heat and nostalgia for the sweets I ate when I was young. He invites me to spend some time on his stall today if I have the time. Something tells me Alex will be cracking the whip too hard for that, but it's great to see him and his wax topped bottles all laid out in his alchemy cave.

I then bump into Victor Nwosu, the Nigerian chemist and owner of Wiga Wagaa I'd met at the Suffolk Food Festival. He's still fighting the good fight with his chilli oils, dips and sauces. He drove for six hours to get here yesterday and stayed at some awful place last night. It claimed to be a hotel but ended up being a dingy pub, he says. Yeah, I know the one.

As the sun comes up – and the Wetherspoon's opens for its first drinkers – very slowly people begin to come into Penderyn Square. I've no idea where they come from, because there don't seem to be any actual houses anywhere in Merthyr, but come they do. First in a trickle, then in a flow, then by late morning a torrent. The weather ambles between hot and scorching, and there's not a few men sporting bare pink torsos.

From the front of my stall, I try to give the impression of swan-like calm, but beneath the surface I'm paddling like a maniac trying to keep the samples topped up, the tortilla chopped (in the right sized pieces), the towers stacked, the bags packed with leaflets, the right money taken and the right change given.

Among football- and rugby-shirted men, women with flowing dresses, tattoos, hair of various bright shades, and various teenagers with various piercings, the chatter all revolves around pretty much the same question: "What's to that 'ot one then?" This roughly translates as 'could you possibly point me to the spiciest of your curry sauces?' It doesn't matter much anyway because a reggae band has struck up in another corner of the square and none of us can hear each other. But pretty much everyone wants to go straight to the hot Naga sauce.

The sauces sell well. By noon I'm knackered, my throat hurts from the shouting and my feet ache. Alex has been popping by all morning, helping out at crowded times and offering me sage advice about my sales. The British, he states, are unlike any other nationality in the world. They'll happily sit at home in their underpants, pretending to sing into a hairbrush in front of the fridge (no, I didn't get that either), but put them in public and they're all shy and need to be persuaded. I need to be reaching out to them, flirting with the girls, joking with the boys, and always always upselling any single purchase into a three for £10.

I'm feeling a little too British myself for the hard sell, but it is true that the more relaxed I am the more tubs of curry sauce get sold. I discover that if you can get someone to take a sliver of tortilla, even if you have to reach out and shove the bowl under their noses from five metres away, then they're bound to try the sauce. The conversation is started and you're on your way to a sale.

Alex has an extremely easy way with people and his sales chat comes across as endearing and funny rather than overbearing. He's extremely charismatic, and the good people of Merthyr lap up his 'you'll regret it if you don't' line about buying three rather than one tub, or 'the tasting is completely free, but I'll gladly take some money if you like' that he offers to anyone who looks sceptical about taking a dip. He's frequently joking with me (as well as at my expense), elbowing me in the ribs and patting me on the back. You can tell he enjoys this: meeting new people, seeing his event unfold, getting them to try his sauces, soaking in the vibe and making himself the centre of attention.

At 2 p.m. I just have to eat. I've been surreptitiously nabbing slivers of tortilla all morning but they don't do the job. Alex tells me to bypass the huge queue in front of his parents' food complex and nip round the back. His dad shoves a massive pile of curry and rice into a bowl and stuffs an enormous recently fried samosa on the top.

How often have I queued for half an hour at food festivals only to get a tiny tray of congealed tasteless noodles or a limp undercooked paella for £4.50? There's nothing rushed or stack-em-high, sell-em-cheap about the food from Auntie Jee. It's all cooked on site, is plentiful in the giving and extremely tasty in the eating. I hide myself on a bench behind my curry sauce tent and take as much time as I'm allowed (about five minutes) to enjoy it. The curry is made with lentils, aubergine and hot Bullet chillies which have been split end to end, leaking their heat into the sauce and onto the fluffy yellow rice below. The samosa is crisp and greasy, filled with a mix of potato, peas and spices, and is luscious as I use it to scoop up what's left of the curry sauce. I'm sweating.

I go back to work and then get an unexpected friendly arm around my shoulder. It's Chilli Dave, who also greets me like an old friend. He and others from the Clifton Chilli Club have arrived to sell their sauces and plants and to run the Clash of the Titans chilli eating competition later this afternoon. There are loads of punters here now – Alex is estimating around 1,500 people will pass through today – and Chilli Dave has no problem recruiting ten people for his competition.

The sun has been out all day, the cider, chilli infused vodka and lager is flowing and there's a real buzz in the air.

The locals are in good spirits and are effusively friendly. Many of them swap seamlessly between Welsh and English. Someone from the council comes over – one of Alex's VIPs – and she's delighted with the event. She's never seen so many people in the centre of Merthyr, giving the impression that people must have come in from miles around (and out here in the Welsh valleys, that *does* literally mean miles and miles).

Rather than resenting our presence the Wetherspoon's seems to have been encompassed into the chilli festival, with its patio doors flung open and the crowds inside bobbing up and down to the music. When I dash to the toilet inside I notice the pub is packed with chilli shoppers and almost everyone inside is singing at the top of their half-cut voices to a Bob Marley number blasting out from our live reggae band.

The Clash of the Titans is won by a chisel-chinned guy with a red face and a severe haircut. A few dropped out after just a Jalapeño making me finally admit something I'd been trying to ignore: I cannot really write a book about the British chilli scene without having a go at a chilli eating competition myself. I resolve to sign up for the competition at the Hertfordshire chilli festival which is coming up in a month's time. The one to which I've already invited a whole bunch of friends for a day out. Gulp.

After the competition, the crowds start to dissipate. Within half an hour Penderyn Square has begun to go quiet again. My whole body aches and I'm relieved to be given permission to take down the stand. But before I do there's eating to be done. Stallholders and friends come up in little groups to the Auntie Jee stand and are dished up bowls of curry and rice, lentil balls and samosas, anything that's left over from the day's trading. There's a feeling of camaraderie and everyone agrees it's been a good day. Well, everyone except the olive guy who's still grumbling about his position.

I get talking to Dan Reed of Chilli of the Valleys, one of only two Welsh suppliers at the festival. Dan's day job is with a firm of solicitors, while his evening and weekend job is selling his sauces, jams and plants over the internet. He's from Merthyr and the chillies that go into his sauces are grown through a Merthyr community garden scheme, another part of the town's regeneration strategy and, I think, a lovely touch.

"I've never done a live event before," he says. "I'd never have attempted anything like this if the festival hadn't come to Merthyr. They're really throwing money at regenerating the town centre now, but no-one knew what would happen with a chilli festival or whether people would come. But it's been a success."

For the event, Dan had brewed a 'Heading Up to Merthyr' sauce to complement a little YouTube video that the town's businesses created to promote tourism – it's a take on the late-nineties Vengaboys hit 'We're Going to Ibiza'. Apparently the Merthyr version went 'viral' in the valleys – which I think means it went further than the Wetherspoon's – and people were coming up to his stand singing the song. He sold out of the sauce before lunchtime.

"People just came up and said they really wanted a bottle of the Merthyr chilli sauce, which is so rewarding. I've got the bug now for festivals, so I'm going to think about which other ones to do."

Luke Baines, another Welshman who runs The Duke's Chilli Emporium, said he was surprised that a stall like his – barbecue chilli sauces and pickles – would do so well when there were so many other suppliers offering similar things.

"There's a great love of chillies in Merthyr, obviously,"

he says.

The food is finished but the work is far from over. I spend the next two hours packing, pressing, lifting, shifting and tidying, occasionally breaking off to wish Steve or Victor or Jay or Dan well as they leave. Chilli Dave says he'll get me into the chilli eating competition in Hertfordshire and we share a firm handshake as we say goodbye and see you soon.

Most of the stallholders are gone now, and it's just the Auntie Jee complex we're slowly taking apart. Everyone's tired and Alex ends up parking his not inconsiderable backside in the side of the van and directing us all like an enormous sweating conductor as we buzz around him, cleaning, shifting and collapsing equipment and shoving it into vehicles. Apart from me, everyone knows what they should be doing but there's still haranguing and teasing from Alex. He's offering anyone a foot rub if they're feeling tired, which I regretfully decline. This is a family that has been doing this for a long time and, with Alex at the helm, it really works.

For him, chillies are not just a hobby, or even a business venture. He sees the fruits and the communities they can help to build as almost a religious calling.

"You know," he says wistfully, "my dad used to tell me about two armies lined up against each other. One is clearly going to give the other a hammering and a soldier says to his teacher: we're bound to lose this battle. The teacher says the battle isn't about the results but about doing your duty.

"That way of thinking has been inspiring for me." He's pretty much talking to himself now. "We don't think about the results, we're just doing our duty. We don't think about how many people are going to come and how much money there's going to be, it's getting the chilli community together and you can't buy that."

Me, I don't see chillies as a religiously inspired duty, I just like good food and a good atmosphere. The festival had that in spades. I've no doubt Alex and his passion will be back here again next year, and I hope he will continue to bring people to this corner of Wales that, despite falling on difficult times of late, has acres of potential.

I leave just as the last of Alex's little corner of the little village he created in this little town is being taken down. I walk across Penderyn Square, now almost as empty as it was when I first saw it last night. The Wetherspoon's is full again but the rest of the town is approaching eerie quiet once more.

Once again, I leave with a real sense of the chilli scene in Britain being a tight-knit community. Chilli Britain is a place where friends are made, suppliers support each other and, after it's all over and done with, there's hot food and a warm atmosphere to share. I know it's only a silly little fruit, but it feels good to be here. I hope this feeling of comradeship was at least one of the things good old Dic Penderyn was thinking about as he dangled from the gallows in the place where I've been touting Naga masala hot, wild and mild curry sauce all day.

We need to talk about ladybirds.

Last year, my chilli plants suffered an infestation of greenfly that covered some of the plants so comprehensively, you couldn't tell where the insects ended and the plant began. So far, I've avoided any such plague but pests are a fact of life for any chilli grower. Unless you're going to use harsh chemicals on the fruits you're about to eat, then you have to accept them. Then do as best you can to prevent infestation from spreading. You could cover all plants with a thin fleece, but you'd be trapping out the nice pollinators and it looks pretty cruddy too. Last year I followed popular advice to spray leaves with soapy water, but all I got was aphids that looked happy enough to be taking a bath.

The advice is that when you get the first of the greenfly – they look tiny flecks of green – you should pick them off and crush them between your fingers before they get a chance to lay eggs. Don't let them get a foothold. If an infestation does creep up, then wash the plants with a hose regularly, though this is unlikely to wash away the eggs and also sounds like a hell of a chore.

What sounds much nicer is the introduction of ladybirds, which feast on the critters. Last year I bought a little tub of forty ladybirds and released them onto the plants, hoping they'd gobble up the greenfly, multiply and all would be well. But next morning, the greenfly were still there and the ladybirds had either gone, or were lying dead on the windowsill, their little legs poking into the air. I had reluctantly used some pesticide on the plants. It hadn't worked on the aphids, but was apparently fatal for the poor old ladybirds.

Adrian Nuttall tells me one of my mistakes was to introduce the ladybirds while their tummies were full. The ladybirds had been feasting on the nutrients in the tub while they were in the post. Instead, I should have transferred them to a new tub and put them in the fridge for a good few hours. That would make them docile and slowly growing hungrier. Then I should have transferred them by hand to the plants while they were still snoozy. When they wake up, there'd be a ready supply of greenfly for them to eat, so why would they go anywhere else?

"You don't sit in a restaurant with a steak and start

looking around for another restaurant, do you?" he says. I kept quiet about the pesticide.

At the Suffolk Chilli Farm Adrian showed me what he called his sacrificial lamb, a chilli plant that was absolutely teeming with greenfly. He'd put it underneath some very thin gauge netting and introduced ladybirds into the enclosure too. An epic insect battle was taking place under that cover, which Adrian assured me the ladybirds were bound to win. And as they gradually took the upper hand, they'd be laying more and more little ladybird eggs – which unhelpfully look exactly like greenfly eggs – producing loads more ladybirds for spreading around any other chilli plants that show early signs of pest invasion.

19th June – With their abundance of flowers, Lemon Drop, Vampire and Purple Tiger are tall and top heavy. My marigolds are in full flower now, and there are lots of flowers on almost every chilli plant – though not on Habanero 7, obviously; that would be too much to ask. My hydroponic Prairie Fire has really surprised me with how well it's doing. It has loads of flowers. It's definitely not as tall as its soil-bound sister, but it's prolific with leaves and has a few chillies growing. I've not once had to worry about its hydration either. Maybe next year I'll go 100 percent hydroponic.

Vampire is still the most beautiful plant. It's nearly three feet high with four or five branches reaching up and outwards. It's topped off with the most attractive deep purple flowers, each with cream centre. Joe's Long Cayenne is also tall and branchy and now has a smattering of flower buds hanging down on long stalks.

24th June – I have an abundance of fruits on Masquerade. Vampire has a load of purple chillies growing too, and Prairie Fire has *some light green noses poking out from behind spent flowers. Joe's Long Cayenne has loads of drooping stalks and I know these will turn into long red fruits.*

1st July – Joe's Long Cayenne, Etna, Lemon Drop and Red Missile have joined the party, all now proud with fruits. Half of my chilli plants have at least a few fruits growing, with the usual suspects of Masquerade, Prairie Fire and Vampire in abundance. I try a Vampire fruit, but so far it has no heat at all.

Spice island

BEFORE LEVI ROOTS was made to sweat under the *Dragons' Den* spotlight, just about the only Caribbean cook in the public eye was bubbly 1980s breakfast TV chef Rustie Lee; she of enormous hair and gigantic belly laugh. Back then, the Jamaican-born Rustie tended to hold back on the chillies in the dishes she cooked. Presumably to prevent us culinary conservative Brits from choking on our cornflakes and toast.

It's just a couple of miles south of where Rustie Lee once had a Caribbean restaurant that I've come today, up a quiet Birmingham residential street. I'm in the home of the two Caribbean cooks who make up the food company Tan Rosie. They're on their own little mission to educate us all about traditional food from back home. And they aren't afraid to add a little spice, as long as that's what families back on the Caribbean islands would do.

You get the impression that the dining room table of Lee Sylvester and her mum Monica Cudjoe sees a lot of action. On the day I visit, it's piled high with chilli fudge ready for a local farmers' market stall tomorrow and the Lakes Chilli Festival on the weekend. The pair were up late into the night cooking because the fudge has to hit the market stall as fresh as possible.

"I remember Rustie Lee serving me fish and chips when I was about seven," says my host Lee as we take a seat on the veranda of her terrace house, looking out onto a colourful suburban back garden bathed in afternoon sun. "She served me crinkle cut chips which I'd never had before. I thought they were the most exotic thing in the world."

It's in search of something exotic that many others have stepped over this threshold and into Lee and Monica's home, to enjoy one of the Caribbean supper clubs the pair run each month. They clear that dining room table, add another put-up table and serve the Caribbean food which Monica cooks for up to a dozen paying guests, most of them strangers. They come to meet new people, learn about Caribbean cuisine and, of course, to eat it. The idea was Monica's and it came from visiting a farmers' market someone had set up in their home in Kilburn, north London. There were stalls in all kinds of weird places, says Lee: under the stairs, in cupboards, in the garage. It made them wonder what they could do in their own home.

"My mom does all the cooking, while I tend to do the marketing, welcoming and serving," says Lee in a soft Brummie accent. Her use of *mom* rather than *mum* reminds me I'm back in the Black Country.

Monica speaks with a soft Caribbean accent, extending her syllables. She's wearing an apron when she greets me, as well as a striking silver and red brimless African cap called a kofia. She came to the UK with her family in the 1960s aged just fifteen, and spent most of the rest of her life as a midwife.

Cooking for the supper club, as well as creating the pastes, jams, hot sauces, meat rubs and chilli fudge for Tan Rosie market stalls, is something she decided to do to "keep me busy" after retirement. Judging by the many boxes of produce and tall towers of pots tucked into corners, it's kept her retirement very busy indeed.

Her daughter Lee couldn't be more different. She's tall,

wears a red pinstripe power-dress, thick-rimmed bright-red PR glasses and is every bit the excited entrepreneur. She's spent over ten years in fashion design, travelling the world for major sports brands. After dipping into lecturing, running a handbag label and freelance design work, Lee eventually decided four years ago to try something completely different.

"She's forced me to keep working and tells me what to do," says Monica with a gentle laugh.

"Mom was always talking about wanting something to do in her spare time, so I wanted to help her," says Lee, batting off her accusations as we all move to the kitchen.

Lee was born in Birmingham, but her mom is from Carriacou, one of the three islands that make up the Caribbean state of Grenada. The island of Grenada itself is the big brother; Carriacou − pronounced *carry-a-koo* − is the middle child; and at just over two square kilometres the sparsely populated Petite Martinique is the very little sister. Together, the islands are affectionately known − and I'm sure it does island tourism no harm either − as 'The Spice of the Caribbean'. A clove of nutmeg spice is included as part of the Grenadian flag. The islands are also famous for growing cloves, cinnamon, mace, cacao, ginger, turmeric, vanilla and, of course, chilli.

Levi Roots has done great things to raise the profile of Caribbean cookery in the UK, says Lee, but one of the negative things is fostering the idea that all Caribbean food is the same as Jamaican food. And that it is overwhelmingly spicy. In fact, Caribbean islands − and there are 700 of them in total − have quite different ways of preparing dishes, and sometimes radically different types and intensities of chilli heat. Like Zambians and Mexicans, most Caribbean islanders prefer to have a hot sauce on the table and to use that to add extra heat if they want it. Even the three islands that make up Grenada have their own cooking traditions.

"Grenadians don't like it too hot," says Monica as she finely chops two whole Scotch Bonnet chillies. Admittedly, she does discard much of the pith, along with the seeds. "It does have to have something in it though," she smiles. Myth has it – even repeated by celebrity chefs on TV and in their cookbooks – that the seeds are where the heat in chillies lies. But it's actually the pith towards the stem where most of the capsaicin killer heat lurks. The seeds just get a coating of the chemical because they sit in the pith.

She's cooking me a very traditional Caribbean dish: cou cou with red snapper in a creole pepper sauce. Cou cou is a polenta paste that's cooked all over the Caribbean. Presenting it with fish is done across most of the islands. Each might also traditionally prepare creole sauce in subtly different ways, but it almost always involves Scotch Bonnet chillies as well as milder peppers. The fish used depends on the island location: on Grenada it's most likely to be red snapper, but further south in Barbados it is flying fish that would be swimming (and flying) off the coast. Cou cou with flying fish is the national dish of Barbados.

Monica drops fine strips of sweet peppers and the diced Scotch Bonnets into a hot pan of butter and olive oil, along with some chopped tomatoes. The smell of the Scotch Bonnets rises from the hob immediately and I'm reminded that the chilli, which is native to Jamaica, has a very specific taste and aroma. It's unlike many other chillies, which can have a slightly acidic and tight heat to them. Scotch Bonnets have a much more complex, flowery, almost citrusy smell. They're creasingly hot, but so distinct in flavour that chilli connoisseurs can tell them a mile off.

Lee and Monica have invited me into their home to

watch the dish being made and to talk Caribbean cookery. Inviting strangers through the door to eat, and to talk food, is second nature.

"Food plays a very large part in our culture. When you step into a Caribbean house, the first thing you get offered is something to eat and something to drink," says Lee. "We've always had large family gatherings who have brought along strangers to join us for food; the supper club is just an extension of that really."

Each month the club has a theme such as barbecue jerk, Caribbean curry or street food, or it's based around a particular country: Antigua, Jamaica, Trinidad and Tobago, and Cuba have all recently appeared on the menu. The evenings attract a broad range of people, of all ages and hues. This part of Birmingham is rich with people of different backgrounds – African, Asian, Caribbean, English – and the club brings them all together, single people as well as couples, to share what they all have in common: an interest in food and an open mind about the flavours they're about to try.

"It's always interesting to watch them arrive because they tend to be nervous and don't quite know what to expect, or who they're going to meet," says Lee. "After all, they are coming into someone's private living room to eat with a bunch of strangers. But when they've sat down they tend to relax and soon get talking and excited about the food."

"And it's bring your own booze, so that helps obviously," chips in Monica. She's now chopping okra, the green star-shaped finger-length vegetable that's also grown across the Caribbean. She puts it with some onions into another pan, to sauté in hot oil for a while. Then she adds a can of creamy coconut milk. When it starts to bubble she adds a little extra water and some vegetable stock.

Lee continues: "Our guests tend to have either been to the Caribbean and want to revisit the taste of the foods that are available there, or they're planning to go and want to know what to expect. There's not a great deal of Caribbean food out there in the UK and so they say they've come here for the authentic flavours."

Lee's often surprised how poor the knowledge about Caribbean food is in this country. The questions she's asked at the supper club reveal only a very basic knowledge of what Caribbean dishes are like. Many islands, for example, cook a mutton curry and each has its own version. It's a Caribbean staple. But guests come saying they can't eat it because it's so hot: trying to cook it at home they've piled in chopped Scotch Bonnets, seeds, pith and all, and it's become impossible to stomach. She tells them the chilli is supposed to be put into the curry pot whole – like my Habanero 7 – and you have to be careful that it doesn't burst. Then it's taken out again once the dish is cooked.

Jerk chicken and pork are another example. People sometimes come back from a holiday in Jamaica expecting all Caribbean meat to have that same barbecue jerk flavour. But jerking is a particular way of barbecuing, and is almost entirely Jamaican rather than more generally Caribbean. It involves rubbing the meat with a very specific and very hot jerk rub, then cooking it over an open fire or, even better, a charcoal made from wood from the allspice pepper plant.

Diners and visitors to Lee and Monica's market stalls are also surprised to learn that Caribbean islanders traditionally eat lots of fruit jams and chutneys, and even fudge – one of Tan Rosie's biggest sellers. The islands are rich with fresh fruit and vegetables, and there's no better way to preserve them and protect them from a withering sun than to boil them up with sugar and make them into a jam. And some of the key ingredients of a tasty fudge – sugar, cacao, cinnamon, nutmeg, cow or goat milk, rum and raisins – are exactly those spices and foods that are abundant on the islands.

"We have to get over the idea that all Caribbean food is hot, because it does scare people off," says Lee. "The TV and the media make people think if they approach a Caribbean stall at a market or festival that the food is going to be curried mutton, rice and peas, jerk chicken, and that all of it is going to be unpalatably hot.

"They've only heard of those dishes or Jamaican hot sauces, so that's what they expect them to be like. Or they think that's how they *have* to be, otherwise they're not authentic. But in Grenada the food and sauces are only medium hot. At the supper club, and at our stalls, we try to give people those different standpoints."

Lee creates short menus with tasting notes and bits of history for each supper. She keeps the chat going and tries to answer questions from her guests. If there's anything she can't answer, she drags in Monica at the end because she's the real expert.

"We want to share our heritage with them," adds Monica.

Her kitchen is clearly her castle and she moves around it with grace but authority. It's only around four by three metres and I have to continually dodge out of the way as she reaches for pans, ingredients, into fridges and the oven. She gives an impression of immense calm. It is in this small space that every single Tan Rosie product is made.

"I don't spend that much time in the kitchen," says Monica, but Lee corrects that modest impression.

"She's very organised and she just loves to do it. Once

she's in there, that's it: it's where she's most comfortable, it keeps her relaxed."

I say I'm surprised Monica cleans and washes up as she goes along. It's something I've never managed to do when I'm trying to create some culinary opus in my own kitchen.

"I think that comes from being a midwife," smiles Lee. "Always having to mop up and keep everything sterile and clean."

"I thought you were going to help me?" Monica says.

The kitchen sports the usual trinkets. There are magnets on the fridge, a clock with fruits around the edges instead of numbers, recipes and shopping lists pinned to a cork board. But there are also family photos taken on pristine white beaches, with a silver-blue surf behind. As I admire them jealously, Monica lifts the lid from the pepper mix and a waft of the Caribbean rises up and around the kitchen. She stirs a little, then takes a taste.

"Oooh, that does taste hot. Maybe I should have only used one Scotch Bonnet."

I gulp.

Like the peppers, the okra-coconut pot is bubbling away nicely so Monica turns to the fish. They're hand width sized fillets with silver-pink skins. She scores both sides of each fish with a sharp knife, before patting them dry with kitchen paper and then sprinkling them with a pre-prepared mix of cornmeal, flour, salt and pepper.

"Can you just give those peppers a stir, please," she says. It's an instruction, not a question. But I'm at least glad to have been allowed close to her oven and to get another waft of the Scotch Bonnets. She lets me smell a home-made garlic and ginger paste, before adding it to the okra.

Apart from the food – which from just watching its preparation I can see is bound to be a huge attraction – Lee says people come to their supper club with genuine curiosity about Caribbean culture and history. There are a host of culinary and cultural influences on the Caribbean islands, including African, French, Portuguese, Dutch and British. Cuba is very Spanish, says Lee, while Trinidad has strong Asian influences. Grenada has a predominantly British and African background, though the Brits wrestled the islands from the French after the First World War.

A glance at the map of Carriacou actually reveals a decidedly Scottish thing going on. Along with French place names, the largest town is called Hillsborough, with other locations named Dumfries, McIntosh Point, Craigstone Point and Mount Pleasant. It occurs to me for the first time (yes, do keep up Gideon) that even the 'Scotch' in Scotch Bonnet might be connected to Scotland.

And indeed it is: the chilli is so named because of its resemblance to the traditional Scottish hat or 'bonnet' called the Tam o' Shanter. They're the tartan hats you sometimes see Scots wearing at football matches or out on stag nights, usually with fake ginger hair dangling all around the rim.

On Carriacou a rich culture and love of food come together each year at the Maroon festival. Monica went to the festival in April and came back bursting with ideas for new dishes and experiments for Tan Rosie market stall products. They also hosted a supper club based around the celebrations.

"There are lots of smoked foods at the festival: we cook cou cou and rice, and stewed pigeon peas, all things that are grown on the island; chicken and pork stewed, all kinds of vegetables," says Monica fondly. "It's like a harvest festival, and there's also music, drums and dancing, and we carry torches at night that are meant to invoke and honour the spirit of our ancestors."

"Yeah, that's done with rum basically," says Lee. Monica giggles.

The okra is ready and Monica pours in the polenta. Caribbean food tends to be rich in starch thanks to an abundance of yams and sweet potatoes, plantain and cassava. Monica pats her belly and tells me she's on a diet. Very quickly the okra and polenta mix goes the consistency of a thin porridge, which Monica stirs vigorously to stop it forming lumps. One more check on the peppers and we're ready for the fish.

She heats up another pan and pours in a heaving gulp of olive oil. One fillet at a time, she lays in the red snapper. It immediately starts to curl at the edges as the heat sears in the flavour. As soon as the fish is ready we can eat, so we go out onto the veranda to lay the table. The sun is just peeking from behind the clouds, creating a very peaceful and warm place to eat. It's not quite Hillsborough Bay, but it'll do.

The company Tan Rosie is named after Monica's grandmother who she grew up with in Carriacou, who was familiarly known as Rosie. The 'tan' comes from *tante*, the French for aunt.

"Tan Rosie has an emotional resonance for me," says Monica. "She died when I was ten, but I do remember her very well."

Tan Rosie's face has been incorporated into the brand that bears her name, along with the Grenadian flag's colours and the nutmeg shape to offer the Tan Rosie packaging a feel of authenticity and history. I can detect the touch of Lee's design background and PR nous at work.

"I've learned more about her since we started the business than I knew before, because people are always asking questions about her and why she's on our packaging," she says. "It's been really interesting to get to know her. It's like she's been brought back into the family."

Heritage is obviously very important to Lee and she's forever nagging her mom to write down recipes and teach her the culture of Grenada. Through the food, she says, it's like the two of them are writing a little history of their family and country together. Like with the Kankun Luchador, the Grenada tourist office has seen the potential of what Tan Rosie is doing and has been in touch to see how they can work together.

Monica brings me a glass of what she calls 'ginger drink', a ginger beer without the fizz. It has a mild ginger spiciness that increases slowly but pleasurably the more you drink. It's tasty and perfect for supping in the sunshine. When I ask her how it's made she laughs and says it's a trade secret. I think she's joking, but she ambles off with Lee to go and get the plates.

When they return, the food is beautifully presented. The polenta makes a firm rather than mushy base, with the pan fried red snapper draped over the top. It's covered in a glistening red and orange creole sauce in which I can see the flecks of the Scotch Bonnet. This is going to be good.

The meat is very light and not overpoweringly salty or fishy; it comes with a decent crunch to the fried skin, but the flesh is softer and more subtle. The creole sauce is warm and tomato-y, but it's not as wild as expected from that doubling up of chillies. I can taste the Scotch Bonnets and their flowery heat comes through more pronounced as I eat, but at no time is it uncomfortably hot. I'm glad, because I want to taste the fish. And it really isn't as hot as I expected a Caribbean dish to taste.

The real star of the show is the polenta. It's like a congealed cous cous, but it's coconutty, creamy and sweet. The chopped okra has gone soft – it's been slimy every time

I've eaten it before – and it falls apart in the mouth. With the ginger drink, the heat of the Scotch Bonnets, the subtle garlic and the cream and sweetness of the polenta, it's a lovely balanced lunch. I can see why many supper club guests keep coming back.

Over lunch we talk about the other side of the Tan Rosie business: the sauces, meat rubs, marinades, jams, chutneys and, of course, the fudge they make and sell at market stalls and festivals.

Monica had always made hot sauces at home for her own use, as well as an aubergine and mushroom pesto. She started sharing them with friends and family, and the people she worked with.

"She started selling them," corrects Lee, with a smile.

"I was raising money for a hospital in Carriacou," she says, turning to me.

The two created a few meat rubs and jams too, and took the whole lot to a farmers' market in nearby Mosely. The food went down well and the pair enjoyed selling it so much, they realised there could be a business in selling Caribbean flavours this way. The supper club came a little later, but there's a huge crossover between the two. Often, Monica will create something for their guests and it will be such a hit that she'll create a version of it for selling at markets.

Now the business is the mother and daughter's full-time work, though Monica still insists she's retired. During the winter, they create the preserves like the jams, chutneys and sauces, and during the summer they spend the week making the fresher products: chilli fudge, ginger fudge, plantain crisps and seasonings. Most weekends, and some weekdays too, are taken up with sales.

Lee in particular likes the selling, saying the production is the hard part and the weekends are like a holiday. She loves meeting people and talking about Caribbean cookery and, as well as at the supper club, this is where she really gets the chance. She gives a little giggle as she tells me shoppers often get a shock when they try her chilli fudge.

"You can see their faces as they initially enjoy the fudge because it's sweet, but then you see their faces as they walk away and the heat from the Scotch Bonnets comes in.

"Usually, though, they come back and buy some."

She offers me a bag to try. The chunks look soft and pliable, and there are no flecks of red chilli to be seen. In the mouth it has the texture of a near melted butter and the taste is immediately creamy on the tongue, with just a hint of chocolate. But she's right about the Scotch Bonnet. I can feel its flowery sweetness slowly build, then behind it the heat. And it is a strong heat, much stronger than in the creole sauce. If I hadn't been eating chillies pretty much non-stop for the last few months, I'd probably find it difficult to swallow. Though I'd still have a pretty good go at it.

Duly accustomed to the heat, I find the Scotch Bonnets in the fudge offer a moreish sort of burn. I take another chunk and this time wait for it to melt on my tongue, then I swill the creamy fudge around, easing out the sugar and chilli, fully coating my mouth and throat with it. It is beyond delicious. Later on the train home, I polish off the whole packet – just so my kids don't get unnecessarily excited, thinking I've brought back a bag of sweets for them, you understand.

Before I go, we chat about the growth of street foods and artisan food producers like Tan Rosie, and how they're coping against the smash-and-grab dominance of the supermarkets. Particularly now that the big multiples are getting further into the hot foods market.

Lee says she's optimistic. Even in the nearly five years

they've been running Tan Rosie she's seen an increase in stalls selling authentic foods at markets, rather than just the ingredients for them. The growth of chillies, chilli dishes and hot foods, she says, has been astounding and her Caribbean cookery has only benefitted from that.

"I think street food is overtaking farmers' markets; it's the next big thing," she says. The recession has meant more people are launching food businesses. That's because food is a relatively easy way to go it alone. A shrinking of the world, thanks to easy travel and the internet, means more people are wanting to try new things.

"People's tastes are changing, and especially they're getting a taste for hotter foods. They're experimenting more," she adds.

Foodies want to get up close and personal with the people making the foods, just as I have today, rather than pulling anonymous bottles off anonymous shelves. It's shopping and tasting as experience and lifestyle, rather than as a function. The supermarkets might be able to mass produce and sell cheap, they may even be able to get the quality and taste, but they can't recreate that personal experience.

It's a reminder again that the chilli sub-culture in Britain is really about the community, as well as the taste and heat. As my friend Dan said at Mezcal Cantina, it's like a little secret we can be let in on. And it's worth protecting.

For a number of years, Caribbean food has sat on the edge of Chilli Britain with only a few Caribbean influenced sauce sellers around. Even Tan Rosie tries to stay relatively local, because they also want to attract diners to the supper club, though they will do the larger food and chilli festivals. Lee thinks Caribbean cookery in the UK has lacked role models. Rustie Lee was a larger-than-life character and Levi

Roots was picked by the Dragons not on the basis of his grasp of the numbers or the business model, but on his personality. But there's been very little since.

"Caribbean food is one that's not really taken off until now. Perhaps we've lacked confidence in the Caribbean community, or the financial stability," she says. "But that is changing. I feel immensely privileged to be part of what's going on at the moment and to be educating people about true Caribbean food and flavours."

I suspect the little corner of Caribbean influenced Chilli Britain can only grow. With a belly full and warm with cou cou and red snapper in Scotch Bonnet creole sauce, followed by very hot chilli fudge, I head for the train feeling very privileged myself. Not only have I had a tasty meal in the afternoon sun, but I've enjoyed it with two very smart and inspiring women.

9th July – In a matter of a week, we've moved well into fruiting season. Previously Vampire had dozens of thin, purple slightly bitter tasting fruits with no heat at all. Now it has dozens of two inch long chillies that have suddenly gone and got fat, and they now come with a serious burn. Joe's Long Cayenne is living up to its name; the longest fruit so far is a lanky sixteen centimetres and still growing fast. Lemon Drop, Purple Tiger and Vampire have got so tall, easily three feet each, that I've had to introduce canes to prop them up. Friar's Hat is just as tall, but has a sturdy stem so I haven't bothered.

But it's the small things that matter. Sweet Pepper Sunshine, Purple Tiger and Lemon Drop all have tiny buds. Friar's Hat has an abundance of flowers but no fruits. But get this: Habanero 7 is in flower! It has two fully opened flowers, and up to a dozen other buds on their way. This is way further than I've ever got with Habanero 7. I've gingerly knocked the flowers a few times, hoping for a little self-pollination. There are loads of hoverflies in the vicinity too. But if the Habanero's flowers begin to die off without any fruits, I can and will resort to the paintbrush.

15*th* July – It's been an amazing week for my chilli collection (did I just write that?). Drum roll, please: Habanero 7 has fruits! At the beginning of last week there was a handful of little flowers, then in the middle of the week the petals of a few dropped and behind them were little stubs: definitely fruits. And now there are three actual Habanero 7 chillies growing in my conservatory. Each is about the size of a peanut, deep green and just about the ugliest chillies I've ever seen. They're wrinkled and far from symmetrical, but they are there. Whatever I did wrong in previous years (like not giving the plant enough attention) I've managed to get it right this time. If I can keep them going then I'm going to have one of the hottest chillies on the block, grown from seed. For chilli producers the UK over that's not much, but it makes this one deliriously happy.

I also had a bit of a chilli epiphany in the week. Friar's Hat and Lemon Drop are very beautiful plants. They're tall and branchy, have lovely wide leaves and lots of flowers. But still no fruit. All they seem to do is put on more height and more flowers. So before the weekend I decided to take a risk. With a pair of scissors I cut off the new, highest tips of the plants to prevent them going up any further. And by the next morning – incredibly, the very next morning – both had pushed out little fruits. By Monday morning, Friar's Hat had sprouted six or seven wonderfully shaped little green bells that seem to have grown a few millimetres every time I check. Which is pretty often. I'm kicking myself now because if I'd cut them earlier (I think gardeners call it 'pinching out') they'd be more fruitful. But then again, I wouldn't have the tall, broad plants I have now. It's a happy medium and I'm loving it.

The longest fruit on Joe's Long Cayenne is now twenty three centimetres. Prairie Fire – both soil and hydroponic versions – are so *heavy with pale inch long fruits they're both threatening to fall over. And Etna has clusters of green chillies in two groups right at its highest points – I can't wait for them to turn red. The tiny Sweet Pepper Sunshine, like a little chilli bonsai, has fragile thin and pale green chillies dotted all over it. The sheer diversity of the plants, the size and shape of the chillies, is really satisfying.*

Three. Two. One... Eat!

I NAIVELY THOUGHT they'd start us off with something mild. Perhaps a heat free Bell Pepper or something with only the slightest sting like a Pasilla. The Clifton Chilli Club, which has come to run the Hertfordshire festival's chilli eating competition, obviously has other ideas.

The competition goes straight in with the Bullet chilli, the same fruit that had been used to spice up the pretty hot curry I'd eaten for lunch at Merthyr Tydfil. And they just get hotter from there.

A bunch of my friends have come along with their kids to the chilli festival at a Hertfordshire country club. I'd secured a place in the chilli eating competition there, my friend George had signed up too, and they've all come along to watch the suffering as a little pre-entertainment before we all retreat home for a summer barbecue.

Right now, as George and I sit at opposite ends of a long table in front of a crowd of onlookers, that barbecue seems an awful long way off.

Jim Booth, of spiked cider fame, is compering. He's busy explaining the rules to the expectant crowd. Chilli Dave is filming the event for their YouTube channel. Dave Mac is on chilli selection duty. Volunteers from the Red Cross have come to the sides of the competition table; they're wearing disinfected blue gloves and brandishing cardboard sick bowls.

George, eight other contenders and I sign a waiver form,

assuaging the club and the festival from any legal responsibility for anything we're about to do to our bodies. It concludes with the words: "Furthermore, I understand that chilli peppers are hot and I am an idiot for entering the contest!" We take a deep breath, then it's down to business.

"Three. Two. One… Eat!"

The Bullet chilli, checking in at between one and three thousand Scovilles, goes down surprisingly easily. I bite into the light flesh and feel nothing so chomp the rest down in a couple of bites, grinding it between my teeth and then swallowing. There's only a tiny sting in the tail and I'm unsurprised to look around and see all ten of us still in the competition. My initial nervousness has gone now, so I take a moment to look at my immediate neighbours.

I'm sat next to František on my left and Simon and Steven on my right. František is Czech and, according to Jim, has hitchhiked all the way across Europe. He's wearing a skull and crossbones bandana, has a long matted beard, chunky silver rings and battered clothes that he's clearly been wearing since Prague. Simon looks like a hardman with mirror sunglasses, gelled hair and a smart sleeveless shirt. His mate Steven is in a polo shirt and his eyes and nose are all battered up. He's a rugby player or a boxer, I think. All three of them seem formidable opponents. On looks alone, I suspect any one of them could triumph.

The next chilli up is the Aura. It's slightly hotter, but still not so hot that I can't taste the flesh. The back of my mouth is tingling, but I'm far from in trouble yet and everyone else is still in the game too. After the red Jalapeño, which comes with what I'd call a normal chilli heat, and then the Finger chilli, a long, thin, green fruit about 25,000 on the Scoville Scale, my familiar hiccups start and I begin to sweat. I look up at the crowd to see a big bloke resting a pint on his belly laughing and pointing at me, putting on mock hiccups for the benefit of his pals.

"I reckon he ain't going to be able to do this," says Hardman Simon into Jim's microphone indicating me, inducing delighted 'oooohs' from the crowd. Then he leans to me and speaks off-mic: "Only joking mate, behind these glasses my eyes are streaming."

The crowd's attention turns elsewhere as Jim hovers over Luke, a spindly boy in a cap who looks about fourteen (but must surely be eighteen to have entered). He's struggling and the look on his face is one of incredulity, as if heat in the chillies was the last thing he expected when he signed up.

"You don't need that my friend," says Jim, as he relieves the boy of his cap. "It's getting hot down there, isn't it?"

Dave Mac hands out the next chilli, a Cayenne Pepper, as Jim announces it hits 50,000 Scovilles. Steven, Simon and I hold the chillies in each other's direction, as if to say *'en guarde'* and relatively easily chomp them down to the stem. The hiccups have gone now, replaced by an uncomfortable heat in my throat and mouth. My lips have gone all spiky. OK, I say to myself, now we're entering the hurt locker. A cheer goes up as Luke rises from the table and spits bits of half-eaten Cayenne into one of the cardboard bowls. He's done well for a teenager and the crowd knows it. One down, I think. The competition starts here.

I try to concentrate on the table in front of me, and the next few chillies are a blur. My mouth is in pain and I'm starting to feel the heat in my stomach too, but the following two chillies come so rapidly – a Super Chilli and a beautifully curled and crimson Bangalore Whippet's Tail – that I can take them because my mouth is already burning hot. Piling more heat into an already painful mouth will have no effect, I tell myself, as long as I can stay focussed.

But soon after I decide a little knowledge is a dangerous thing when it comes to chilli eating competitions. Having spent the last six months around chillies, I know well each fruit that comes out for the rest of the competition. And each time Jim announces their names, I look to the sky and shake my head. There's an audible intake of breath as Jim announces the Scotch Bonnet. That's some serious heat, I think, but at least they're small.

But the Scotch Bonnet that Dave Mac presents us each with is three times as big as any that I've ever seen. They're as broad as a child's fist, deep red, plump and fleshy. On the count of three, we all take a bite and the heat hits immediately. But it's not just the incredible fire of the thing that's the problem, it's the thickness of the skin. This can't be quickly chewed and gulped. It takes some biting to even get into it and then real jaw action and a work around the mouth before it's ready for swallowing.

After the first bite, I find myself staring down into the body of the Scotch Bonnet. It has wide fleshy skin and a deep ring of seeds nestled in the white pith where most of the capsaicin is lurking. For the first time, I start to struggle.

At the other end of the table, I see one guy lean behind the table and spit the chilli out, grabbing for his milk. Then to my left Frontišek starts chucking up red sticky bile into a bowl. I glance over at George and he looks in pain, but he's still there. Seven of us left.

I want the next chilli before the heat of the Scotch Bonnet wears off, but it's not forthcoming because another guy then drops out. He sets off a domino effect and in 20 seconds Steven and Simon have pulled out too. I ought to feel smug after the ribbing they've given me, but I'm thinking nothing but heat right now. I hear over the loudspeaker that George has pulled out too.

I look up with surprise to see there are suddenly only three of us left in the competition: Laura, a larger woman in a leopard-print top; a round and ruddy guy called Kevin; and me, all sweaty and trying as best I can to maintain a poker face. We're presented with a Chocolate Habanero – a close cousin of the Habanero 7 – which I know is just scorching.

Jim is telling the crowd: "These are 350,000 Scovilles. They are a *hot* chilli."

I try not to listen as I eat it down to the stem and glance at my wife whose eyes I've been avoiding. She's shaking her head and calling 'pull out'. But all other eyes are on Laura. Her face has gone bright red and puffed up. A 'friend' from the crowd says she looks like she's giving birth. She's holding the back of her hand against her mouth. In her other shaking hand she's holding her Habanero. I see a medical volunteer kneeling by her side as if she's trying to talk her down from the ledge of a high building.

"All I'm saying is: 'is it worth it?'," I hear her say. Jim reiterates – with a tone of encouragement it seems to me – that contestants can drop out at any time. Rather unkindly, I'm thinking: "Either jump or get back through the window, just make a decision."

Laura reaches for the milk, but then puts it back and bites the Habanero, chews and swallows. The crowd go crazy. But then she throws it back up again. The Red Cross volunteer is holding her hand.

Jim announces the next chilli is the Green Ghost Pepper, at about 900,000 Scovilles. I've seen YouTube videos of people keeling over after eating Ghost Peppers, so its announcement is genuinely scary. But after such a hot run up to it, Kevin and I clear it in a few bites. I can tell we both want to keep moving on as quickly as possible. As I finish the

Ghost, I can feel my arms beginning to shake and notice Kevin seems to be hanging onto the table for dear life. He's struggling with his chilli. My temples begin to pulsate and it feels like I'm cut off from the outside world. I can only barely hear the cheering crowd now, and it echoes as if I'm listening from the other end of a long tunnel.

For some reason, I've decided Kevin and I are cyclists in a final battle to win the Tour de France (the final stage of the Tour is on today). It's no longer a battle to win, I want to say to him, it's just a matter of who has the legs to stay the course. One of us is going to take the Yellow Jersey. Clearly I'm having the mild endorphin induced illusions that Darth Naga had told me about.

Kevin eventually finishes his Ghost Pepper and we are handed Dorset Nagas. A few years ago, this held the world record for the hottest chilli.

"These are evil," says Jim.

Kevin is shaking. We're on an Alpine climb and I just know he's going to crack any minute. I gnaw the thing down, but Kevin is again struggling to finish. But when Jim gives him the count of fifteen seconds, he eventually does.

Unbelievably, we then plough through a Green Dorset Naga and then a 7-Pot Bubblegum in quick succession. Then we're given a Naga Viper. This time it's Kevin who's eaten the whole fruit down and me who's hanging off the back of his wheel. I'm suffering badly. Approaching the end of the Naga Viper I'm suddenly ready to give up. It's no longer the heat, it's the mental pressure I can't take. My body has decided it doesn't want to do this anymore and it's a conscious act of will for me to keep biting, chewing and swallowing.

I shake my head, throw the final bit of Viper onto the table, slowly lean over and pull the milk towards me. Shouts emerge from the crowd and I look up at Sarah and she's shouting: "Finish it!"

I push the milk away, pick the Naga back up and take the remaining bite out of it, swallow and hold the stalk up into the air to the crowd's delight. Soon, the Yellow Jersey will be mine. Then I hear what seem like the worst words I've ever heard in my life. Trinidad Scorpion.

"They're the hottest chillies we can find at the moment, only surpassed by the Carolina Reaper," says Jim. "These are super hot." I feel my stomach go into cramps at the very mention, but it's only a small crinkly red thing and it's only a matter of holding on.

"Three. Two. One... Eat!"

In the end it isn't a conscious decision. I take only one bite of the Scorpion and haven't even got down to the business end when, from afar, I watch my arm pick up the milk and drag it to my lips. I drop the part eaten Scorpion on the table, stand, swill and spit the red-dotted milk into a cardboard tub someone has handed me. People are cheering and patting me on the back as I walk away.

In the far off distance – very far off, it seems – I hear Jim declare Kevin as the winner of the competition. He didn't need to eat the Scorpion, but he does anyway. The crowd whoop as he is handed a bag full of chilli goods from around the fair. I take a moment to compose myself then head back to the table to shake hands with Chilli Dave, Jim and Dave Mac, to congratulate Kevin and then to chat with a few well-wishers. Though I'm too sky-high to listen properly to what they say.

"You did bloody well," says Russell Williams, founder of Grim Reaper Foods, grabbing my hand. "Well done! I know you don't feel like it right now, but you deserve a runner-up's prize."

He hands me two bottles of his hottest sauces: Evil One Deathly Hot sauce and Evil Twin Deadly Hot sauce. Both are made with Scotch Bonnets and Naga chillies and he's right. I don't feel like trying them right this minute. I thank him, but I have other things on my mind.

There's something I've discovered about country clubs. It's that there's nowhere to spew. I'd already decided before the competition that it would be immediately followed by Darth Naga's poke and puke strategy. With my stomach already in cramps I know it's something I have to follow through with. When I go in search of a suitable place, I'm only marginally satisfied to hear that Kevin is already in the only available toilet cubicle. But it means I have to find somewhere else, and that means wandering around the whole country club – past the packed children's playground, past the cricket pitch with a match in full flow, around the pristine manicured bowling green – until I find a suitable place.

That place, it turns out, is crouching behind a compost heap next to the groundskeeper's tool shed. But it's to no avail. I won't go into detail, except that while the mind may be willing, the stomach is not. Instead I return to my friends with my tummy twisting, fearing the worst for later. My wife greets me with an ice cream which does, for about three minutes, neutralise the cramps.

"You did really well," says my mate Mike, supportively. "That bloke was on the brink all the time, but you looked dead composed throughout."

"Ah, you big wuss," says my other friend Jonny, somewhat less supportively.

"What the hell were you thinking?" asks Sarah, less supportively still. "Why didn't you pull out?"

"Hold on," I reply. "You said 'finish it' after the Naga

Viper, so I did."

"No, I said 'don't finish it'. Pull out."

"Oh," I say. "Er, sorry."

Back at Mike's house, I do manage to purge. But I miss most of the barbecue, electing instead to lie down in a darkened room, my hands gently resting on my stomach, trying not to move. I only rise an hour later when the neighbour decides on a little late afternoon lawn mowing and I have to head downstairs to murder him.

Jonny presents me with a cold veggieburger in a bun. I can't even bare to look at the selection of sauces on offer to accompany it.

22nd July – Habanero 7 now has three plump, though rather ugly, gnarled fruits and they continue to grow apace. I think it's because the weather has been so warm. Too warm: I'm continuing to struggle to keep the chillies hydrated. The hot summer has seen me dipping them in and out of a bucket, constantly spilling dirty water all over the conservatory floor. But, hey, Habanero 7 makes it all worthwhile. Lemon Drop has surprised me with its fruits. I expected them to hang low and long like Joe's Long Cayenne, but the beautiful lime-green pods actually point upwards.

Friar's Hat now has a full complement of weird shaped bells, so replete at the top of the plant that it now keeps falling over. Sweet Pepper Sunshine is blooming with little handfuls of yellow-green lanterns. My chilli crop is officially a success.

1st August – I'm excited that there has now begun a creeping ripening of most of the fruits. The lovely yellow-white fruits on Prairie Fire and Red Missile have started to go red from the tip towards the stem, creating a stunning upside down sunset effect. Friar's Hats' hats are turning from merely light green to the same, but just tinged with a hint of orange. Purple Tiger's fruits are now a shimmering bright purple, as if they're glistening with water. I'm surprised to see Vampire's deep purple chillies have started to go crimson at the ends: the effect is like creeping blood leaking into the darkness above. So, that's where it gets its name. I definitely tasted them too early. The clump of chillies at the top of Etna are starting to go a very deep and fiery red, another obviously named chilli. The pods on Lemon Drop have gone an almost translucent lime-green. They're a beautiful fruit, all squished and bumpy but with a little tip that flicks up like a quotation mark. There's something really special about that plant.

But most attractive as it ripens is Joe's Long Cayenne. They're very long deep green fruits, but the tips of many of them have turned bright red and the colour seems to be creeping up a few millimetres every hour. Habanero 7 has grown another little ugly fruit, but the three already there are now very crinkly, like green ping-pong balls that someone has stepped on. It feels like we're getting to the end of the growing season. In a few weeks these will be ripe too and, for this year at least, my chilli growing journey will be over. I'll be relieved and sad in equal measure.

But at least there'll be lots of hot eating to be done.

6th August – Lemon Drop is in irrecoverable trouble. The flat pods have started to go mushy in the middle and keep dropping off the plant. It could be that they've already ripened and are starting to rot, or perhaps there's something else going on: the constant overheating of the conservatory? Either way, there are only a few chillies left. I've harvested a few – they're hot only right at the stem end and do indeed have a strong lemon bite – but there's only three or four left on the plant now. It was beautiful while it lasted, but I think that plant has had its day.

Now I'm turning to harvesting, there are far too many chillies coming off the plants for me to consume each day. I have a couple of choices. You can either freeze them, making sure their skins are dry, in a plastic bag or container. When you take them out, cut them while frozen *and throw into your cooking without thawing. Or you can hang them up to dry. Thread them onto a piece of cotton using a needle, poking the end through the stem not the flesh. Then hang them up in a dry but not stagnant place: the conservatory with a window open is perfect. Don't rush them, and when they're fully dry they can just go into a tub for using as and when.*

What goes around...

WHEN CAR PARKING attendants are wearing huge sombreros to show you to your space, and do so by shaking maracas in the direction you're supposed to go, you can be sure this is no Royal Horticultural Society flower show.

I'd prepared for the worst for the West Dean Chilli Fiesta. After admitting to my wife that I hadn't booked the stone floored cottage I'd (kind of) promised, I'd said we wouldn't stay long at the fiesta. It would probably be a wash-out anyway, given the torrential downpours we'd enjoyed sitting on the M25 for three hours yesterday.

"We'll just stay for an hour, I'll say a few hellos, then we can head back to the hotel and the indoor swimming pool," I say. A little later I try a tentative: "Maybe I'll stay a couple of hours and you can come and pick me up later?"

This is the third chilli festival I've dragged the whole family to this year. Both the others had pretty much offered chilli sauce stalls and not a lot else. I need to tread carefully. But for one day in August, everything falls into place. The weather is so good that we've already spent a few hours on the beach and we're all in good spirits. At the fiesta, there are long queues of people waiting to get in. But I've booked ahead and so we sail through. Priority boarding.

As soon as we get inside, the kids are bounding up and down with excitement at the bouncy castles and the Ferris wheel, the merry-go-round and sweets and fudge stalls. A smile (of relief?) spreads on Sarah's face as she spies the homeware, nicknack and card stalls, the beautifully laid out gardens of West Dean College, *ordinary* food available and *ordinary* people eating it.

Me, I'm just wide-eyed at the size of it. I knew West Dean was the biggest chilli festival in the UK, but I can't believe how huge it really is.

There's a full size music stage, surrounded by hot dog, noodle, taco and curry stands. There are chilli themed entertainers on stilts and a Latin American band playing pumping music. There are women in chilli dresses and chilli earrings, kids with chillies painted on their faces, and dozens upon dozens of grown men walking round in multi-coloured chilli shirts.

There are three fields full of chilli product stalls: plants and seeds, sauces and jams, brownies and fudge, chocolate and pancakes; there are burgers and booze, chilli extracts, rubs and shakers. There are a dozen bars, some advertising chilli infused cider and ale. There's a demonstration tent with a full programme of chilli cookery, and horticultural presentations.

And I can't even get close to most stalls to taste their wares. There are long lines of punters desperate to be parted from £20 notes. Everyone is doing a roaring trade. Except for the guy selling lavender soap who perhaps expected the Chilli Fiesta to be some kind of genteel craft fair.

If you are planning death-by-chilli, the West Dean Chilli Fiesta is the place to do it. And I'm already a little emotional that this colossal celebration of all things capsicum will be the final staging post on my journey. I leave Sarah and the kids at the funfair and set off in search of some total strangers to talk chillies.

"We don't like hot foods," say the first couple I approach. They're sitting miserably behind a fence, licking ice creams.

"Oh, so have you come for the atmosphere?"

"Don't know, really," says he. "We just turned up."

A cracking start, So, I decide to go for a far easier win. I look for the biggest, fattest bloke wearing a chilli shirt and a sombrero that I can find. There are more than a few available and Paul from Basingstoke more than fits the bill.

"I've been coming here every year for the last six years," he says, waving around a half empty pint of beer. It's not his first drink of the day. "It's great. I've organised a coach trip for 32 people. Look," he says, pointing at another fat chap in a sombrero and matching chilli shirt, "there's my father-in-law." The crowd he's with let out a huge cheer.

"I always come to try something really really hot," he says. "The thing about chilli is that it's addictive and you always want to experiment with something hotter. We're all challenging each other today."

But what's behind our growing interest in Britain?

"I think there's just so much more out there, and it's the influence of other countries. We're all going away further and trying things from different places."

I move to a slightly older and pretty mismatched couple. The woman is petite and straight out of the loiterers at *Antiques Roadshow*. He's somewhat larger and wearing a pirate T-shirt with the slogan: 'What goes on board, stays on board.' He's carrying bags and bags of produce.

"I love chilli, I just *love* hot food," he says. Tony has travelled around Africa and everywhere he's been he's tried the hottest foods. "I think chilli is one of those things that you either love or hate, and if you love it then you have to have it with everything." That does sound pretty familiar.

"I like hot foods too," says his partner Anna. "It's a question of getting acclimatised. Once you've tried one hot thing, you can go up and try something even hotter."

"The only thing I didn't like today was the chilli beer," says Tony. "It was a waste of good chilli and a waste of good beer."

I go off in search of more opinions and catch two teenagers laughing conspiratorially: "Don't put too much in George's drink," says one. "Just enough for him to get a shock." Little Clifton Chilli Club apprentices.

I'm drawn across one of the fields towards a woman in a full length chilli frock. "I love your dress," I say to her, as a way of breaking the ice before I stick my notebook in her face. "Where did you get it?"

"Oh, Debenhams, I think," she says, a final indication that chillies have well and truly hit the mainstream. Her name is Pal and she's of Punjabi descent. "I've been coming here every year, I just love chillies," she says. "I grow Scotch Bonnets at home and for me, it's the hotter the better."

"I'm more into the flavours," says her friend John. "I am into the heat, but I also like to taste what I'm eating. We as a nation are taking more and more heat. It's because of the growth of cookery programmes. We've become a nation of food lovers, much more interested in flavours than we ever were."

Their friend Andy chips in: "People are going abroad more, going out to dinner more. In Britain we're becoming connoisseurs and chilli is one of the latest trends in that."

With a few punters interviewed, I go off in search of some of the people I know at the festival. Chilli Dave is the first familiar face I bump into. He's at the Upton Cheyney Chilli Farm stall, selling jams and sauces and, of course, promoting the Clifton Chilli Club, their YouTube channel and their super cool merchandise. We greet each other like old friends and he's totally in his element. In between serving customers, he tells me I'm in for a treat today: "There's nothing like West Dean."

He tells me that interest in chillies only continues to grow; it feels like it's limitless. "When we met back in May, we had 3,000 subscribers to our YouTube channel. Now we've got half that many again."

Jay Webley, the Chilli Alchemist, hobbles up to the stand to join him. He's had an operation on his leg so his alchemist's wooden staff has been temporarily replaced by a pair of NHS-issue crutches.

"This is the real heart of the chilli industry," he tells me. "Even after the customers have gone home, it's where we carry on talking to each other, doing deals, sharing ideas.

"Are you going to be around for long?" he says, suddenly having a great idea. "Dave and I are planning to do a chilli review while going round on the Ferris wheel," he says, pointing his crutch towards the funfair and the rapidly spinning wheel. Broken leg or not, these guys are up for anything. I excuse myself, but no doubt I'll see that video later in the week: five minutes of shaky camera work, spilled chilli sauce, painful howls and near vomiting on the kids in the seats below them.

Next I see the inspiring mother and daughter team of Tan Rosie. Monica immediately calls me over with a huge grin. After the peace of their Birmingham kitchen and back garden, it's great to see them in busy flow. Monica has lost her hat thanks to the sweltering sun and is dishing out tastes of her hot chilli fudge and jams which customers can't wait to try. Lee has the stall under chaotic control. She's serving ginger drink with one hand, handing over meat rubs with another and impossibly taking cash in another. She gives me a friendly wave with a fourth.

Just up the way is Grim Reaper Foods and Russell

Williams. He'd handed me my runner-up prize in the wake of the Hertfordshire chilli eating competition a few weeks ago and I wasn't really in a state to thank him properly.

"Gideon, hey great to see you," he says.

"I just wanted to say sorry for not really thanking you for the great sauces you gave me after the competition."

"No problem, you definitely deserved them. Have you recovered yet?"

"Just about," I reply. "I had to go and lie down in a dark room for a couple of hours afterwards. But things are just about settling down now."

A bloke standing next to me pipes up, "Wow, lie down in a dark room?" He pulls out a tenner. "I'll have whatever he's having." Russell winks and hands him a gift box featuring The Grim Reaper's Evil One. I feel a slight welling up of pride.

I'm especially pleased to see Steve Woodward from Mushemi Fire. My brother and I had such an enlightening time in his Rugeley kitchen. Keen, sharp and passionate businessman that he is, I'm rooting for him to make a success in the chilli industry.

"Do you know," he says, pulling me to the side of his stall, "this year is the first anniversary of me registering Mushemi Fire as a business and I couldn't be happier. I've got more new products on the stall this weekend, and they're just selling and selling."

My favourite Zwao! (Pain) has become one of his leading products and I'm delighted to hear that Mother's Ruin is still flying off his shelves too. An American customer comes to the table: "You make all these yourself?" he asks. "That's amazing."

And it is. I leave Steve as he turns to a Zambian woman who's turned up to his stand and they begin chatting animatedly about Lusaka, African chillies and how he got started. His familiar history sales story.

When I approach the Wiltshire Chillies stall, it's like I'm going from one familiar sales patter to another. Jamie Sythes – well tanned, no doubt from spending every hot summer weekend in the sun doing exactly this – is grinding crushed chilli-salt into potential customers' hands. He's mirroring his dad's approach from when we worked on the Bath stall together.

"This is great on steak or on roast potatoes, maybe char-grilled vegetables straight out of the oven. Just pull them out from under a hot grill still bubbling, grind a little of this on top and serve straight away. It's a truly delicious experience."

And then there he is: Darth Naga. He grabs my hand and shakes it vigorously as someone calls from the waiting crowd: "I love your videos."

"Gideon, welcome," says Tony Ainsworth, aka Darth. He doesn't waste a second. He has unfinished business. "I've got the video camera here, and Lisa has agreed to film us, so I thought we'd do another tasting video if that's OK with you?

"I think we should revisit the Burning Desire Foods range, from the one you tried with me in the last video. Jason who runs the company was up until 11 p.m. last night brewing up something special. It's a Ghost chilli sauce and he's been saving a bottle for you.

"We'll just wait until Lisa returns from the bar, he says, then we'll get on with it."

"You did bloody well in that chilli eating contest," says Lisa from behind, a very short few minutes later. I feel a little embarrassment at becoming a tiny, albeit temporary, celebrity in the chilli world. It's quickly replaced by fear at doing another sauce tasting video with Darth Naga. This time without a sick bucket in sight.

Tony takes me over to the Burning Desire Foods stall. Jason is pleased to see me, though we've never met. He's been keeping up to date with my journey over Facebook. He actually thanks me for the review video I did with Darth Naga on his 7-pot Scorpion Insane Hot Sauce.

You can see on his face that he shares the same passion (or is it obsession?) with the chilli world as everyone else I've met. He's recently developed a chilli infused butter, the first on the market.

"I always like to do something different," he says. "I wanted to create something that people could use in their own way; go into the kitchen and get cooking and clever with their own dishes. You could put it on popcorn, or over chicken, or prawns."

Jason was raised across Africa and the Caribbean, which gave him a taste for heat, but also took away any fear of it. Like many I've met on the chilli scene, he gave up a corporate career "that wasn't fun" to follow his heart. As an amateur he entered one of his home-made chilli sauces into a competition at the Brighton Fiery Foods festival a couple of years ago and was surprised to come away with the top trophy. At around the same time he was made redundant from American Express, a coincidence which he describes as "destiny, a dream come true".

"Winning the competition blew me away," he says. "Reviewers liked the sauces and that gave me the confidence to start doing it. I came up with Burning Desire as a name for my company, because it encompasses everything I love about chillies. It's the heat, of course, but then that desire to keep coming back for more.

"This festival is a showcase for chilli producers from all

over the country," he says. "People come here knowing
they're going to see the very best chilli companies doing the
very best chilli products they can." He swings his arm
around to take in the hundreds of stalls. "This is the best of
the best."

He grabs a spare teenager from someone else's stand to
hold the fort on his, then takes a bottle of the sauce we're
going to try and we all retreat behind the tents to film the
video.

"Tony asked me to do something really special for you,"
says Jason. He hands me the bottle. "This is a Peach Ghost
sauce" – which would sound rather strange in any other
context – "so it should be hot, but also quite sweet."

The sauce has an off-white colour, rather than the red or
crimson of most chilli brews, and has the lumpy consistency
of apple sauce. It's made with Peach Ghost chillies (rather
than peaches *and* Ghost chillies), so I have no idea what to
expect from the flavour. But I know it's going to hurt.

"I haven't even tried this sauce yet," says Jason, rather
worryingly. So Tony invites him to join the video too.

Lisa starts the camera and Darth does his usual chilli
padowans routine, welcoming me back to the Darth Naga
mothership and introducing Jason as the creator of the sauce
we're going to try.

We both take a dollop of the sauce onto our spoons.
Jason advises us to scrape about half of it back into the
bottle. He's at least got an idea of how hot the sauce is likely
to be. But – incredibly – I find myself refusing. I'm after the
full monty this time and after the contest a couple of weeks
ago, I feel like I've earned my place among the super hot
tasters.

One, two, three and it's down the hatch. The sauce
comes with an immediate citrusy bite that's pleasant, like a

lemon sorbet, but straightaway backed by that Ghost chilli heat. There's a hint of florally grassiness in there too. See, now I'm at the end of this journey even I've learned the culinary vocabulary of the seasoned chilli taster.

The Ghost chilli is particularly hard on the back of the throat and that's where I feel it. But it's warming, rather than overtly painful and allows the fruitiness to come through at the front of the mouth. Though it's hot, I think Jason's Scorpion Insane sauce comes with a much bigger punch.

Tony is coughing and his eyes are watering (as usual) and he reaches for his pint. Jason and I talk for a bit about the sauce, then Jason offers us both some more. Tony refuses but I'm happy to accept. If anything, the sauce isn't quite hot enough for me. Jason tells me it will get hotter as it matures. Given it was only made last night, this sauce has a great future ahead of it and I'm delighted as he hands me the bottle to keep. Darth signs off his video and shakes his head at again having failed to defeat me. The force is strong with this one. Or maybe the last six months has just blown my capsaicin tolerance sky-high.

I leave Tony, Lisa and Jason and make my way to what I know will be one of the highlights of the fiesta for me, if a little jealousy inducing. A whole glasshouse has been given over to a display of hundreds of varieties of chillies. It's the kind of display that got me growing chillies in the first place, but this is far more comprehensive than anything I've seen before.

It's tucked off the main drag so it's quieter here and I've got time to properly look at the varieties in detail, each with its own neatly written label. I am, of course, looking for the chillies I'm growing and there are a few varieties of Friar's Hats, a Vampire, a Prairie Fire, an Etna and a Masquerade.

Each of them seems brighter and sturdier than mine, and they definitely have more fruits. But hey, they're the professionals and I'm not. And the plants are bound to have been specially pruned and presented for the occasion.

There are also a wealth of chillies I've never heard of. And some look just as improbable as they sound. Hot Banana chilli anyone? They are long, broad and yellow, of course, but they hang down individually rather than in bunches. What about Beaver Dam? They're huge, fat and have a single deep valley in one side that looks like... Well, I think they were named by someone pretty mischievous. The Cherry Pimento has lovely bulb-like fruits hanging down in red, yellow and green. The Poblano, from which dried Ancho chillies are made when smoked, has luscious brown fruits as big as a fist, so shiny they cast your reflection.

As I pass through the long glasshouse, I'm amazed by the variety and the colour. There are Chinese Ornamental plants with hundreds of tiny chillies that are so small you can barely see them. There are long purple chillies; orange, yellow, green and striped chillies. There are loads of reds, of all different hues and shapes. There are chillies pointing down, chillies pointing up, chillies curling round and round, or sitting like round peaches or wrinkled plums. There's a whole section of chillies that are super-long and some of them would easily bring my own Joe's Long Cayenne up rather short.

When I come out of the glasshouse at the other end, I can't help but walk back to the front and start the whole journey again. And I only see it on the second trip round. There, tucked at the back of one of the rows, almost out of sight behind some of the leafier plants. It's a foot high, rather limp looking Habanero 7. I check the leaves and look at the fruit. Yes, it's definitely exactly the same plant as mine. But, well, mine is... better. Much better.

My Habanero 7's leaves are much greener and broader, the plant is taller and more vibrant. And the best bit, the most satisfying bit of all, is that my Habanero now has at least four or five golf ball sized sturdy Habanero 7 chillies. This one, the one grown by the pros, has two. And even those look precarious. I'll say no more, but I leave that glasshouse a second time a more excited and satisfied chilli grower than I have ever been.

When I finally meet up with my family, I'm only an hour or so late but they don't seem to have noticed. Sarah's been at the fudge, my daughter has had braids put in her hair and my son has a chilli painted on his face. All three claim to have eaten chilli ice cream. My wife tells me they've spent a fortune going on rides, playing hook-a-duck, eating pancakes and generally having a great time. I can hardly complain. They've indulged my obsession not just for today, but for the last six months. Actually, much longer than that.

My two kids beg for just one last ride before we go. They want me to go on the Ferris wheel with them. My wife smiles mischievously, as if she's put them up to it. She knows I may have developed a stomach for the very hottest chillies, but I'm a total wimp when it comes to fairground rides. Especially ones that go very high and creak and rock in the wind and probably have never had a health and safety check in the forty years since they were poorly constructed from wood and packing tape. I put on a brave smile, check that Chilli Dave and Jay aren't getting into any of the carriages above us, and allow them to drag me aboard.

As we rise up into the sky, my kids rock the carriage and wave their hands as the wheel begins to turn. I cling tightly onto the handle in front, grit my teeth and look out onto the festival as we go up and over it. There are hundreds of sombrero hats floating around on a sea of thousands of Chilli Fiesta-goers. There are dozens of chilli helium balloons hovering above them, the occasional one rising right up to our level, then further up into the sky. The music stage has a huge chilli, in bright red neon lights, illuminating a Mexican band playing to a decent crowd. Steam and smoke rises from the barbecues and hot food stalls.

In the near distance wherever I look there are rows and rows of stalls, each still crowded with customers. And inside each of them are clever, entrepreneurial, enthusiastic and inspiring people. Each with their own little portion of chilli passion to share.

11th August — All of my chilli plants, except the ones my dad gave me which never did fruit, are abundant and ripe. But there's only one star of the show here. Habanero 7, you have done me proud. The plant has seven, yes seven, chillies. There are even more buds on the way. Last year, I didn't even get any Habanero 7 flowers. This year, I already have four fully ripe shining red wrinkled chillies, each the size of a small mouthful. I tried eating one like that at the chilli eating competition and don't want to repeat the experience. And anyway, I intend to give Habanero 7 as much attention and love in the eating as in the growing.

My chilli growing is over for the year and, with a few dips along the way, I've achieved my aim. I've reared my Habanero 7 to reach its full potential, fulfilling my own potential as an amateur chilli grower. I've raised a dozen plants of all shapes, sizes, colours and heats.

It is indeed a display. An exhibition. An exhibition you can eat.

With the chilli season coming to a close it's time to think about next year. In the UK we tend to sow chillies from seed every year, but in fact chillies are perennial. For non-gardeners like me, that means they come back year after year. The problem is keeping the plants warm enough over the winter to flower next year, called 'overwintering' in Monty Don speak. But for those who are determined, I asked Adrian Nuttall what to do. Once the plant has fully fruited, he says, cut it back with scissors or secateurs to about a hand width above the soil, essentially just leaving the dry stick.

Then keep that plant indoors, maintaining it at no less than ten degrees throughout the whole winter. Leaving the house cold while you go away for a winter ski break is a no-no. Any particular cold snap, or even an open window allowing cold air to come through, will kill your chilli. If you keep a close eye, use a thermometer, and ensure the plant is in a sunny position – and doesn't suddenly suffer when there's frost lapping at the windows – then you might, just might, get that ugly brown stick to leaf, then flower, then fruit again next year.

Or you could just plant new seeds.

One more thing

I HOPE YOU'VE had fun reading Chilli Britain. You've probably guessed: I'm not some huge publisher with a vast marketing budget. I'm just a guy who loves writing and loves chillies. That means I'm hoping readers will pass word around about this book and tell people what you think.

I'd love it if you left an honest review of Chilli Britain on Amazon, Goodreads or any other book review site you use, as well as posting about it on any Facebook and Twitter account you have. It would make a real difference to me and might help me to write better books in the future.

I like to hear from my readers too, so please do connect with me on Twitter @chillibritain. Or contact me via www.facebook.com/ChilliBritainBook.

You can view pictures and videos from my Chilli Britain journey at www.chillibritain.com, click on the 'Gallery' tab.

Thanks so much for reading and hopefully for reviewing. Happy (and hot) chomping!

Gideon Burrows

Thanks so much to all the wonderful people I met on this journey, including those who I didn't find space to mention. Thanks particularly to Chilli Dave and all at the Clifton Chilli Club who have been so supportive of the whole idea, and to www.scufoods.com for allowing me to use their clever Scoville periodic table.

It's been incredible fun, I've learned a whole lot, my own chilli crop has exceeded my expectations and my obsession for chillies has deepened even further. I *think* that's a good thing.

I hope the chilli community in Britain will continue to flourish and it's been great to be part of it. Regretfully I couldn't get a Northern Ireland angle into the book, though I did try. The only chilli festival there this year was cancelled.

Thanks to my wonderful copyeditor Barney Jeffries and to my toughest critic (and massager of my ego) Sarah Mole. Thanks too to John Chandler for another great cover design. Any errors, especially those arising from a pretty dodgy understanding of world history and plant genetics, are mine.